# THE
# DESIGNER'S GUIDE TO
# DOING RESEARCH

# THE DESIGNER'S GUIDE TO DOING RESEARCH

## Applying Knowledge to Inform Design

SALLY AUGUSTIN | CINDY COLEMAN

WILEY

John Wiley & Sons, Inc.

Published by John Wiley & Sons, Inc., Hoboken, New Jersey.
Published simultaneously in Canada.

LIBRARY OF CONGRESS CATALOGING-IN-PUBLICATION DATA:
Augustin, Sally.
 The designer's guide to doing research : applying knowledge to Inform Design / Sally
Augustin, Cindy Coleman.
    p. cm.
 Includes index.
 ISBN 978-0-470-60173-0 (cloth : alk. paper); 978-1-118-09961-2 (ebk.); 978-1-118-09962-9
(ebk.); 978-1-118-10378-4 (ebk.); 978-1-118-10379-1 (ebk.); 978-1-118-10380-7 (ebk.)
 1. Architectural design—Research. I. Coleman, Cindy. II. Title. III. Title:
Applying knowledge in practice for design excellence.
 NA2750.A94 2012
 720.72—dc22
                              2011010961

Printed in the United States of America

10  9  8  7  6  5  4  3  2  1

# CONTENTS

# The Necessity for Research

THE HALLMARK OF A VITAL PROFESSION is its *body of knowledge*. In law, it's clearly defined as precedent, found in the great tomes and used, daily, by attorneys. In science, practitioners admit freely that they "stand on the shoulders of giants." Those employed in the many subsets of the physical and behavioral sciences build their work on the findings of those who came before them, those who work next to them, and those who toil, simultaneously, in competing institutions. Although much of this body of knowledge is gleaned in the course of everyday practice, such opportunistic research is not enough to keep the professions at their cutting edge. It is the deep dives and the intense focus on confounding problems that lift each profession to its highest level of performance and increase the value of its contributions to the growth of human intelligence and betterment of the human condition.

In an age of climate change, global materials shortages, aging populations, technological sophistication, and a worldwide web of connections between people and ideas, the design professions—those best equipped to shape the built environment—are searching for ways to fine-tune their responses to these complex issues. The well-being of humanity and the Earth that supports all living things is at stake. This is a big assignment; it requires a collaborative approach to problem solving. This complex problem solving needs many different professionals, each at the top of his or her game, to bring their unique skills and extensive knowledge to the table.

Clearly, architects and interior designers, whose work comes in close contact with our bodily and emotional needs, are essential participants in this growing and evolving public dialogue. They stand to make significant contributions to human well-being everywhere, to every culture and every economic group, not simply to well-funded institutions, multinational corporations, and wealthy home owners. The prospect of this new clientele predicts a broadening of the designer's work options, even as it calls for a new understanding of this uniquely varied population. At the same time, the profession's fine-grained sensibilities, once defined by such skills as choosing colors, textures, and styles, as well as devising spatial adjacencies and lighting schemes—those things that continue to humanize our most intimate surroundings—need to be refined, expanded, and redefined.

Material toxicities, energy performances, and emotional connectivity are only a few challenges faced by architects and interior designers today. How should they dive into these topics while carrying on the duties of a midstream career? How can they understand problems that were, by and large, previously ignored by the professions? What tools are needed to bring today's spatial designers up to the high level of performance expected of them? Research is a good place to start.

Research can become the solid cornerstone of the profession. The processes and approaches defined in this book are a strong beginning. But, like any worthwhile beginning, this moment, defined so skillfully by the authors, must grow and evolve if the profession and the world at large are to reap its full benefits.

Starting with the familiar, on-the-job research, a habit of relentless inquiry needs to be learned. Its clearly defined goal is to build a solid body of knowledge, a foundation on which future research will be based. This kind of information collection and analysis will be at its most powerful when the professions, as a whole, share their findings through publications and educational programs with ever-growing audiences. At the same time, practical knowledge accrued within firms must be shared freely, through available technologies and the many ways we are learning to use face time. Added to this effort, the professions must engage relevant specialists such as biologists and behavioral scientists in original research on human interaction with the interior environment and how our interiors connect to nature and the surrounding built environment. We intuitively know that it's all connected, that it's all part of a great system. The research will prove the hypothesis.

So, start here and start now. It's the beginning of a wonderful, productive journey in laying a solid foundation for the twenty-first-century design practice. That foundation will make your work indispensable. Your embedded knowledge will make you a valued member of any team. And your contribution to the body of human knowledge will be noted, celebrated, and appreciated by those who are fortunate enough to occupy the spaces you'll be designing.

—Susan S. Szenasy
Editor in Chief, *Metropolis* magazine

# ACKNOWLEDGMENTS

THANK YOU TO ALL the architects, designers, researchers, and experts who have contributed their time and knowledge to this book: Roshelle Born, Perkins + Will; Joseph Connell, Perkins + Will; Malcolm Cook, Loughborough University; Christian Derix, Aedas' Computational Design Research Group; Bill van Erp, Gensler; Megan Fath, Conifer Research; Judith Heerwagen, PhD, U.S. General Services Administration; Todd Heiser, Gensler; Thomas Jacobs, Krueck & Sexton; Cary Johnson, Gensler; Keelan Kaiser, Judson University; Jan van den Kieboom, Workshop Architects; Peter van den Kieboom, Workshop Architects; Lynn Kubin, Gensler; David Ogoli, PhD, Judson University; Leah Ray, Gensler; Holly Roeske, Conifer Research; Jennifer Smith, The School of the Art Institute of Chicago; Carolyn Stuenkel, PhD, Conifer Research; Adisorn Supawatanakul, Conifer Research; Nicholas Watkins, PhD, HOK, and Claire Whitehill, HOK.

We extend our appreciation to: Conifer Research, Gensler, Keelan Kaiser, Krueck & Sexton Architects, Perkins + Will, and Workshop Architects for contributing their time and resources to the Stories of Practice.

We are grateful to Susan Szenasy, editor in chief of *Metropolis* magazine, for contributing the foreword to this book—we are honored.

We extend a special thanks to senior editor John Czarnecki at John Wiley & Sons, Inc., for his skillful guidance.

Finally, from Sally to Denny: Thank you for making all the effort worthwhile. And, from Cindy to Neil and Emanuela: Thank you for making all the effort fun.

# Before You Do Design Research

*RESEARCH* IS A SPECIAL sort of word. It is simultaneously a noun and a verb. As a noun, it represents a collection of insights and facts—a jumble of the long-time known and newly learned. This "research" is a tool to inform future decisions. As a verb, *research* represents the process of moving questions that are important enough to require answers toward those answers. At the early stage of a project, it can help to generate new ideas, and at later points in a project it can be used to assess them.

*Design* is also both a noun and a verb. When acting as a noun, it is a physical manifestation of a series of decisions about form and function. The verb forms of *design* and *research* are synonyms—both are a question-answering process. Designers for millennia have been doing research, but it is only in the last few years that people have begun to speak of design and research in the same phrase. Being a "design researcher" is among the hippest professions around—but the job title is redundant.

In this book, we will show you how to apply the processes and tools you have learned as a designer to answer project-related questions in ways that ensure competitive advantage and your own professional satisfaction.

## RESEARCH VERSUS INSIGHT

Research alone is not all that important. It might get someone tenure at a university or spark conversation at a party, but research does not acquire real power until it is integrated with conscious and unconsciously recognized knowledge. Knowledge combines professional experience, abstract knowledge, common sense, and inspiration. Knowledge becomes intensely valuable when it can lead to an insight that inspires the resolution of an unanswered question. Insight is, according to Microsoft Word's dictionary "the ability to see clearly and intuitively into the nature of a complex person, situation or subject."

Developing a multifamily housing complex that enhances the lives of residents, while minimizing the literal and green footprint of their homes grows from a research base to an inspired insight. A school cafeteria that encourages camaraderie among its young users while minimizing bullying springs from the same process.

Insight is really useful to space designers. In this book, we show you, our fellow designers, how to move from questions to insights. It is important that you do research and develop your own knowledge because the people who can most effectively apply knowledge are those who generate it—no one else understands its nuances as well as they do. In this introduction, we talk a little bit about knowledge and insight, to ground our later chapters on research. After reading the introduction it'll be clear why time used to do research is time well spent.

## THE RESEARCH/DESIGN RELATIONSHIP

We discuss research in the flow of the design process because research is an inherent part of each stage in that chain. Designers are always posing questions and answering them in the physical forms of the spaces they develop. They are continuously translating both project-specific and generalized expert information into a language understood by clients and others through projected physical forms. This book is not introducing designers to a new process but to new tools that can be used to make the current ones they use to answer design questions more effective and efficient.

And it's about time that process was streamlined. Designers are being asked to develop more spaces more quickly. Our colleagues come to us exhausted, with questions such as these:

- What precedents are there for the design of preschools where young people succeed cognitively and socially?

- Who are the experts on sales-record-breaking retail design? How do I find out from them what I should know about designing gourmet, organic food stores?

- What's known about stores where people buy things they need or cherish?

- How can I use a survey to collect the information I need to program the Massive Company headquarters?

- How should a space be designed to maximize the productivity of a work team? (And the even thornier question: How should we define productivity, anyway?)

- How much community space is just right in a new multifamily residential complex? What should it look like? Feel like?

- What're the secrets of writing a good survey? What about a survey to collect information from the people in the offices ringing a civic center who use its public space every day for lunch?

- How can I be sure that the new hospital patient room we're presenting will increase patient, visitor, and caregiver well-being? That the surfaces won't harbor germs and the carpeting won't trip up unsteady feet?

- What do people actually do when they visit a farmers' market or a county fair? What can I learn from that experience and apply when I'm developing a new store or shopping mall? While we're at it, what could the design of indigenous villages teach me that should be applied to the design of that new multifamily residential complex (the one mentioned in my earlier question)?

- Where should I suggest a new school be located? How should it be oriented on the site selected?

- Which potential diners should I talk to about the design of a new restaurant? What should I discuss with them? What are their expectations about eating out, and how can those hopes/desires/requirements be reflected in design?

- OK, I've learned a lot about people, materials, and social trends while doing this project—how do I save that knowledge so that my coworkers and I don't have to go to the effort of learning it all again?

Reading this book will teach designers how to answer these questions.

## WHY THIS BOOK?

This book identifies ways to acknowledge the information generated by the design process, as well as how to analyze, apply, and store that data. The insights gathered from the process and products of design strengthen efforts to develop spaces that are informed by relevant knowledge, whether that knowledge is culled from previous projects and research efforts, or from project-specific investigations. This book is about research that enhances design.

When you've completed reading it, you'll see that for as long as you've been designing you've been doing design research. Since designers are continuously generating information on one project that is used by both themselves and others on future projects and also using input beyond their own expertise, they research. Designers deal with complex issues that can be resolved only through the integration of material developed by people with different areas of expertise and through their own professional practice and place experiences. The ability to integrate this information is a hallmark of an effective designer. Both the design process and product are research activities in and of themselves that teach us about our world and ourselves.

In the pages that follow, we present the most effective ways to align research methodology with the design process and maximize the influence of the information garnered during design. The book supports the designer's efforts to effectively access new, relevant information at specific milestones as design progresses.

This book lays out a process that a designer can adapt to his or her practice requirements. It outlines a practical approach that demonstrates, at each project phase, how to integrate a systematic research-based methodology into the basic scope of design service. After reviewing the information that follows, you will make design decisions with the confidence that comes from having greater insight about the context of those choices.

Key to the acquisition of new knowledge is learning how to appropriately analyze and apply the available information. This book includes firsthand accounts—stories of practice—that narrate effective methods, the lessons learned, and the outcomes of a research-based design application. Each story of practice focuses on a research strategy accomplished during a particular project phase. Beginning with project initiation, research is a means to market a project. Project investigation is when research is employed to build a statement of need. In the integration phase, research establishes a project's philosophy of use and refines design thinking. Implementation is when research becomes a means to evaluate and document measures of success.

**FIGURE I.1**
The design process cycles through four main phases: initiation, investigation, integration, and implementation.

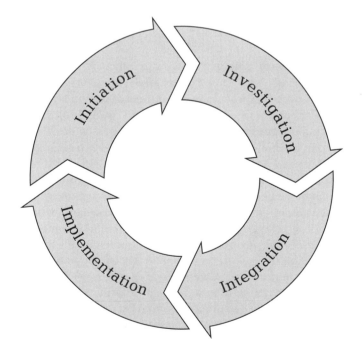

This book is written for all practices and people concerned with the built environment, from architects and interior designers, to facility managers, landscape architects, and urban planners. All of these groups will be referred to collectively as *designers* throughout this book. Students can also use the contents of the book to inform, and guide the development of, their design careers.

The authors have been doing design research for several decades; Cindy Coleman has been practicing in the field of interior design and Sally Augustin has been practicing in the field of applied environmental psychology. We have a good idea of what you need to know to move forward with a design project. We have organized this book so that the chapters focus on the phases that a design project moves through: project initiation, programming, conceptual design, design development, contract documentation, and project completion.

You can use this book in two key ways:

1. It can be read chronologically, either independent of a particular design project or as you work through a project.

2. It is a reference book. Each chapter stands alone and can be referenced as needed over the course of a project.

In the text that follows, we have not specified sources or references for research's standard operating procedures for social science studies discussed to encourage you to do your own research. We do provide references, whenever possible, to unique methodological contributions by design and social science researchers.

## WHY RESEARCH?

Increasingly, a designer or design firm's center of knowledge is a key resource and important source of competitive advantage. This core knowledge generally flows from two primary sources—first, from a designer's previous experiences, education, and intuitive sensibilities. The other source is the new data and research that a designer uses to supplement this initial knowledge base— derived by conducting experiments (both actual and conceptual) generally and acquiring new information to inform a particular design response more specifically. Whatever its source, the value of this knowledge stems from effectively applying it and creating higher levels of understanding for the designer and his or her clients that provoke new ways of thinking and innovation.

Research for design is important. It is a fact: design has the power to affect human behavior, and research can identify the probable influences a space will have. Research (and practice) have shown, for example, that certain environments are better suited to socializing because they promote casual conversation. Sick patients respond more quickly to treatment in environments that reduce stress; lowering stress levels improves the functioning of the immune system. For certain tasks, a quiet and enclosed space heightens a person's ability to concentrate. Classrooms that promote a student's ability to move and release energy while taking in new information increase his or her capacity to learn, particularly for kinesthetic learners or those with ADHD. Broad research findings such as these inevitably need to be supplemented with the answers to project-specific questions to ensure design success.

The power to influence the behavior of the people who use a space or building or to optimize their performance in a place is fundamental to a design's value. Design is valuable when its outcomes can create desired situations and potentially alter the performance of a space's stakeholders. Design is fundamentally about change—change in behavior, attitudes, income, and so on. Good design encourages good changes.

Today, real estate investments must perform well financially. They require a significant outlay of an organization's financial resources, and in return must make an active contribution to an organization's cultural, social, professional, and financial success. Regardless of whether the real estate in question is residential, commercial, academic, medical, or civic, it is someone's strategic asset—and its performance is crucial to this organization's viability. Therefore, the design team's primary obligation is to develop project-specific solutions that assure that clients' strategic assets support their perceived and implied goals. Effective research makes a positive outcome much more likely.

## DESIGN AS RESEARCH

Design is simultaneously a product and a process. Design as a product and design as a process rely on a sophisticated language to communicate—a language that negotiates between ideas that are presented as completed objects, places, and things; ideas systematized as experiences, emotions, and values; and ideas informed by social scientific data and theory.

The information needed for valuable design surrounds us, and is often a byproduct of the design process itself. Designers learn about new cultures within their home country and around the world. While waiting for a meeting to begin at a client office, designers notice that people walking by seem to show one sort of a behavior (culture) or another. With proven research tools, designers can not only quickly access and consider what they've learned through life and previous design work while making design decisions but also probe new areas.

### Good Design Process

For many, the act of designing a place or a thing is in itself a form of research. Design as research acknowledges the similarity between the design process and a research methodology. From problem identification to the application of new information, a good design process, like an effective research methodology, is well informed and employs a range of techniques to derive a project-specific solution. Both require the integration of diverse information streams as expeditiously as possible. Design as research recognizes the important roles that emotion, intuition, and experience play in informing the design response. It establishes a methodology that a designer can use to proactively seek out additional sources of new information through the review of material learned earlier, investigation, experimentation, and establishing meaningful collaborations with specialists inside and outside of the design disciplines.

For practicing designers, ideas are more often presented in objects and places than they are in words and theories. Therefore, when the process of design is approached as a type of research, the process itself becomes an extremely useful analytical tool that informs the form of ideas, objects, and places.

Research, like design, is an evolved process. Both processes are nonlinear; they occur concurrently and simultaneously require multiple frameworks of analysis. For example, design researchers actively gather and interpret new information or begin a process of extracting and analyzing what is already known in the context of user needs, available resources, organizational values, and organizational goals. Although this is where the process often begins, it need not become the limit of design research.

The goal of design research is to enrich what is already known or understood and to actively seek out new information. This enhancement may require a series of well-crafted questionnaires to understand how the different stakeholders or users perceive their independent interests relative to place—something very familiar to the process of design.

To take the research role further, and to supplement the questionnaires, a design researcher might use observation to challenge and understand subjective concepts about space (how a stakeholder perceives he or she uses or should experience space) and objective reality (how a stakeholder actually uses or should experience a place). When a designer inserts data collection and analysis into the design process, it often shifts the working concept of the design firm from preconceived notions and stereotypes toward more clearly defined and explicit concepts—a more effective and knowledgeable base for design decision making.

Design research, as an experimental technique, is a proactive tool that demonstrates the effect of a design strategy while there is still time to refine or modify the design plan. Experiments and mock-ups provide opportunities to evaluate, reiterate, and modify design concepts using the information collected.

For example, during large workplace installations, when an organization is considering the benefits of furniture systems, design firms will frequently undertake an extensive mock-up and evaluation process to uncover which option yields the most efficient and effective response. However, the benefits of this type of experimental design research are often more extensive. A place-based experiment or mock-up can uncover many social, environmental, or physical conditions that may not have been considered without the benefit of the experiment or mock-up.

Research methodologies supported by the design process make it possible to incorporate the expertise of people with a wide range of backgrounds into the solutions suggested. Integrating this knowledge and then giving it a physical form is at the core of effective design. The research process not only provides a vocabulary and syntax for problem identification and solving but also roughly lays out the roles and the goals of different potential participants.

Established methodologies show each of these team players the part they will perform in the design process and can resolve many problem-solving turf battles. These methods provide the basic direction for a research program to which participants can apply the specific training they've received. As client teams have become more diverse, design solutions that reflect a variety of intellectual disciplines are increasingly important and highly valued. Insights from culture and technology experts, psychologists, and sociologists, among others, are also becoming increasingly important as the problem-solving contexts rapidly evolve. Materials experts and suppliers can also be valuable team members.

Different sorts of professionals have different approaches to defining and resolving complex problems. Psychologists, for example, look for answers at an individual or relatively small group level, while sociologists are concerned with much larger groups, and anthropologists regularly focus on cultural issues. Material scientists generally think more about how well a substance behaves mechanically than psychologists, who generally would focus on the emotional response to the color or texture of that material. All of these viewpoints and knowledge bases are important, and many are crucial for project success.

Design researchers aware of the important knowledge bases developed by practices, as well as individuals, store and retrieve this collectively derived information. It is a valuable component of what a designer *knows*. It gains its value when the designer has access to it, can reference it, and can demonstrate its effect. Some firms create databases of benchmarked information to organize what the individual employees generally know, as well as what the organization as a whole has learned; other design researchers maintain intranet sites that store specialized databases on project types, conditions, and goals. Some of the collective practice knowledge is stored outside firms, in published records.

## Benchmarking

Benchmarking, like using design precedents, allows information to be compared across different projects. These comparisons can be stored and accessed within the firm or may be shared with clients and potentially published in professional journals. Benchmarking and comparing pertinent project parameters adds considerable knowledge to a firm.

Benchmarking is a process that continuously quantifies and measures aspects of a project ranging from energy consumption per unit to square foot ratios of staff to overall square footage. The goal of benchmarking is to establish a metric by which projects and processes can be analyzed and comparatively evaluated. When benchmark data are collected (to the extent possible) both before changes are made to the environment and afterward, they become particularly valuable. When several aspects of the physical environment are changed, it is impossible to isolate the influences of a single one on the benchmarked data, but before and after data still provide useful insights to designers.

Design researchers add to the knowledge bases within the firm and external to it by seeking out greater understanding and information. This greater insight may be achieved through the research methodologies described in this book, or from reading, attending conferences and lectures, or seeking out information (which might be more data driven or more anecdotal) from other practices.

Establishing systems to seek additional insight is an active process. It moves the knowledge source beyond what the typical act or process of designing delivers. It reaches beyond a designer's internal source of knowledge to build greater understanding and perception through investigation, reading, learning and exploration—all components of a proactive research methodology that effectively informs design decision making.

Research-derived design knowledge includes the vast amount of information uncovered by answering project-specific questions—for example, when considering the materiality of a project, the acoustical attributes desired in a specific space, codes and compliance, thermal and energy conditions in a building or place, sustainability issues, site conditions, and so on. Individual sets of site-specific information are particularly valuable when integrated with other collections of similar material.

A system that analyzes, retains, and accesses this information for future projects is a key firm asset and plays a critical part in building a designer's (or design firm's) body of knowledge. Librarians have developed effective systems to retain and distribute information that can be used with physical and electronic files and artifacts, and those that are relevant are profiled in Chapter 7.

## Application of the Information

Once you've obtained the information, how do you apply it? Effective analyses ensure that the critical information gained from the research process can be applied constructively and is appropriate for the situation at hand. Here, the data are tools and not simply part of the project history. Designers who conduct research know what sorts of answers they need and when they need them. It is therefore vitally important that designers control the research process as part of the design process. Control isn't enough, though—when designers collect the information themselves, they need to answer outstanding design questions and analyze what's collected. Through this process, they understand what's been learned in a visceral way that immensely enriches design.

The way the collected data are evaluated and measured will also flow out of the research process. Looking for patterns in the frequencies of responses is a valuable way to assess information available from quantitative tools, for example. Looking for consistencies in the responses to qualitative discussion questions posed is also important. Reviewing observation videos for specific project-relevant behaviors transforms a meaningless stream of images to applicable information. Clear-cut statistical analyses can also provide information collected through surveys and simulations with a lucid and usable structure.

Each methodology aligned with the design process lends itself to particular and straightforward analyses, which will be profiled in the pages that follow. Collecting the information you need, and analyzing it with the appropriate tools, dramatically increases the likelihood that you can effectively apply that data.

## KNOWING

Writer, poet, and philosopher Henry David Thoreau quoted Confucius in this familiar saying: "To know that we know what we know, and that we do not know what we do not know, is true knowledge."[1] Thoreau seemed to really understand the "knowledge dilemma" currently facing designers. What designers know, as Thoreau put it, is, in fact, their core competency. It's what gives a designer his or her competitive advantage. Sometimes, this knowledge can be articulated and sometimes it can't, but it is present and valuable, in either case. What a designer doesn't know, however, does not need to stand in the way of success. It gives a designer an opportunity to expand his or her body of knowledge. The stock of things that are not known is always evolving—new information answers existing questions, providing the foundation on which new questions are posed. Data collected are analyzed and used to structure an evolving discussion.

Everyone comes to the proverbial design table knowing "stuff." When designing interior office spaces, most designers know that placing a desk with the worker's back to the doorway might be problematic for that worker because it is distracting not to know who might be approaching from the rear. Most designers understand that living spaces require separation between private and social activity and that a doctor's office requires a reception area that accommodates both the healthy and the sick—without too much contamination of the former by the latter.

Mostly, this knowledge is gathered through life experiences. Education, travel, relationships, and personal/professional experiences all develop the designer's ability to understand how life is lived. We learn about many cultural variations in the use of space through visits to other countries and through conversations with colleagues born into other cultures, for example.

Additionally, designers often draw from their intuitions. A designer might not have personally experienced a condition but still have the intuitive capabilities to predict certain outcomes because of their own professional and personal experiences. Designers generally realize, for example, that people must be able to relax somewhere in their home and that different shopping experiences encourage the purchase of different sorts of products—the big box store is for shoppers looking for bargains or routinely purchased items, whereas the boutique is more appropriate when shoppers want to acquire something unique or special and to have a pleasurable experience.

Learning through experience and intuition can be described as learning by observation—whether that observation is conscious or unconscious.

Philosophers, psychologists, and epistemologists (people who study knowing) spend a lot of time trying to answer questions such as who knows what and how they know what they know. They have learned that when we encounter some new information that we value, we integrate it into our mental networks of similar information. These knowledge networks are stronger, and accessed more confidently, when the information they integrate is consistent (as opposed to inconsistent). When unexpected material becomes available, we work hard to reinterpret or modify it to remove any doubt. Whether we actually call our entire integrated data network to mind at a crucial time depends on a number of things, such as the cues we are encountering in our environment as we are trying to remember things.

Designers are information integrators of the highest order. The focus of their work has always been developing a design response that reflects knowledge that they have before a project begins, project-related information that they collect through a review of previous academic and applied research, and new material that they gather as they move a project toward completion. Often, this integration requires coordinating the thoughts of multiple individuals. Sophisticated syntheses of this information push the boundaries of design forward and assure that it not only remains viable but also respected. It also distinguishes design from more purely artistic and technical fields.

## The Complexity of Knowing

In 1992, Richard Buchanan, then head of design at Carnegie Mellon, described design as a "wicked problem," amplifying the concept originally developed by Rittel in the 1960s.[2] Rittel first defined *wicked problems* as a "class of social system problems which are ill-formulated, where the information is confusing, where there are many clients and decision makers with conflicting values, and where the ramifications in the whole system are thoroughly confusing."[3]

Buchanan uses the nonlinear nature of design practice, among other factors, to classify the act of design as a wicked problem. He explains that a problem-solution phase follows a problem-definition phase, which, in turn, leads to additional problem definitions. Although wicked problems do not have solutions that are easy to define as correct or incorrect, applying a design research methodology gives designers a way to structure and organize the wickedness and develop a framework for the design process that keeps it focused on key issues, clear goals, and a way to evaluate success. All designers have undoubtedly experienced the dilemma of a wicked problem and likely have found that when dealing with a wicked problem, greater information and knowledge brings clarity—and a solution.

A design research methodology also provides a mechanism to deal with the fact that complex problems often do not have clear-cut solutions and that it might even be difficult to determine what issues need to be resolved. A design research methodology supplies a way to effectively weigh alternative options while determining what problem or problems must be addressed.

## Integrating What We Know

People are more confident about knowledge when it is supported by a network of previous experiences or firmly established facts. They are more accepting of new information when it is consistent with information that they have already accepted and when the support for the new information is strong, based on criteria they find important. A statement from a respected professor related to their area of professional expertise contributes more powerfully to a knowledge base than a remark by a colleague without training in the pertinent topic, for example.

The importance of a designer's existing knowledge networks for building new knowledge can't be underestimated. Our minds integrate all of our sources of information—but each of us coordinates that material in our own way. One person values a certain type of supporting argument more than another. Some people treasure information that they derive through direct investigation; others are more amenable to accepting information based on extrapolating findings from other disciplines.

Some knowledge is more tacit (understood without being stated in words—in fact, difficult to express in words) and other knowledge is more explicit (can be stated clearly in words leaving no room for confusion). What's tacit and explicit varies from person to person, due often, but not exclusively, to their professional training. Incorporating all of the tacit and implicit knowledge that should be reflected in design is the opportunity and challenge of design research.

Tacit knowledge is carried in our heads and gut, often without us even being aware we know it. We regularly gain tacit knowledge through exposure to other people, often through face-to-face interaction. Culturally specific issues in design are usually understood tacitly—at least by the cultural group of the ultimate users of a space. Cultural groups exist at organizational and national levels as well as among specific sets of people, who may share a religion, profession, or hobby, as examples.

For example, Middle Easterners designing healthcare facilities in the Middle East tacitly know that patient rooms must be big enough to accommodate the large family groups that will visit patients and that exam rooms must be large because patients rarely venture there without social support. Without special training in cultural sensitivity, even the Middle Eastern designers might not be able to state how they have determined appropriate patient and exam room size. Without education in how to discuss tacit information, it generally remains unstated, not even thought about consciously. To continue with the example, the information on Middle Eastern practices that must be reflected in room sizes is not tacit to North American designers, a culture in which visiting groups can generally be expected to be much smaller and family or friends do not accompany patients into exam rooms. North American designers can create spaces that accommodate larger family groups when knowledge of expected number of people that will be in a space is made explicit, however.

When knowledge is consciously acknowledged and organized, it becomes explicit. When knowledge is made explicit, it is much easier to transfer between people and to discuss in a meaningful way. Although the design process attempts to communicate underlying intentions in an explicit way, it often fails to do so. To the untrained eye, or a nonvisually minded client, it might be difficult to understand or accept all of the knowledge being presented.

Ikujiro Nonaka, a Japanese philosopher and management expert, has developed a widely accepted model that details how knowledge is used and how it can move between tacit and explicit forms.[4] Nonaka's model profiles how tacit information can be shared between individuals—for example, if two people are socializing, one can learn tacit rules through observing the other party's gestures and body language. Tacit information can be made explicit when it is consciously focused on and directly stated, which makes it easier to discuss. Explicit information can be combined with other explicit information to build a stronger and richer base for action and reflection. Explicit information can be internalized, which can make it tacit, although readily convertible back into explicit form.

The process of converting tacit information to explicit information is regularly important, as well as difficult, for designers. Nonaka famously details the process of designing a bread-making machine. Through careful observations of master bakers, the designers of the machine were ultimately able to fully incorporate all of their tacit and explicit knowledge into a machine that consistently creates great bread.

For a designer, the value of research is making the tacit explicit so that it can be shared with others. Gathering, organizing, and sharing the information that supports a design decision gives designers a way to clearly present and discuss important topics. Tacit information is difficult to apply consistently, or give a physical form—explicit information can be clearly stated and is easily accessible to project stakeholders. Deciding what information to "explicit-ize" is an important part of the design research (and problem-solving) process.

Another part of the process of making the tacit explicit is ensuring that design issues are addressed within the correct context. Life is always in context. A common understanding of that context is essential for resolving sophisticated design research issues. Informed project-specific design decisions are just that, project specific, and much of the art of design is correctly evolving what has been learned in another context to that of the current project.

## THINKING AND KNOWING

A Thomson Reuters advertisement trumpets "The end of think. The beginning of know." Everyone in the design business agrees that knowing about users, materials, and processes is a good idea. Designers also agree that research should be conducted effectively and efficiently, with moderate debate about what *effective* and *efficient* mean. Tenets of social science research and design practice can be merged to provide definitions of those terms that are useful to uncover and resolve context-specific, design-related questions.

As Rick Robinson details, design is a process of moving from a current concrete situation to a new concrete reality, with the two concrete phases interrupted by a journey through the abstract.[5] It is insight distilled from research that keeps a project on target toward happy resolution, as opposed to wandering aimlessly through an abstract vision. That research suggests the final physical forms that projects can take, but in no way defines them. Research may reveal that a particular group of employees needs acoustic shielding, from themselves and others while they do their job, but does not detail how it is to be provided. It might indicate that a color of moderate saturation and brightness should be used on the walls of a space, but thousands of colors meet those criteria. The opportunities provided by research are detailed later in this chapter. Design research does not restrict creativity, but focuses it into broad, desirable avenues.

Design research is a process for answering the questions that people creating new objects and spaces must resolve before they can comfortably finalize a design and make decisions. The work process followed by a particular design researcher is illustrated in Figure I.2. It is grounded in the designer's existing knowledge and experience but moves beyond that base to reflect either research conducted specifically for a project or applicable material developed for another project by the same or alternate designers or academic researchers.

All design research takes place in the context of a particular design question—the first design question forms the initial horizontal plane in Figure I.2. As the research process proceeds, the design research question also evolves—the action spiral created as the design researchers moves purposefully through the thought/knowledge quadrants cuts through different planes as time moves on.

Tacit knowledge is unstated and often so fundamental that it is unstatable, while explicit knowledge can be clearly expressed and presented to another person. Analytic thought is characterized by collecting research findings, knowledge, and insights from different projects that the design researcher has worked on or that other designers or academic researchers have done. Project-specific research is also relevant. Analytic thought often involves isolated and siloed material. Synthetic thought is holistic and reflects a nuanced integration of many relevant factors.

All design research begins when the designer refines the design question using his or her tacit knowledge of successful designs of the place-type being developed and the salient attributes of the client group. This review is subconscious and leads the designer to identification of explicit knowledge related to an issue. As the research process continues, information is collected from other appropriate sources, academic or practitioner, and project-specific research can be conducted using the techniques presented in this book. The synthesis or integration of tacit and explicit knowledge is necessary for design researchers to know what questions must be explicitly researched. The integration of explicit knowledge must be rooted in tacit knowledge.

Design researchers move from quadrants 1 to 4 in Figure I.2 in the course of answering any particular research question, and as the initial question evolves into the next, parallel "question-planes" surmount the initial one diagrammed. Each of these research phases is cumulative and completely integrated with those before it. New questions and issues are continuously revealing themselves, but ultimately the designer has enough information that they feel comfortable moving forward, or the time available for research is exhausted. Eventually, design action must be taken with the design resources available. Insights develop as personal professional experience and knowledge of research done by others are critically assessed and integrated.

**FIGURE I.2**
The design researchers'
work process involves
resolving current issues
and identifying new ones.

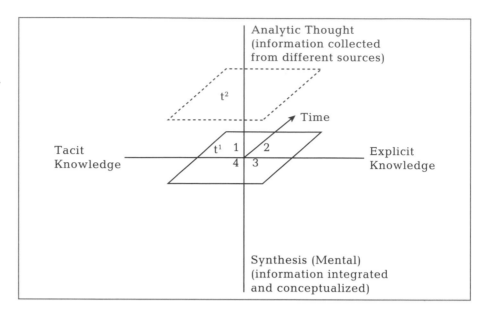

An example: Put yourself in the place of someone designing a multifamily living complex. This multifamily living complex is the broad context of the design problem, when it is moved from the theoretical to the concrete, by introducing some aspect of its marketing plan—for example, that it will serve the needs of Orthodox Jews extremely well. Designers tacitly know that homes need to serve a variety of needs, such as relaxation, eating, and self-development (e.g., children study). Explicitly, they also know a variety of things about home design. In the analytical thought phase, designers use their explicit and tacit knowledge as a base to collect information related to specific aspects of the multifamily home, such as places that facilitate kosher cooking or religion-appropriate socializing. Some data gathering is necessary even if the designer is an Orthodox Jew, because it is not entirely certain that the designer's own experiences are actually representative of the target population at large. After information is collected from available animate and inanimate sources, it must be synthesized. The design research process continues as the issues to be resolved evolve. This synthesized information ultimately finds expression in the physical form of the place created. Appropriately conveying to others all of the nuances of the information learned during the research process is a primary reason why designers must conduct their own research.

Explicit knowledge can derive from multiple sources—perhaps time and resources mandate a straightforward literature review only. Alternatively, interviews and discussion groups with potential purchasers and/or surveys might be possible. Interviews of experts might be appropriate if experts are known and available. Explicit information is integrated with tacit knowledge about fundamental human needs that must be satisfied through a space. Tacit knowledge might have been acquired through past research projects— whether those projects are professional or personal, formalized as research or implicit in the process of living life.

## A SCIENTIFIC METHOD

The process of design answers questions with physical forms. The first design-related dilemma is to identify the audience, stakeholder, or user groups and what experience the space, place, or object should provide to them. Designers resolve this first issue, and all of the subsequent ones that flow from it, by developing a research plan. The resolution of these issues takes the physical form of a building, a space, or an object. By contrast, academic research usually culminates in a verbal product, which may be oral or written. The designer coordinates a conversation that integrates a variety of professionals while resolving multiple issues at differing scales. The scientific process is more similar to an uninterrupted monologue.

Even though there are differences between design research and the classic scientific process, designers can benefit from the processes and ground-work laid by the scientific community. Scientists have, over hundreds of years, developed effective research methodologies that collect information needed quickly and efficiently. Scientists have learned the effect that language has on communicating intent, what sorts of words warp responses to survey questions, how to assess whether people at meetings being observed are working well (for example, if positive and negative situations are occurring in the right ratio), and different strategies to probe the changing nature of how people use spaces and what the differences signify. For designers, this body of knowledge is extremely relevant and offers credible ways to answer questions about how and why a space performs in a particular way. Designers can use this information that scientists have rigorously learned, be it study findings or research tools, to inform design research and decision making.

Often, the built form is evaluated based on its aesthetics and its functionality—attributes that are easy to see and understand. The true value of the built form, however, is the knowledge that informs the design response. That knowledge is less obvious than aesthetics and functionality but is likely more instrumental in creating an outcome that is aligned with the desired goals for the project.

A well-planned research program provides both the system and the framework to inform design. A design-based research plan establishes a valid foundation for design decision making.

## ASKING THE RIGHT QUESTIONS

The design research techniques outlined in the chapters that follow meet the criteria established by scientific researchers, but they are discussed in terms that resonate with the design process. The purpose of these discussions of tools is to introduce you to a systematic approach to informing design decision making. It includes effective processes that enhance the value of design services by encouraging project-specific, well-informed design thinking.

A design research plan assures that all questions—simple, complex, holistic, and technical—can be answered in an efficient way with relevant information that is applicable to the design response.

Effective research questions are based on the context of the project. As an example, at the Seattle Public Library, if the project was intended to encourage diverse generational use, expected research questions in the context of the project are: Who are the different generations of library users? How are they being defined? (For those who access the library for information) Why does each seek out information? How do users wish to access the information? How much time does each generation spend accessing information? At what time (of day, day of the week, etc.) do they access information? How does atmosphere influence each generation's perception of public space? Note that these questions are broadly defined to gather information that will influence the design process. They are not focused on specific design questions such as these: Where should the fiction section go? How much space should be dedicated to shelves versus seating?

When Rem Koolhaas's OMA/LMN set out to design the new Seattle Public Library, the firm established a plan that allowed it to reconsider the social and functional attributes of a public library. Not satisfied with the notion of a library as an institution dedicated to the storage of books, OMA/LMN's design team determined that new digital forms of media made the classical library concept obsolete and altered the paradigm for library design.

According to the 1999 Seattle Public Library proposal by OMA/LMN, the notion that the library relies on one type of literacy (reading of paper-based books and magazines) has prevented the modern library from accomplishing more than repackaging of earlier ideas.

Whether the OMA/LMN designers were familiar with library design or not, the Seattle Public Library project required an extensive knowledge base to answer fundamental questions relevant to the design of the new library (see Figure C.1 in the color insert).

The design team needed to think broadly about the historic influence the library has had on society and to identify the cultural, social, technological, and functional issues of today and tomorrow that alter this historic perception. Some of the questions for consideration included understanding the audience of users, their demographic profiles, and what is unique to each group. How do issues of flexibility, new acquisitions, or shrinking financial resources influence the project? What will attract new populations of library goers while holding on to current users? Beyond books, what other forms of media belong in a library? And, what is the social role of the library?

Although designers are skilled at asking questions, having a well-formed research plan ensures that the questions being asked garner the information that is actually needed for successful design. Good questions collect information that can be applied, and they do not impose on users to provide information that time or tasks prevent the questioner from using.

In a well-formed research plan, researchers organize their knowledge-gathering objectives and write succinct, straightforward questions and goals. They consider their clients as well and review the sorts of information they will need to be comfortable with decisions that have been made—and make sure that it is available and reflected in design proposals. From this organization, selecting information collection methods/tools and implementing effective research plans follow in a logical, systematic way. Structuring good research questions is something we will discuss in subsequent chapters.

# CHAPTER 1

# Design Research and Its Influence on the Practice of Design

AS THE PRACTICE OF DESIGN seeks to find ways to gain relevance in a changing economy, designers and design firms understand the important role design research programs will have in their future.

Today, *design excellence* is synonymous with *design knowledge.* In order to be an effective design leader, designers use vision, knowledge, understanding, and communication. They develop a clearly stated and cogent design discourse based in knowledge.

Building a research expertise can have a powerful effect on design futures. It alters the perceived value of both the products and services provided by designers. A research orientation promotes greater insight into viable practices and methods. From the profession's view, it enhances the body of knowledge that becomes the foundation from which all professionals derive solutions. Its potential is enhanced by associations to other fields of knowledge. By facilitating cross-disciplinary collaboration, the design research approach encourages greater acceptance of design as a political, economic, technological, material, and cultural activity.

Today, it's no longer viable for the discipline of design to rely on preconceived design processes. Issues of globalization, speed, technology, sustainability, and more are transforming how design is practiced. Since LEED certification has focused attention on quantifiable goals, interest in numeric objectives can be expected to increase. Designers are reexamining current design methodology with a goal of creating new processes with greater access to sources of knowledge. Nondesigners have also recognized the ways that *design thinking* can help resolve fundamental economic and social issues.

## GENERALIZING DESIGN THINKING

Designers' focus on holistically resolving complex problems by integrating information from diverse fields provides them with an approach to problem solving that is receiving increasing attention and respect as more and more business, medical, and other professionals see the benefit of applying this approach to the "wicked problems" in their own work processes.

Roger Martin, dean of the Rotman School of Management at the University of Toronto and the author of *The Design of Business: Why Design Thinking Is the Next Competitive Advantage*, feels that the thinking style that designers perfect is key to the success of businesspeople—and that businesspeople must learn to think the way that designers do.[6] He is far from alone in this sentiment. Martin believes that future economic greatness is more likely to flow from thinking about possibilities (or *abductive reasoning*) in ways that integrate new and current knowledge than from proof-based analytical thinking. Designers are masters of abductive reasoning:

> *Abductive logic.…[is] that it is not possible to prove any new thought, concept, or idea in advance: all new ideas can be validated only through the unfolding of future events. To advance knowledge, we must turn away from our standard definitions of proof—and from the false certainty of the past—and instead stare into a mystery to ask what could be. The answer…[will] come through making a 'logical leap of the mind' or an 'inference to the best explanation' to imagine a heuristic for understanding the mystery.[7]*

In the June 2008 issue of the *Harvard Business Review*, Tim Brown discussed using *design thinking* to solve nondesign problems.[8] Brown, CEO of IDEO and author of *Change by Design: How Design Thinking Transforms Organizations and Inspires Innovation*, understands that while design thinking relies on empathic, intuitive, and emotional capacities, it must be balanced with rational and analytical skills to make it truly effective as an integrated thinking strategy.[9] He describes design thinking as the skill that designers possess because of their professional mission to match human needs with technical resources within practical business constraints. IDEO has even developed a complementary guide to design problem solving for leaders of social action groups.

The growing realization that the design-thinking process is valuable has, as Brown describes, much to do with the changing economic climate of the developing world. As the shift from industrial manufacturing to knowledge creation and service takes hold in the world economy, innovation is critical for success. Innovation is no longer relegated to the physical object or place alone. Now, innovation is reflected in new processes, services, experiences, ways of communicating, and working.

Design thinking is an exploratory research process. A systematic approach to design, which centers on a research-based methodology, is self-adjusting, thoughtful, analytical, integrative, and highly valued today.

## DESIGN RESEARCH AS A MEANS FOR ATTRACTION AND RETENTION

When design and research are overtly linked, the practice of design becomes a laboratory of experiences that attracts the most curious and the sharpest minds to the field. Actively incorporating research into the design process provides a range of fresh, exciting design opportunities and energizing collaborations.

Design supported by a research methodology aligned with the design process becomes an active field that can inspire both its own practitioners and the general public. The information generated from research supports both the designer's and the client's needs to understand how a design strategy influences the performance of the object, place, or space. It validates a design recommendation using data, resources, and social scientific concepts.

A design research methodology is also an educational tool to mentor young designers. By establishing systems that help young designers better understand the human condition and/or how a design response may influence a user's experience or perception, for example, design research establishes a mechanism to gain better insight into unique project specific goals.

## DESIGN RESEARCH AS A MEANS FOR SOCIAL REFORM

An effective research program supports design as a force for social good. The global issues of environment, water, energy, and food resources have significant influence on housing, commercial developments, education facilities, and public spaces all over the world. With a design research approach, design questions change from what will the object or space look like to who will use it? How will they use it, and why? How will it be used in five or ten years? Will it support the sponsoring organization's goals for the object or space?

Design as a social *and* spatial practice is experiencing a global revolution and requires an effective research base to feed and further key objectives. Large-scale cultural, social, environmental, and economic issues excite great thinkers and energize meaningful collaborations. Anecdotal evidence indicates that the primary driver for the people currently entering design schools is their ambition to have a positive effect on the world.

## DESIGN RESEARCH AS A RESPONSE TO THE NEED FOR DESIGN SPEED

Design research provides design practitioners with a systematic process and an effective way to have the information they need, when they need it. As a result, the design process becomes less iterative.

Although some design firms believe this is a reason to abandon research, which is perceived as an addition to the already burdened design process, in reality, the opposite is true.

Today, when speed has become a driving force in design and a means of competitive advantage, firms that can commit to a shortened project schedule without compromising the care and knowledge that goes into the design response win.

A systematic and proven research process expedites the practice of identifying and applying needed information. Asking good questions that, when answered, provide needed information, speeds design decision making. Using a process that confirms, but does not assume, the answers to the questions being asked, and knowing how to evaluate and use the data collected, also speed and streamline the design process.

John Maeda, the president of the Rhode Island School of Design, has effectively described the influence that knowledge has on design in *The Laws of Simplicity*. As he succinctly states, "Knowledge makes everything simpler."[10] As Maeda describes, it eliminates focus on unnecessary concerns and spotlights issues that need to be carefully addressed. Far from restricting design options, knowledge keeps the designer on the right sort of general path and ensures that he or she can confidently move forward.

Staying on track leads to a situation that Maeda discusses as the ability to marry function with form to create intuitive experiences that are understood immediately:

> *Good design relies to some extent on the ability to install a sense of instant familiarity.…[T]he most successful product designs, whether simple, complex, rational, illogical, domestic, international, technophilic, or technophobic, are the ones that connect deeply to the greater context of learning and life.*[11]

A design research process establishes this context and identifies ways to simplify and effectively communicate complex issues to expedite the design decision-making process internally and externally.

## DESIGN RESEARCH TO BUILD A SUSTAINABLE KNOWLEDGE BASE

Design research enables designers to become more effective stewards of natural resources, both directly and indirectly. As a profession, design consumes large amounts of both financial and natural resources. Designers have a professional responsibility that extends beyond their clients and services to consider the effect that design processes and products have on society and the environment. This professional responsibility requires that designers be prepared for both the more subjective and more objective demands of sustainable development.

Understanding the systemic issues and lifecycle effects of the built environment is a fundamental responsibility of all designers. The evolving nature of earth-sustaining information requires designers to fuel their design thinking with the most current data. Although demanding, the challenge provides an amazing opportunity for designers and design firms to build internal research agendas to stimulate more informed and responsible design responses.

The design process is inherently a laboratory for sustainable research. By establishing a design research process to access, apply, document, and store the environmental impact of design decisions, designers are able to effectively apply this knowledge in new conditions. This information source becomes part of a designer's core knowledge and a competitive advantage.

## DESIGN RESEARCH TO GAIN UNDERSTANDING OF CULTURAL DISTINCTIONS

Through design research, designers are better able to recognize and respond to demographic, economic, and social changes. As world cultures become more integrated, it assures that spaces psychologically and physically support people of different traditions, values, and experiences. Different cultures perceive and use their environments in different ways, for instance. Through research, designers access information that builds a framework of knowledge and insights to draw from when responding to culture-based challenges.

Design research identifies true cultural differences. Access to demographic, psychological, sociological, and anthropological research studies, along with the knowledge developed through life experiences such as travel, provides the core information required to create environments customized to optimize the experiences of diverse groups of people. This is especially valuable when those diverse groups will use a space concurrently.

For example, designers often develop spaces intended for the simultaneous use of several generations of workers. A body of psychological research (e.g., from the lab of David Meyer at the University of Michigan) shows that members of generation Y and the baby boomers multitask equally well, although intuition might indicate that this is not the case.[12] Although generations multitask similarly, they have differing place-based expectations and respond uniquely to nonverbal cues in their environments. In this situation, having access to grounded research information leads to the design of more effective environments—for all users.

## DESIGN RESEARCH AS A SOURCE OF VALUE

Design research also helps designers qualify and quantify design's value. There is increasing focus in the client world on the return on investments in design, and research provides a way to establish that value.

Design research can support the process of creating a project-specific design agenda that is aligned with an organization's stated and perceived goals. This process can then be used to identify the appropriate performance measures or benchmarks to establish for a project and a framework that allows the design and client team to later assess whether those objectives have been attained.

Integrating pre- and post-occupancy analyses into a design research process is key for validating the design product. The research process and the information obtained through that analysis not only increase the designers' knowledge base with data about outcomes, measures, and performance but also give stakeholders an opportunity to evaluate their investment and the value of the services provided. Publicizing the value to be gained through effective design transforms increased client value into increased firm earnings.

## CORE CONCEPTS

Design generates and applies knowledge, culminating in a contextually appropriate, physical embodiment of those accumulated insights. Accessing, augmenting, and preserving the knowledge underlying design is an important core competency for designers and design firms and is a significant way to competitively differentiate firms.

Designers need information that helps them lead cross-disciplinary teams working to resolve wicked problems. Using their accumulated knowledge of previous design solutions and design research tools, they can tap into important pools of tacit and explicit knowledge. Designers have access to an array of more qualitative or more quantitative research tools, ranging from surveys to interviews to discussion groups to observations (among others) that they can apply to most effectively leverage the information already available and obtain the data that can best inform the design decisions to be made. The insights designers can generate through the research process inform the design of effective spaces—with the definition of effective also flowing from the design and research process.

The support for design decisions that flows from the design research process increases your comfort (as well as your client's) in design recommendations made. Insights generated, however, do not direct or define decisions— instead, they simplify them.

The following chapters will identify the information generated by the design process as research. The chapters will also demonstrate how to analyze, apply, and store information generated through the design process in a way that follows the basic scope of services for most design firms dealing with the built environment. They establish a pragmatic approach to design research that conforms to the basic scope of design services.

## ENDNOTES

1. Henry David Thoreau, "Economy," *Walden; or Life in the Woods* (Boston: Ticknor and Fields, 1854); available online at thoreau.eserver.org/walden1a.html.

2. Richard Buchanan, "Wicked Problems in Design Thinking," *Design Issues,* vol. 8, no. 2 (1992), pp. 5–21.

3. C. Churchman, "Wicked Problems," *Management Science*, vol. 4, no. 14 (1970), pp. B-141–142.

4. Ikujiro Nonaka and Noboru Konno, "The Concept of 'Ba:' Building Foundation for Knowledge Creation," *California Management Review*, vol. 40, no. 3 (1998), pp. 40–54.

5. Rick Robinson. Plenary Address. Design Research Conference, Illinois Institute of Technology, Chicago, May 11, 2010.

6. Roger Martin, *The Design of Business: Why Design Thinking Is the Next Competitive Advantage* (Boston: Harvard Business School Press, 2009).

7. Ibid.

8. Tim Brown, "Design Thinking," *Harvard Business Review,* vol. 86 (2008), pp. 84–92.

9. Tim Brown, *Change by Design: How Design Thinking Transforms Organizations and Inspires Innovation* (New York: Harper Collins, 2009).

10. John Maeda, *The Laws of Simplicity* (Cambridge, MA: MIT Press, 2006).

11. Ibid.

12. Claudia Wallis, "genM: The Multitasking Generation." Time, March 27, 2006, www.time.com/time/magazine/article/0,9171,1174696,00.html.

# A Story of Practice: Making the Implicit Explicit

*Information contributed through interview by: Perkins + Will, Chicago, Illinois*

**Context**
Joseph T. Connell, Principal

Project [Name Withheld] Corporate Office Facilities for a Distribution Company

Scope: Programming and planning requirements for a new multi-storey 500 employee corporate facility

Date: 2005–2007

Square Footage: 120,000 square feet

Location: Midwest, USA

## PROBLEM DEFINITION

In 2005 when Joe Connell, principal of the Chicago-based The Environments Group (now a principal of Perkins + Will, Chicago) was hired by a Midwest distributor to design a new workplace facility, it appeared to be business as usual. The client was looking to build a replacement corporate office facility adjacent to their current distribution center and hired Connell's team to conduct programming through design development services as a way to create an "inside-out" analysis of the new building's footprint.

Early into the programming phase of the project, the client asked a simple question that turned into a game-changer. "How can you know what we really do here without spending time to do it with us?" That question, and the rest of the question "How do we know your suggestions are right?" caused Connell and his design team to rethink the programming through design development processes. Personal opinion and implicit knowledge from having spent 25 years in workplace strategy wasn't going to be sufficient. The project required the design team to retool and learn how to expose its process to explicitly demonstrate and prove what informs each design recommendation.

## OBJECTIVES

It should be noted that this project never moved beyond the schematic design phase because of an economic downturn that put the company's new building plan on hold. Connell's team at Perkins + Will is continuing to work with this client, applying some of the research and recommendations to its existing facility.

The objective of this case study is to present Connell's project process. Although the project included a broader scope of responsibility, this case will focus specifically on the workplace portion of the client's building analysis and how this team was able to take the implied knowledge that is the basis for much of workplace design strategy and expose it to become an instrument for developing, presenting, and evaluating design recommendations.

## PROGRAMMING AND OBSERVATION

Beyond a typical workplace programming process where the team received headcounts and questioned key personnel about workplace needs and wants, the design team also conducted a multiple-week study, sitting alongside or shadowing approximately 36 different job types for a one- or two-hour duration to physically observe or participate in different aspects of the organization's work processes. This observation and participation moved through the entire organizational structure from senior management to warehouse operations. Moving from one department to another, Connell and his team set out to examine behavioral issues, environmental factors, and ergonomic conditions in an effort to know the unique conditions and skill sets of each department.

"Our team observed important processes that weren't expressed in the original programming exercises," explains Connell. One example is that the catalog copywriters place each catalog item on his or her desk while writing copy (to accurately describe the product's operation as well as its physical appearance). "This was an insight that was missed when interviewing the copywriting team," notes Connell. No one stated that object placement was integral to the process during the programming interviews, yet all the copywriters work precisely the same way, and it is critical to their process.

The design team uncovered similar discoveries throughout the organization. The safety team's description of work processes was very thin compared to the information that came from observation. Experiencing the speed and weight of the fork truck and the products that move through the warehouse floor was a useful discovery. This experience informed the team's understanding about the need to limit visual distraction in the warehouse facility, maintain clear circulation zones, and look at ways of instilling greater sensitivity to the issue of safety for these multitasking warehouse workers.

Because the organization has high employee retention, there is greater generational diversity within the workplace. "Unlike many other corporations who have a young workforce, this organization has as many employees near retirement as they do new hires," says Connell. This diversity results in more extreme ergonomic considerations—well beyond universal design standards— to provide suitable space for employees who are very overweight, some with missing limbs and in wheelchairs, or blind. "Again, if we just looked at head-counts from the programming phase, we would have missed this observation," he adds.

The information also guided the team's discovery into how the work-stations can better support individual work processes, as well as considerations in issues of safety, lighting, thermal comfort, and access to daylighting—all things, Connell acknowledges, that designers think about but seldom get the time or opportunity to delve into in this level of detail.

However, more than anything, explains Connell, the participatory process gave his team insight into the organization's culture that would have normally gone unrecognized. For example, notes Connell, the people working throughout the entire organization are highly educated, intensely curious, non–status–minded, and amazing problem solvers. Even a forklift operator holds a PhD. "We totally missed this insight when we interviewed the employees," adds Connell, explaining that the organization has a culture of doing things better, continually improving processes, and being truly empathetic to fellow workers and customers. "Mostly," he says, "the organization's culture is about adding value everywhere—from thinking about how to shave a fraction of a second from an assembly process to the sense of pride that goes into packaging items for distribution and the way product is presented to the customer."

## ADJACENCY AND STACKING

At the conclusion of the programming and observation phase of the project, the design team applied these new insights to departmental adjacency and stacking concepts. This second phase advanced the ideal core-to-perimeter-glass dimensions for the new building. In addition, the team assessed how to best site the building as a way to optimize the facility's access to daylight and developed a three-dimensional massing diagram for the building.

From there, the team began more detailed investigations. It developed a strategy of zoning the perimeter for circulation. By employing this strategy, the design team was confident it could simultaneously address daylight penetration and obtain better thermal comfort in the interior environment, as well as reduce computer glare.

In presenting these more detailed recommendations to the client, the team hit the second roadblock. It's here that the client asked: "How do we know your solutions are right?" Connell said, "We realized the planning strategies we were recommending were common practice in the design world, but for the client, they lacked the benefit of knowing what was behind these proposals."

## INSTINCTS ARE GOOD, EVIDENCE IS BETTER

In a relatively short period of time, Connell's team came back to the client with a process for moving forward. The team adopted a working model that broke the knowledge sources—the-what-they-know—into digestible bites. They delivered the information and/or research on one day following up one week later with a workshop to demonstrate how the collective information is transformed into design recommendations. The team filtered the information through three factors: the effectiveness of the use of space, the effectiveness of the dollars, and the effectiveness of the employee experience/organizational performance.

"If it didn't meet the three-part criteria," says Connell, "The idea was dismissed." As an example, Connell recalls how multiple consultants presented the idea of a green roof to the client. First, it was presented as a means to mediate rainwater on the site and later as a way to introduce native plant materials to the location. Although the client agreed that a green roof had advantages, they weren't sold on it for their own facility. Finally, when the collective consulting teams pooled their knowledge sources and demonstrated how a green roof could accomplish the first two measures but also lower energy costs, improve the longevity of the roof structure, and instill a positive sustainable corporate culture, the client was able to then fully realize the value of the investment.


## PLANNING FOR THE EMPLOYEE EXPERIENCE

With the basic massing of the building described, Connell's team began the process of introducing this same three-part strategy for the interior workplace environment. As an organization strategy for all of the information and research, his team established the following list of questions to drive the project's development.

What makes people effective at work?

What prevents people from being effective at work?

What makes people satisfied with their work?

What makes people satisfied with their workplace?

What is the distinction/correlation between employee productivity, effectiveness, and satisfaction in office work?

What features and qualities of the work environment may lead to people being more effective and satisfied with their workplace?

## SOURCES OF KNOWLEDGE

To demonstrate the scope of influence and knowledge that goes into his design team's inquiry surrounding workplace design, the team aggregated each member's source(s) of knowledge—where the individual members of the team go to get smart about the subject of workplace design. The list of sources ranged from environmental behavior research, organizational development, industrial psychology, human resources, facility management, from precedent studies of successful architecture and design projects and research emanating from the medical community and neurosciences.

From this cataloging, the design team's research identified three clusters or groups of factors that influence job satisfaction: (1) management practices, (2) environmental satisfaction, and (3) pay/benefit satisfaction.[1]

Since management practices and pay/benefits are beyond the role and capacity of a build out, the scope of the Perkins + Will assignment focused on environmental satisfaction.

## ENVIRONMENTAL SATISFACTION

The Perkins + Will team presented its amassed research, knowledge, and professional expertise relative to environmental satisfaction. It drilled down into the role that lighting and HVAC and acoustics play in environmental satisfaction. From there, the information turned more finite. The team presented qualitative and quantitative research regarding how thermal comfort (being neither too cold nor, too hot) impacted employee satisfaction. For acoustics, the team identified that satisfaction required distraction reduction, specifically in open workstation areas where telephone calls, team meetings, and impromptu conversations often disturb fellow workers.

Research also supported the adoption of a lighting strategy that matches the work process versus a universal or standardized layout that is generally considered more efficient. The team demonstrated how different functions require lighting strategies that support the different requirements of computer and paper-based work activities.

As the team drilled further into the subject of satisfaction, it identified the knowledge sources that explore other qualities of a workplace that rank high on employee preferences. These qualities include the ability to reduce distraction, spaces that support impromptu interactions, and spaces that promote meetings and group work.

## PROGRESSIVE SCALE OF SPACES

Using this research, Connell's team adapted a working model that addressed the research and recommendations through a progressive scale of spaces. Connell presented the notion of a hierarchy of space— space that ranges from individual space good for solitary work to team and conference spaces, large and small, to satisfy a variety of activities, collaborative or otherwise (see Figure 1.1).

The Perkins + Will's team maintained this progression of space as a consistent format when presenting information to the client. The research, knowledge, and recommendations advanced in the same way, from individual work to team, departmental zones, and circulation. This, in turn, informed the layout and interior massing of the floor plate, and it further defined the massing of the building and its position on the site.

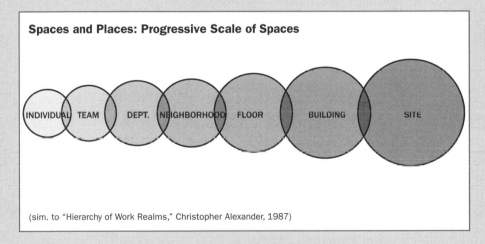

**Spaces and Places: Progressive Scale of Spaces**

INDIVIDUAL | TEAM | DEPT. | NEIGHBORHOOD | FLOOR | BUILDING | SITE

(sim. to "Hierarchy of Work Realms," Christopher Alexander, 1987)

**FIGURE 1.1**
Spaces and Places: Progressive scale of spaces.

## WHERE AND HOW INDIVIDUALS WORK

The earlier programming analysis Connell's team performed on behalf of the client set up the next step of the process. From the analysis of the programming and observation information, the team created a series of diagrams that clustered the client's specific departmental functions and work styles to establish the conditions that distinguish requirements for when spaces should promote concentration, collaboration, training, and leadership (see Figure 1.2).

FIGURE 1.2
Adapted from Christopher
Alexander's "Hierarch
of Work Realms," the
Perkins + Will team
maintained a progression
of space as a consistent
format when presenting
information to the client.

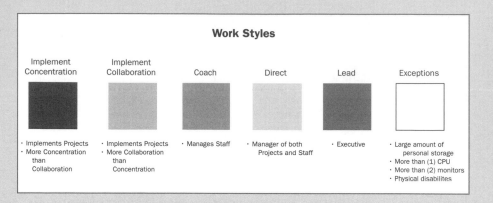

Connell and his team modeled this work style framework over the client's organizational chart, enabling them to visualize the framework's application in each individual department (see Figure 1.3).

FIGURE 1.3
The work style framework
is modeled over the orga-
nizational chart, enabling
the client to visualize
the framework in each
department.

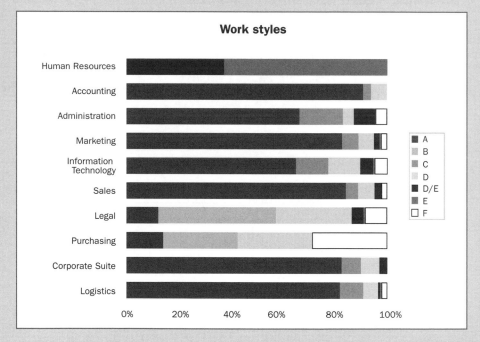

## PROXIMITY AND ADJACENCY

As a next step, the design team presented the research and knowledge that informs modes of workplace communication, specifically how it relates to proximity and adjacency within the organization. "We were able to find research that established the distances office workers are most likely to travel to speak to fellow office workers," explains Connell.

From a MIT study, the team documented how communication reached its lowest point after the first 75 to 90 feet of travel distance.[2] Another Cornell study indicated that researchers and engineers from different departments, but located on the same floor, were six times more likely to work together on projects than employees who were on different floors or in different buildings.[3] Armed with these insights, Connell's team adapted what it refers to as a "field of action," workplace neighborhoods that are zoned to accommodate distances that promote communication and collaboration.[4]

"Equipped with this research, we were able to demonstrate to the client through drawings and simulations the different attributes associated to where and how individuals work and work together," explains Connell. By clustering these groups together in zones of a predetermined size, the team was able to bring together employee workspaces, open meeting spaces, meeting rooms, and accommodation for shared tools and technology, storage and supplies. Special areas were provided for access to a higher degree of privacy, when needed. Like a good urban neighborhood, these workplace neighborhoods were each self-sufficient and were designed to promote a variety of activities and work styles.

## CIRCULATION AND THE FIELD OF ACTION

The "field of action," or "neighborhood" was then further defined by the circulation strategy. The team conducted time studies to see how far the average office worker walks in five seconds (22 feet) to one minute (264 feet). This information informed Connell's strategy for the placement of circulation routes and the width for each:

- Primary, 6 to 8 feet
- Secondary, 5 to 6 feet
- Tertiary, 4 to 5 feet

Understanding the site conditions and position of the sun over the course of the day, the team revisited earlier research presented to the client regarding thermal comfort, daylight harvesting, and ergonomics of computer-based work. Here, the Perkins + Will team diagramed how the collective research and knowledge instructs the perimeter circulation strategy evaluating it and the entire planning strategy on the three-part system of behavior, effectiveness, and economics (see Figure 1.4).

**FIGURE 1.4**
Diagram illustrating how
the collective research
informs the perimeter
circulation strategy.

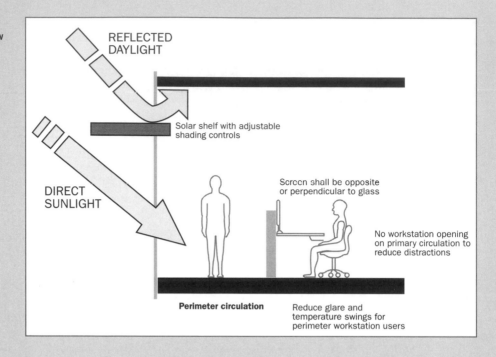

REFLECTED
DAYLIGHT

Solar shelf with adjustable
shading controls

DIRECT
SUNLIGHT

Screen shall be opposite
or perpendicular to glass

No workstation opening
on primary circulation to
reduce distractions

**Perimeter circulation**

Reduce glare and
temperature swings for
perimeter workstation users

## CONCLUSION

"This was an atypical process," admits Connell. "Explicating our process
wasn't part of our scope of services. But, it became apparent early in the project that the client was unable to make or manage any recommendations based
on say-so, alone. Therefore, we had to find ways to take our implicit knowledge
and make it explicit," he adds.

Since the new building project was put on indefinite hold, many of the
large planning concepts went on hold, too. The client team, however, has
retained Connell and the Perkins + Will design team to address many of the
workplace concepts presented in the original scope of work into its current
facility. "The value of the recommendations, when presented as valid sources
of knowledge, is difficult to ignore," notes Connell. "Once they saw the influence these recommendations had on things they valued—effectiveness of their
employees and their organizational performance—they were committed to
implementing the proposals."

## LESSONS LEARNED

"Fundamentally, our clients want to know our recommendations are right. They want to believe us," says Connell, noting that credibility is easier to achieve with third-party validation. "As designers, we skip over a lot of the meaningful learning and principles because it's so obvious to us," adds Connell. But, he notes, these principles are unknown to others, and designers gain reliability by making it overt to their clients.

1. Adapted from Guy Newsham, Research Matters: Individual Control Benefits People and Employers, the National Research Council (NRC), 2007.

2. Thomas J. Allen, *Managing the Flow of Technology*, chapters 4–8 (Cambridge, MA: MIT Press, 1997) (reprinted 1993).

3. F. Becker, Quinn, Rappaport & Sims, *Implementing Innovative Workplaces*, Cornell IWSP, 1994.

4. Fischer Gustave-Nicolas, *Individuals and Environment: A Psychosocial Approach to Workspace,* (Metz, France: University of Metz, 1997), p. 51.

# CHAPTER 2

# Researching: Context, Process, General Concepts

THIS CHAPTER INTRODUCES the practical framework you need to fully utilize information generated throughout the design process. First, it establishes the economic and psychological context in which design decisions are made, then it discusses important elements of the design research process itself and general design research concepts.

## ECONOMIC CONTEXT OF DESIGN AND RESEARCH

Economics is all about choices—choices on how to use available money, time, manpower, and goodwill, based on current circumstances. Different people value different things to different degrees, and thus even individuals and corporations with the same amount of resources, in absolute terms, can have different portfolios of possessions (tangible and intangible).

On the occasions when people have some resources that they're interested in exchanging for different ones, markets develop. Exchanges are made when valuations match—two people or organizations with different things (tangible and intangible) think that an exchange is equitable, and so it happens. And it happens in what economists call a *market*. Markets have traditionally been viewed as intensely rational, but we'll talk more about that later.

Generally, when people talk about markets they are thinking of physical goods and money, but people are even more motivated by intangibles than tangible things. People pay huge amounts of money in excess of the concrete value of physical materials for objects every day.

One of the intangibles in hottest supply is *prestige.* Often, prestige is delineated with a distinctive appearance, the form of which can change over time. The raw ingredients in many make-up products are identical, but some become prestige brands because of the way they are marketed and sold, which creates an allure of value, while other, identical formulas languish as commodity products.

Perceived risk and perceived value are both represented in the exchange price for a perceived good or service. The repetition of the word *perceived* here is not a typo. Exchange value really is based much more closely on what's in people's minds than what can be "objectively" determined. Any rules used to establish an objective value are rooted in value judgments and decisions that have multiple possible generally acceptable outcomes.

Design can be used to establish the value of various goods. Responses to different design options are apparent in the marketplace. Design can affect criteria that are relatively easy to assess, such as functionality, but design also influences criteria that are highly variable from person to person, such as aesthetics. Virginia Postrel maintains that our society is becoming more attuned to design, and that its influence on economic decisions increases as our more basic, survival-level needs are satisfied.[1] Design in each time and place has the ability to make people feel comfortable in a way that is entirely separate from function.

## Design in Economic Context

Design thinking, which is separate from design itself, is capturing the attention of business, and other, pundits and practitioners. Older economic systems are evolving, trying to adapt to current conditions.. The rise of both wicked problems in fields outside design and societywide adoption of traditional design thinking to resolve them was profiled in the introduction to this book.

All design decisions take place in an economic context that provides funds for potential activities or withholds them. The stock market and the banking system are more direct sources of financing for projects. The central banking system influences interest rates and the availability of money to be loaned. The stock market also indirectly influences the availability of money for design projects by influencing investor mood in general—more optimistic investors generally write larger checks.

Government policy also affects design decisions. Real estate taxes and property and furnishing depreciation schedules can influence the flow of funds into a project, because they determine the profits and losses that a project will ultimately incur. Many people attribute the rise of cubicles in the U.S. workplace, at least in part, to the fact that they can be depreciated at a faster rate than the solid-walled offices that they replaced (see Figure C.2 in the color insert). Faster depreciation means that more of the costs of the cubicles can be applied against earnings sooner after purchase, which decreases taxes due. On the one hand, some tax policies encourage particular activities (e.g., investing in solar energy); on the other hand, some laws discourage particular activities (e.g., using fixtures that require incandescent light bulbs).

Values are exchanged in markets, and markets exist because exchange is possible. The standardized technical language of finance and underlying rules of evaluation and recordkeeping facilitate these exchanges. These terms make comparison across situations possible. One of the most straightforward ways to think about value is in terms of *opportunity cost.*

Opportunity cost is the alternate use to which a set of resources could be applied if it was not put to its current one. For example, at least in the old days, 50 cents could be used to buy a Snickers bar, a ride on the bus, or a magazine. You can only spend the same 50 cents once, so everything that you didn't buy is the opportunity cost of what you did. When people think about the trade-offs they face as they make all sorts of design decisions, they are thinking about opportunity costs. When you start to think about how the value of goods changes through the passage of time, opportunity cost becomes a real factor in evaluating net present value (NPV) and return on investment. Net present value is a future value converted to current dollars. How much payback do I need to receive from an investment to make it a better alternative than putting that money in another investment? In accounting terms, the 50 cents just mentioned, and money in general in its various forms, can be described as capital, and the opportunity cost of that capital is used to do capital budgeting.

Evaluating all of the potential good uses of the capital available at the start of a project, and then comparing their expected future values if invested, culminates in important financial decisions that are influenced by all sorts of money flows that are difficult to calculate in advance of when they are realized. These include flows of rental income, store sales volumes, and building operating costs. Often, these economic decisions are radically influenced by how costs are allocated between projects or between tenants in a project. This makes cost accounting a key determinant of business behavior.

## Value

Values are rarely rationally assigned. Dan Ariely, a professor at Duke University, is a leading expert on just how irrational we can be with those valuations. He is a pioneer in the field of behavioral economics. In *Predictably Irrational,* he details some of the hidden influences on our decisions.[2] For example, when we make decisions and assess the attributes of various options, we focus on attributes that are easy to compare and avoid those that are more difficult to compare. Humans also learn a certain set of prices for particular objects and come to consider those prices appropriate in the future, even in dramatically different markets. For example, Ariely notes the way people become used to housing prices in their home city and use those prices as the standard of comparison to determine appropriate pricing when they move to a new city (see Figure C.3 in the color insert). This is true even if the pricing structure is very different in that new city. After time in the new city, people who move there will adjust their comparison point. It is easier to make adjustments when a new experience seems dramatically different from the original one. In general, however, memories of initial choices affect the likelihood of future choices and distort the influences of supply and demand on decisions made.

Ariely's text also explains that our emotional state has a profound influence on our decision making, and if we're not in a particular state, it's hard for us to anticipate the choices that we'll make once we arrive there. He says that expectations also play an important role in our choices—and expectations can be shaped by prices, with higher-priced items appearing to have higher value/be more effective than identical items that have lower prices.

Ariely sums up *behavioral economics* as follows:

> *Behavioral economists...believe that people are susceptible to irrelevant influences from their immediate environment (which we call context effects), irrelevant emotions, shortsightedness, and other forms of irrationality...If I were to distill one main lesson from the research described in this book, it is that we are pawns in a game whose forces we largely fail to comprehend. We usually think of ourselves as sitting in the driver's seat, with ultimate control over the decisions we make and the direction our life takes; but alas, this perception has more to do with our desires—with how we want to view ourselves—than with reality.[3]*

## Choice

In *The Art of Choosing*, Sheena Iyendar details how our actions are sometimes inconsistent with what might be considered totally rational behavior.[4] For example, people have a great need to believe that they are in control of what happens to them, and will act accordingly. People like to have the ability to choose—but too much choice is debilitating. When people see 4 to 6 options, they are more likely to make a choice and feel good about that choice than when they see 20 to 30 options. Choice behaviors are also rooted in national cultures—for instance, how individualistic or collectivistic a group is, according to *The Art of Choosing*. We also make choices that we think are consistent with our self-identity.

The work of Maslow and Reiss, discussed in Chapter 3, provides additional useful insights into the reasons that people make choices, particularly architectural ones. Maslow's classic hierarchy of needs has recently been reviewed by scientists, who find support for it.[5] Reiss's outline of human needs is similarly linked to recent rigorous psychological research.[6]

## DESIGN PROCESS

Designers and design firms each have a unique way of approaching the design process. The *design process* has many elements, ranging from scale of work to the specific focus of the work. The design process is the series of actions that culminates in the delivery of a solution to a design issue. Additionally, a designer's point of view, personality, and style can influence how one practice differs from another. What is common among the different styles and methods is the scope of services and the deliverables required in most design engagements.

## RESEARCH PROCESS

The purpose of research is to effectively and efficiently provide the information needed to support the design process. The flow of the research process is influenced not only by the research questions that you are answering but also by the audience for your research, particularly their expectations and knowledge base.

Design research plans evolve from a process of *problem identification*:

- What knowledge is essential for you and your colleagues to effectively design a particular space or object?

- What information is required for your clients to feel comfortable with design decisions made?

- What sort of information do you have that you can apply now?

- Can you be confident in the material that you have?

- What criteria will be used to judge the success of the project?

Identifying the questions to be answered requires careful thought and clear priorities. Generally, knowing the reason that your client is thinking about undertaking a design project and the criteria that will be used to judge its success will give you a good place to start to determine the research questions to be addressed. If success of the MRI suite is defined as giving smaller doses of sedatives to patients, for example, you know that relaxing patients is of utmost importance, and you can investigate environmental modifications that will support just that. Similarly, if success will be determined by a lower turnover rate among caregivers working in the MRI suite, then reasons that staff members are leaving, as well as environmental modifications that have the potential to increase staff retention, are important. Projects often have several goals and research resources are often limited, so a prioritized list of learning objectives is very useful. Priorities should be established based on the anticipated ability for a design decision to increase the value of a firm or organization. If the research and development team at an organization has the most potential to increase its value (as defined by the client firm itself), then design interventions to that group are paramount.

Research can answer only a limited number of questions based on the human, financial, and scheduling resources available. The questions may be answered with many sorts of research tools—from surveys to observation to experience sampling to use of a simulated environment.

As you begin to identify research questions, it is important to keep in mind that it is possible not to know everything about the situation in which a design will be implemented and be successful at your job—indeed it is impossible to know about all aspects of every context. You do need to know enough to move forward and solve the outstanding issues that relate to the reason that your firm was contacted—and it is also true that these are generally broader than the client states in your early meetings. To clarify: when designing a workplace it is good to know something about how employees are compensated in a general sense, because that lets you know how much individual and group work are really valued. However, it is not important to know the fine details of the bonus structure for each type of employee. Be realistic and prioritize your information-collection objectives so that they align with the importance of the design questions that they can resolve.

Practical experience builds an important knowledge base—but recognize the limits of drawing conclusions based on your own experience and applying them to a particular project. How similar are the contexts in which you have worked before to the one in which the information will be applied? Also, was it possible to objectively measure how well a previous design solution worked, to know if it should be replicated in a new situation? Realize that even if there is a way to accurately gauge the success of a previous design solution, it is extremely unlikely that the conditions for the new project will be identical to the ones for which those measurements were made.

If you have ever had a journalism class or written for a school newspaper, you are familiar with the five Ws (plus an H) that need to be answered as the design process progresses:

- Who?

- What?

- Where?

- When?

- Why?

- How?

These are fundamental questions that must be resolved as part of creating a design program for a space. For different projects, these major questions will splinter into different subquestions. Sometimes one line of inquiry will be more crucial to the design process than another. In any case, your research question must be clearly and tightly defined—for example, it must relate to preschools rather than all educational facilities if you are designing a preschool—and even then, you should focus on cultures and other similar factors that are clearly related to the project at hand.

To illustrate: When designing an MRI facility, you might want to gather all sorts of information about why patients are being tested or why caregivers have chosen to work with this particular technology. The answers to these questions have important implications for the physical and psychological experiences to be created in a space. If people are often given MRIs because of sports injuries, designers will need to make sure that the patients can move easily to the machine, even with a sprained ankle. If the patients are being treated for cancer, access is still key, but absence of potentially nauseating sensory experiences also becomes very important. If caregivers believe that working in an MRI suite is challenging and they relish challenges, the aesthetics of the MRI control room should meet these expectations by communicating a no-nonsense orientation. In addition, while designing that suite, you need to consider patient mood and how the room might best create an appropriate environment under a wide range of testing situations In short, how can place design make the MRI process efficient, effective, and comfortable for the patient?

With the MRI suite example, caregivers' and patients' needs require the most investigation. Established medical practices and procedures specify the safety standards and technical requirements of the suite, but not the experiential and emotional aspects of visiting it as a patient or working there. Questions related to the functionality of the MRI suite are more straightforward. That might not be the case for other designs. For example, questions about libraries activities must take into consideration that five years they might be very different. Library use in 5 years was pertinent to the design of the Seattle Public Library, discussed in the introduction to this book. Clearly, different sorts of questions are important in varying contexts.

After you identify the fundamental questions to be addressed with the research plan, a realistic review of the human, financial, and scheduling resources that are available to answer those questions must be completed. Carefully and thoughtfully consider the resource requirements of various research tools, as described in the pages that follow.

## "GOOD" RESEARCH

Research leads to knowledge and insights, which are important sources of competitive advantage. Your insights differentiate you from your competitors and establish the value of the design services that you provide.

No matter how you are defining research, it is always possible to categorize it as "good" or "not-so-good." *Good research* answers the questions it has chosen to investigate. It is appropriate to the situation. If the design goal is to create a space that supports an organizational culture, that organizational culture must be identified using credible techniques. Even good techniques can be flawed if used incorrectly:

- Time utilization studies and behavior mapping uncover where people are, but not why they're there or if the place they're in is working for them or against them.

- Confidential survey questions, answered by well-meaning respondents, will give you an idea of what people think they do, but people regularly do not remember their own actions accurately. For example, if you want to learn how people respond to particular colors, study participants must see those colors and experience them in context; it's not enough to just describe them with words.

- It is great when people volunteer to participate in a research project, but collecting information from too many volunteers is also a red flag that something may be amiss. Volunteers sometimes have a hidden agenda (e.g., they want to prove their employer is abusive) that they will pursue relentlessly throughout the research process (e.g., perhaps sacrificing truthful responses to particular survey questions).

- People analyzing the behaviors of groups from another culture need to acknowledge their own cultural biases. Our individual knowledge and prior experiences influence our subsequent thoughts and actions, even about how others perceive the design.

When research is done well, researchers identify any personal factors (theirs or clients') that might have affected the approach that they took to developing the research plan or that might have influenced their analysis of the data.

The most successful design research studies people who are most like those who will ultimately use a space. Clearly, using college freshmen to determine how professionals will respond to a new workspace requires several leaps of faith. Likewise, mothers giving birth/caregivers/friends and family all react differently to a birthing suite—and all those reactions are different from those of the single male architect designing the space. Extrapolating from the experiences of North Americans in a particular sort of healthcare environment to those of Middle Easterners in the same sort of environment is not prudent, as discussed earlier.

In a good research report, all of the details of the research and analysis tools are presented in clear, straightforward prose and diagrams. This makes the research process transparent to observers. A good report also discusses sources of information and appropriate design implications. This means that the research work that is the foundation for the current project is documented, and ways that the collected information can be applied in the future are enumerated.

Insights that add value and stand the test of time are based on "good" information. Good information comes from investigations that are, in science-speak, reliable and valid. Reliability and validity are related to the way that the investigations are done and not the specific research tools applied. No matter what the methodology, the reliability and validity of a study can be determined.

Good information is drawn from valid studies. That means the tools and analysis methods used are appropriate for the questions being asked. Researchers define all different sorts of validity, but the core idea is the same for each type—people are learning about what they think they're studying in sound studies—a questionnaire probing organizational culture really is finding out about organizational culture, for example.

Several specific types of validity will be particularly important to you as you read and conduct research: If a study involves observations in a real world location, it has ecological validity—the situation investigated is so close to everyday life so that you can be comfortable applying the information leaned. The number of odd bits of data introduced into peoples' responses by tests in a laboratory, for example, would be minimal in this case. Internal validity describes the logical consistency of the reasoning within a study (is a finding logically consistent with the sort of people who participated in the study, the ways that data were collected, etc.), while external validity is the extent to which study findings can reasonably be applied in the real world. They are generalizable. Content validity is the extent to which a study thoroughly addresses the issues in question.

It is also important to consider:

- Changes in instruments/methodologies can influence results. If researchers compare two sets of responses to a questionnaire, the survey questions need to be identical, for example, or any differences seen might be attributable to differences in the questions asked.

- Selection related issues may affect study outcomes. If researchers compare answers/responses of two sets of people, those people need to be identical on relevant criteria (e.g., national culture but not hair color)—results can also be distorted if members of one group were more likely to quit a study early or not comply with the conditions of the study. Study participants should also be randomly assigned to different test conditions whenever possible, so that the assignment process isn't responsible for differences seen. In design research this would mean assigning different sets of work teams to different sorts of test environments by drawing their names out of a hat, not having all accounting groups work in one sort of space for a period of time, all marketing teams in another, etc. If it will be possible to customize work areas for groups doing different sorts of work, the level at which randomization must occur moves down a notch, to types of accounting and marketing teams.

- Sometimes the Hawthorne effect is present and changes in participant behaviors are found because they were involved in a study, this is difficult to determine from the research reports of others but you may be able to spot it in your own work

- Subjects behaving in ways the experimenter wants them to behave are another way that information collected may be corrupted.

- Subjects may be concerned about being evaluated, so they respond in a "desirable" way. In this situation the importance of anonymity (versus confidentiality) of data collected come to the fore.

- Changes in the pre- and post-test or as a study progressed that might have influenced the information collected need to be considered. A change could be a society-wide influence, such as 9/11, or something more specific to situation, such as the death of a company executive and resulting modifications in standard operating procedures.

- Pretesting of survey instruments and other tools can result in modification of behaviors by the people they were pretested on. Answering survey questions on a particular topic can move it top-of-mind, even though it is not generally consciously considered.

- Misunderstandings about findings can lead to incorrect ideas about causation. For example, findings of correlation between factors cannot be used to determine which factor caused the other. Also, when multiple factors in an environment are modified, it is not possible to attribute any resulting changes in behavior to a single one of those changes; the entire set must be credited.

Reliability basically means repeatability or consistency. An investigation or instrument is reliable if duplicating it or using it again would produce the same results. Since studies don't often get repeated, discussions of reliability in the applied world quickly turn to the idea of concurrent validity. *Concurrent validity* is seen when studies/instruments that, because of their similarity, should get the same results, actually do. Concurrent validity is found when the same thing (national culture or morale, as examples) is measured using several different tools and the same classification results in both cases.

When a study is done that seems similar to other studies in terms of how it was conducted, but it reaches different conclusions from those of other studies, it deserves special scrutiny. The conclusions drawn might be entirely appropriate—methods advance, the world changes—but those different results might have arisen because of an error on the part of the researchers. Regularly, newer studies find and correct issues in the ways that earlier studies were conducted. It is also true, however, that newer studies might define problems differently than previous ones, which leads to differences in findings. The more recent researchers may also be studying a slightly different population than previous researchers or using a different sort of research methodology, for example—which might be more or less appropriate and applicable to any design effort. Good practice suggests design researchers should remain open-minded to changing how they think about objects, spaces, and places, but be critical as well.

Knowing about reliability and validity will make you a more informed reader of study critiques and give you a mental framework to structure your own reviews of investigations that you do yourself. When you're reviewing research that other people have done, ask yourself if the study seems appropriate based on what you know about the field and if reasonable conclusions are being drawn from the work done.

There are some additional general rules to use when you're deciding if a study you are referencing is strong or weak. A thorough discussion of the topic of interest is a good sign, and so is a head-on discussion of other studies or common professional practices that are inconsistent with the study results. If you can identify topics that should have been addressed but were not, it's time to resume the literature review.

More recent studies are more desirable than those that are older—but sometimes, classic studies stand the test of time. When people repeat an earlier study and get the same results as the original researchers, that's often not very interesting to people who edit journals, so those corroborating studies often don't get reported. Older studies shouldn't be dismissed out of hand—particularly if you can't find more recent ones on the same topic. Also, research topics go in and out of fashion—a subject, such as the effects of ceiling height on behavior, will be hot for a few years, and then related research may die off for a decade. More recent studies will reflect recently completed research by the authors of the article you are reading, as well as their peers. They also might utilize more recent data-collection tools—brain MRIs instead of participants' impressions of their responses, for example.

Good science also recognizes that not all human actions and feelings are logical and consistent—sometimes valid research findings may seem illogical.

## OWNING THE INFORMATION

The types of applied research discussed in this book generally do not result in patentable intellectual property but rather, data and methodologies to better inform and initiate an effective design response. Copyright laws protect all written material whether publication is electronic or physical.

The source of information that has been published electronically or physically is generally acknowledged in prepared materials by including the researchers' names and the title of the source publication. Deviations from this policy should be expressly mentioned. There are laws governing the use of copyrighted materials (length of quotes allowed without formal permission from the publisher, etc.) and those laws are described on the website of the U.S. Copyright Office (www.copyright.gov).

When both applied and theoretical research are conducted, it is important to understand who owns the data collected and the conclusions that are drawn after those data are analyzed. Generally, the person who funds or sponsors the research owns what is learned. The funding documents usually lay out all the details of who controls what, in which ways, for how long. Data that are owned by someone else can only be used when that ownership is acknowledged and any required payments are made and/or permissions are provided.

Using published data-gathering tools pose a particular dilemma. If you use a survey that has been published in a journal for your own nonacademic project, it is best to obtain the written permission of the journal that published the survey because it owns the copyright. Some surveys are only available if a fee is paid to the firm that owns them. For example, the Myers-Briggs test belongs to CPP, Inc., and any use of the questions contained in the test that are not cleared by CPP is a violation of copyright law. Sophisticated anti-plagiarism software is increasing the frequency with which material used without permission is identified.

When a firm has a body of knowledge and has written even short publicly available papers presenting it, those articles can be cited in reports to clients and other similar materials. Those citations increase the perceived value of working with a firm.

Questions of ownership can become murky. When in doubt, seek legal counsel.

## PLANNING AND ORGANIZING A PROJECT-SPECIFIC COMPREHENSIVE RESEARCH PLAN

A good research project needs a plan. Without a plan, information gathering moves from an orderly march to a clear destination to a frantic and disorganized run through a baffling maze.

Different research tools also require different skill sets, and a research plan should be developed after considering the available skill sets. A researcher who is not a native English speaker may have difficulty conducting qualitative interviews because of the metaphors and nuances in spoken language, but if they have lived in their current country of residence for five or six years, they might be familiar enough with its national culture to behavior map certain types of activities or users instead.

The descriptions of the research tools that follow detail how different techniques are used, so that you will know which tools are best to select in which situations. Although certain tools are recommended for particular research phases, if the resources are not available to feasibly apply them, substitute another one of the research tools profiled. As an example, observations may be useful during the programming phase of a project, but if no one on the research team has a security clearance that is high enough to allow them into the site occupied by the users of the space, add more specific questions to the survey to collect some of the useful information that would have been most effectively gathered through observations.

Before conducting any research, think about whether the results will be published in a peer-reviewed journal, which is defined in Chapter 4. If they might, you should have an institutional review board (IRB) certify that your research methodology is not harmful to study participants. Some publications require this certification before they will publish findings. Often, a local university can assist you with the IRB process; an IRB review needs to precede data collection. Also, the U.S. government has developed regulations to ensure that research in healthcare settings is conducted in a way that does not compromise patients. Check with healthcare facilities at which you will do research as well as government authorities such as the National Institutes of Health (www.nih.gov) for the latest regulations.

Research tools are discussed here with different levels of detail because, honestly, some are more rule-intense than others. Scientists have learned, for example, all sorts of things about how the wording and structure of survey questions influences the information collected—and we'll present a reasonable number of those rules. When doing a visual content analysis of the living spaces favored by future residents of a place under development, there are fewer operational rules to report, although both techniques are rigorous and respected in the research world.

Any research effort needs to be coordinated between teammates. The research plan needs to identify the person or persons who will ultimately be responsible for organizing and executing particular research activities. Designating responsible parties makes it easier for people not initially involved with research activities to join the research efforts, or to understand activities undertaken by the research team. Clearly defining the roles of everyone involved in the research project prevents confusion over responsibilities and streamlines the research process. A coordinated plan establishes when, how, by whom, and where information is collected, analyzed, stored, and applied.

A research plan makes researchers feel more comfortable that they will achieve their objectives; gives them confidence, and credibility among the project stakeholders and sponsors of the research; and provides valuable information that informs and brings greater certainty to a design response.

## OVERVIEW OF TYPES OF RESEARCH

Research tools can be divided into categories using several sorts of criteria. Often, people use the terms *qualitative* and *quantitative* to define research types. There are many techniques that fall into each of these broad buckets. Qualitative techniques include interviewing, discussion groups, and observing. Experiments, surveying, and behavior mapping are examples of quantitative techniques.

Quantitative tools more clearly establish the information that will be collected, while qualitative techniques are more open ended. Qualitative tools may gather data the researcher did not initially expect to uncover. For example, a written survey gives respondents a fixed set of choices to use to answer a question and researchers who have developed those questions carefully can be confident one of the choices provided will be appropriate. Some questions may not supply a set of answers, but the topic to be addressed has been determined by the experimenter; however, these open-ended questions are more qualitative in approach. When an observation process begins or a question is asked during an open discussion, the researchers can never be completely sure what will be seen or heard. They often supply unexpected sorts of project-relevant information. These new avenues can be explored because it is possible to change an interview or an observation protocol "on-the-fly." By contrast, survey questions, once distributed, can't be changed by a researcher.

Quantitative findings alone can be stark and lack context; qualitative methods when combined with quantitative ones can add that context. Qualitative research is a valuable way to explore an issue before fine-tuning understanding of the topic with a more traditional quantitative tool, such as survey research. Qualitative research tends to more broadly collect information, which is key in early exploratory studies, while quantitative techniques lead to more narrowly focused efforts. Qualitative information is generally assessed by looking for themes and patterns in the data collected. Qualitative tools are often effective ways to access tacit information, while quantitative tools excel at exploring more explicit issues.

Both qualitative and quantitative research are done using carefully developed protocols. Qualitative research has just as clearly defined research plans as quantitative research—observing is not just hanging out and interviewing is not just talking. Qualitative research is based on a plan determined by the type of research questions to be answered. The same statistical tools can be used to analyze the data collected with either quantitative or qualitative methods—if qualitative data go through an initial coding phase before those analyses begin.

Both qualitative and quantitative research are rigorous and scientific, and if either set of tools is used incorrectly, the information collected can be misleading.

*Primary research* is another term used to define research. When people are doing primary research, they are actively generating new knowledge through surveys, observation, and other research tools. Its opposite, secondary research is completed by drawing conclusions from and integrating research published by other people.

*Market research* focuses on forces and conditions in the business markets for products and services. Market research can guide the development of the design of a condominium structure—it can inform the plan of the structure as well as indicate the likeliest prices at which those homes will sell, for example. This last factor can influence material choice and size of floor plan, among other decisions.

*Material research* relates more directly to the physical properties of items to be used in the construction or manufacturing process.

*Sustainable design and engineering research* examines strategies to create ecologically efficient design solutions.

## DIFFERENCES IN TYPES OF RESEARCH: APPLIED OR THEORETICAL

Applied research is directed at resolving a practical, real-world issue, while theoretical research is not as closely tied to a near-term, real-world use. Applied and theoretical research strategies are similar in many ways—they include researcher training, tools, and ethical responsibilities, for instance. They differ in the motivations that drive people to gather and analyze information.

Applied research products are often put to use immediately by the research sponsors, while theoretical research may never be directly utilized in the "real" world. Often, practitioners and others working in industry perform applied research while theoretical research is done by academics. Applied research, when completed, can be used with little, if any, tweaking, to resolve a particular issue of interest, while completed theoretical research generally is most useful as a component of a future research program.

High-quality applied and theoretical research can be published in well-respected scholarly journals, adding to the professional knowledge of the industry. However, applied research might not be published, at least initially, because its results provide a competitive advantage to the group that conducted it. Publication makes what has been learned at significant cost available to all interested parties, which reduces the period of time it can be applied exclusively (by the researchers) for financial gain. Although theoretical research can also be used to generate income, it is more often completed to enhance professional reputation, promote sharing of information, and expand the profession's collective body of knowledge.

# COMPARING RESEARCH TOOLS

Although certain research tools are particularly valuable at specific points in the design process, it is also possible to generalize about situations for using individual research tools. The flow chart presented in Figure 2.1 is a quick guide to the research issues that, in general, might lead you to select one research tool instead of another.

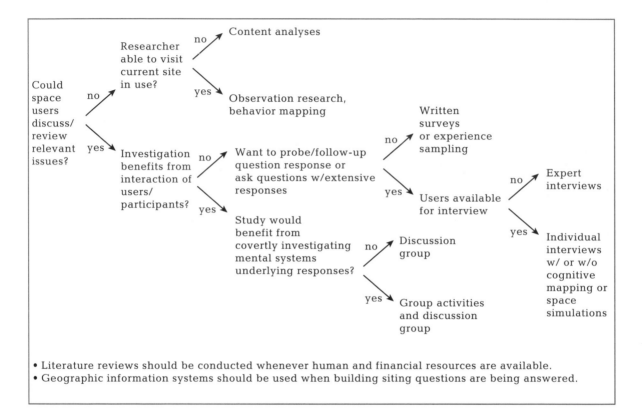

- Literature reviews should be conducted whenever human and financial resources are available.
- Geographic information systems should be used when building siting questions are being answered.

**FIGURE 2.1**
This is an overview of some of the research issues that may lead you to select particular research tools.

The reason that some research tools are more appropriate in some situations than others is the strengths and weaknesses of the tools themselves. Each of the tools described in the next few paragraphs will be presented in depth in the chapters that follow.

Written surveys have been an integral part of the design research process for decades, and for good reason—they efficiently and effectively (and relatively inexpensively) gather a lot of useful information. Surveys have credibility and legitimacy with client groups, making them a valuable resource. When you are using a written survey, you collect the same information from each respondent, whether they are from the same client group or even the same project, and that consistency means that you can compare material you collect in one situation to data gathered in another.

You will wait a long time for data if you do not effectively manage the survey distribution and collection process. Reminders are key, and it is important to preview the data gathered before the final data collection deadline to make sure that nothing is amiss with the process.

Written surveys are not a panacea, however. There are certain situations where people just can't answer questions that designers would like to pose. Nondesigners are notoriously bad at describing "ideal" sorts of environments, for example. Lacking a design vocabulary, nondesigner respondents can only rehash spaces they have seen or visited in the past. People's expectations about future places are strongly influenced by their past place experiences.

In some instances, respondents don't have the information required to answer a question. For example, people might have been doing certain tasks for so long that they have forgotten what they actually do in a particular situation.

The problem with asking people questions that they can't answer well is that respondents (who generally want to help researchers get the information that they need) will answer questions posed and won't volunteer that they don't know, can't recall, or can't respond. In these situations, a survey is better replaced by an observation technique that allows the designer to watch the activity to understand the actual situation.

For example, asking an office worker how many informal conversations he or she has in his or her workstation each day is problematic. The office worker might not really know, since these discussions are unplanned and often very short or seemingly unimportant, or the person being interviewed or surveyed may know that these conversations can annoy nearby workers and therefore not want to acknowledge them. However, gaining insight into this question is important input into the development of a future workspace. In this situation, a researcher's ability to observe the frequency of this behavior would be useful.

When you ask survey questions, you also can't probe intriguing responses or resolve apparent inconsistencies in answers—particularly if survey respondents are anonymous. Following written surveying with observations or discussions (single interviews or group talks) can help rectify this situation.

Written surveys can also seem inappropriate in some circumstances. If a one-off single family home is being created, a survey of future residents may seem inappropriately "mechanical." It can also be impossible to survey some user groups—patients in some healthcare settings may not be willing or able to complete surveys, for example.

Developing a survey, particularly one with multiple-choice questions, requires enough information about the situation being studied to write effective questions. A lot of knowledge of what nurses might be doing in a nurses' station is needed to develop a multiple-choice question about their activities there that provides appropriate response options.

Most surveys are now administered electronically and data that are collected flow directly into an electronic spreadsheet, but if you are distributing a survey in paper form, entering and analyzing the data collected can be time consuming.

Real-time, real-place sampling of the experiences of stakeholders is little used, but is often an effective research tool. It is known as the experience sampling method, or ESM. Study participants receive pagers or are contacted in some other way at randomly selected times while in a space to be redesigned. Each time participants receive a page, they are asked to answer customized questions about the specific activity they are engaged in, their psychological state, aspects of the activity, or other topics of interest. This technique has become increasingly viable as small handheld terminals for relaying the answers to these questions have become more available and economical. The resulting data sets are comprehensive and very rich in useful information.

Speaking with people face to face is another valuable way to collect information. Not only do open discussions help resolve many of the cloudy issues raised by survey responses, they allow the design researcher to explore topics of interest in more detail. Follow-up questions are possible that are directly related to the answers provided. This is particularly important if unexpected but pertinent information is shared and is not possible when a written survey is used. Within very broad parameters, it is possible to evolve interview questions being asked as the research process unfolds. When you need to collect information but don't have much knowledge related to a project, speaking face to face can be a viable option.

In this scenario, interactions between the interviewer and an interviewee, or interviewees if group discussions are held, often result in fortuitous exchanges that collect crucial information that directly influences the ultimate design solution. Interchanges among participants in a discussion group are a good way to establish overall design priorities. Regularly, during group discussions, interviewees ask each other questions or supply clarifying bits of information that greatly enrich the research process. These interactions are the primary methodological reason for having group discussions. Design charettes are a specific sort of discussion group.

Common research practice demands that certain interviews be conducted. If a residence is being constructed and the ultimate residents of a home are known, they should be interviewed, as should executives and other stakeholders at firms where workplaces are being designed, for example. These executives are an important source of information about an organization's future, for example.

Outside experts are sometimes interviewed in the course of a design project. These interviews are particularly useful when the research schedule needs to be compressed because of time constraints and appropriate experts are available for interviews. There are many types of experts (place type, social science subject, etc.). The criteria used to select the person(s) interviewed are determined by the research project objectives. For example, an interview with a neonatal intensive care nurse with years of professional experience can be substituted for interviews with a range of stakeholder nurses and for observations in situ if a new neonatal intensive care department is being planned. The expert is a good alternative when and if there are no current stakeholders to interview or if concerns about infection preclude observation, for example. It is always dangerous, however, to rely solely on information from a single expert, no matter how strong the expert's credentials.

Collecting information using interviews can be time consuming, particularly when the hours required to select interviewees and actually schedule discussions are considered. Since multiple users participate in discussion groups, they are a little more efficient, but it takes longer for the interviewer to coordinate the schedules of all participants in a group.

Interviewing itself can also take longer than might initially be anticipated because transition time between interviews is always required, and those transition times may be quite long if the interviewer needs to travel between interviews, even within the same building.

It can be difficult for individuals to frankly discuss information that they find sensitive, and researchers need to consider the types of topics they need to investigate before using interviews as a research tool. Some topics, such as sexual issues, are clearly more difficult for most people to discuss with an interviewer, but other topics might be more subtly tough, such as those related to financial or human resource performance.

Group activities have many of the advantages and disadvantages of group interviews, but they often relax participants, so they can be a good way to begin a group discussion session. Group activities involve everyone present in the conversation, and once people participate, they are much more likely to do so again. They include creating collages that address some design-related issues, dramatizing particular situations of interest, and other similar participatory exchanges. They can be used to resolve appropriate use of limited resources, as well as to assess particular design options or preferences.

When people are unable to respond to questions on topics of interest either orally or in writing, observations can be key. Observations can also be useful when there is clearly a "correct" answer to a particular question or a clear motivation to distort the data collection process. In North America today, people at firms undergoing downsizing may be reticent to admit that there are serious issues with their current work environments, but observations of body language, for example, may clearly delineate those issues. Space syntax tools are a specialized form of very structured observation, at the level at which we will discuss them here. Observation is also useful when users don't have experience talking about an issue. They may lack the vocabulary to do so effectively. Sometimes people have been doing something for so long, they no longer really know what they do—imagine your grandmother preparing for a holiday feast—and for those situations, observations can again be useful. When you're observing, it's also possible to note signs of wear in an environment or physical modifications to the space that can help guide future design decisions. For example, a chair that's pristine probably is sat in only occasionally. Other research methods can learn why that might be the case. If conference room windows have paper stuck over them, that might indicate a lack of display space inside or a need for more privacy during meetings.

Behavior mapping is an organized way to collect information about how people use a space for example, how they move through a space, and where they linger. It is a specialized form of observation and discussed in depth in Chapter 6. At a fundamental level, it involves literally recording on a floor plan of a site the travel and place-use behaviors of a project-relevant sample of the people who use a space.

People can be observed and then interviewed immediately when space simulations are used, and the combination of interviews and observations in these realistic settings provides important information about the probable real experience of being in a proposed space. Sometimes, surveys are also used in combination with simulations. Constructing simulated environments is expensive, however, and care must be taken to collect information from a representative sample of potential space users.

Reviews of previous research are a good way to begin any new project. Material can be effectively accessed through the Internet or other publicly available sources when the parameters used to determine research quality, which are fully presented in this chapter and in Chapter 4, are followed. Using the correct search terms is key to effective literature reviews. In the chapters that follow, we help identify effective search terms.

Literature reviews provide a strong foundation for a research program and indicate topics that do not need to be investigated for a specific project because generalizable findings have already been determined.

Content analysis of visual and verbal information is a valuable way to uncover implicit, tacit information, although it is also a good source of explicit material. It involves reviewing written and visual records to identify often unstated but significant issues of importance to stakeholders. Obtaining the materials to be studied can be difficult. Content analysis is discussed in Chapter 5.

Geographic information systems (GIS) store a variety of information that can be used by designers. They present data about the exterior, surrounding environments of structures being built—and those environments may be natural, demographic, and economic, among others. These materials can be used to site structures so that views to natural vistas are maximized and stress on natural resources is minimized. GIS is also useful for selecting sites that provide user-desired nearby amenities. GIS tools are becoming more advanced and common; their use is further discussed in Chapter 6.

We will use ten criteria to distinguish the research tools presented in this book. These criteria can guide your decisions about when particular tools should be used:

1. Some tools are particularly useful in circumstances, such as at the beginning of a project, when little is known about the topics being researched; others are particularly useful in other circumstances, such as at the end of a project to investigate a few remaining outstanding issues. This is summarized in the text as *little known* and *lot known*.

2. Tools may collect information relatively quickly or it may require more time to use them to gather useful information. This is noted using the terms *quick* and *not quick*.

3. The information obtained with a tool might be straightforward or complex to interpret and discuss. This is summarized in the text as *info straightforward* and *info complex*.

4. Data collected can also be distinguished based on whether they are generally textual or verbal or more numeric—noted as *verbal* and *numeric*.

5. Some tools are particularly useful for answering "why" questions and others for "how" questions—hence *why* and *how*.

6. Sometimes researchers need to be at the client site when information is collected and with other tools they can be off-site. The abbreviations *on-site* and *off-site OK* are used to describe this tool parameter.

7. Some methodologies are more well established so they have more accepted protocols and there are more related online resources and others are more innovative—summarized as *well-established* and *innovative*.

8. Tools may be better for collecting information about current conditions (from which future places will be developed) or better for learning about expected future conditions—thus, the terms *current* and *future* are used to describe a tool's rating on this factor.

9. Special software or hardware might or might not be required to collect information (*special, no special*).

10. Some techniques are so generally useful they should be considered for any project, and probably utilized, while others are much more specialized (*generally considered, potentially considered*).

A chart at the beginning of the discussion of each research tool will indicate that tool's rating on these ten criteria.

## MERITS OF USING SEVERAL DIFFERENT RESEARCH TOOLS TO ANSWER ANY RESEARCH QUESTION

Having multiple research tools available for use increases the possibility that research questions can be answered well. Using multiple methods also makes it possible for the data collected with one tool to be compared to that collected with another. Consistencies between findings add confidence and inconsistencies indicate that either the situation is complex or that one or another of the tools used could be applied more appropriately. Multiple tools also ensure that researchers build their research muscles by learning new skills and keeping their existing research strengths intact.

Planning to use more than one research tool allows the data-gathering process to move forward, even if there is a snafu with actually utilizing one of the tools proposed. If both observations and surveys are planned, the research process can proceed even if management decides that potential respondents are too busy to answer survey questions, for example. The ultimate knowledge gained may be less if surveys are eliminated, in this example, but useful information will be collected through the observations done.

Findings from different sorts of research projects resonate with different client groups, so including a range of different tools in each research plan increases the likelihood that people will respond positively to the research project. Some individuals believe research that requires human interpretation, such as observations, is too nebulous or wishy-washy to support a design decision. They find only quantitative research techniques valuable. Other people feel that surveys and experiments cannot holistically investigate human experience, and these individuals favor qualitative research. A mix of research tools can satisfy individuals with each of the orientations described.

## CORE CONCEPTS

Many forces influence design decisions (economic considerations, user needs, preferred aesthetic forms, etc.), but an assortment of research tools are available to guide designers toward optimal solutions. Research tools mentioned in this text can be used at one or several points in the same development cycle.

Designing a space is complicated, and the influence of the ultimate design on human experience is complex. Proper use of research tools can unravel the current situation and inform the design of a future space that is most likely to be successful, however success is defined. Research has to happen because as a designer you need to learn what people need to accomplish in the place being developed and what would make them feel comfortable as they go about doing that.

Many of the tools described in this text primarily collect information on current conditions to guide development of a future space. This assumption of continuity of use can be problematic, which is why it is important to make a real effort to gather information about the future of users and their world.

Different research tools exert different levels of control over the parameters that can influence study findings (e.g., a survey and observations have vastly different levels of structure). In a more controlled situation, conclusions can be more clearly drawn, but those conclusions might not be as rich or useful as those acquired in less-structured conditions. In general, study findings must be evaluated using the *reasonableness test*. Even if a study has been correctly done, as far as you can determine, if findings seem countersensical, more investigation is warranted.

Experienced design researchers have learned that the surest way to alienate a user group is to ask their opinion about something and then seem to ignore the information they supply. If you collect information that for some valid reason, such as lack of funds, can't be recognized in the design of a space in any manner, it is best to tell the people who have supplied the information about the reasons that you have decided to follow a different course than the one that research indicated. This is not so that you can ask the users' approval, but to indicate to the users that you respect them and their opinions. As a corollary—sometimes an aspect of a space is preordained for whatever reason. For example, a certain layout of the apartments in a multifamily complex might be dictated by the desire to maximize daylight in the living rooms, the boss's spouse might have already determined where the new company headquarters will be, and so on. In those cases, do not do any research related to these aspects of the space being developed.

Limited resources may make it difficult to utilize all the potentially useful research tools and to respond to all of the information collected using those research tools. In those circumstances, prioritize the use of research and physical resources based on potential implications on the aspects of the organization that add most value. In a firm, this might mean ensuring that the research and development department functions well, even if that means that others won't. In a healthcare facility, this might mean that caregiving staff has access to an outside view in their respite room, even at the expense of a view for waiting family and friends. It is important to remain impartial as these decisions are made and throughout the entire research process.

Built environments are developed because they somehow enrich human experience. One of your research goals should always be to determine how a developing space can fulfill its mission—which might also require that that mission be unearthed. As you start to analyze the data collected using one or several tools, patterns in the data will help you conceptualize that enriching experience.

# ENDNOTES

1. Virginia Postrel, *The Substance of Style: How the Rise of Aesthetic Value is Remaking Commerce, Culture, and Consciousness* (New York: HarperCollins, 2003).

2. Dan Ariely, *Predictably Irrational* (New York: HarperCollins, 2008).

3. Ibid., pp. 240–243.

4. Sheena Iyendar, *The Art of Choosing* (New York: Twelve, 2010).

5. Douglas Kendrick, Vladas Griskevicius, Steven Neuberg, and Mark Schaller, "Renovating the Pyramid of Needs: Contemporary Extensions Built Upon Ancient Foundations." *Perspectives on Psychological Science*, vol. 5, no. 3, pp. 292–314.

6. S. Reiss, "Multifaceted Nature of Intrinsic Motivation: The Theory of 16 Basic Desires." *Review of General Psychology*, vol. 8, no. 3, pp. 179–193.

# CHAPTER 3

# What to Learn

BEGINNING A DESIGN PROJECT is a lot like taking on a new assignment as a spy. You can prep as the assignment begins, learning something about the language and culture of the group you'll be working with, for example, but there are still a lot of issues to resolve as you get into the action and start to make the many design decisions required.

Some of those decisions are consistent from project to project, although the particulars of the answers may vary. The need to consider comfort and control is important for any project, for example, which we will discuss further in a few pages. In addition, every ethnic group has traditional ways of residing with its family, although the particular rules involved aren't always the same. On specific projects, one of those general concerns might assume more weight as design decisions are made. Organizational culture can make one design choice more likely because respecting it is most likely to add the highest value to the group, or the determining issue might be a task that space users need to accomplish well, or some entirely different factor. Sometimes, you might decide that project-specific conditions (e.g., local customs such as public separation of the genders) will be ignored, but each time you don't recognize and respond to important information, you run the risk of creating a space that doesn't meet user needs.

Each design project, like any country you might be spying on, has a past, a present, and a future—all of which are tightly bound together and which you must reflect through design decisions. You need to learn about the client and the social, cultural, economic, market, and technological contexts in which the place you are developing will be located—after all, you are a well-intentioned spy.

## INFORMING DESIGN-RELATED CHANGE

Design generally involves some sort of change, and the changes enacted need to be consistent with a plan for a space that satisfies the needs (stated and implicit) of the client. If a project moves through to completion, something is different at the end of the process than at the beginning—physically. If you consider psychological state, even projects that never take physical form have the potential to change their world. For example, if unbuilt projects have progressed through a research phase, knowledge gained has altered how people think.

So if change is what design is all about—what should be changed? Information can answer that question—but what information do you need to know to successfully design a space? One of the most significant reasons to conduct research is because it can be really dangerous to extrapolate from your own experiences or from generally accepted rules of thumb to design decisions.

## Hurdles to Creating Good Design

As the work of Jack Nasar (a professor in the school of architecture at The Ohio State University) and others have shown, your design training has altered how you interact with the world around you.[1] Your responses to design elements are more highly developed, for example, than those of people without your background. So you can't design based on your own aesthetic preferences, which are tied to your professional culture, let alone your more individualized place-based experiences (e.g., the ways that you enjoy relaxing at home or interacting with a colleague at work). A few years ago, a certain yellow-yellow-green color was very popular in the design world; it was used extensively in physical spaces created by designers and in the clothing that they wore while doing that designing. This color is, however, extremely unpopular with members of the general public, and color preference tests often show it to be the least popular color of all in the population at large. Be forewarned.

One design project can also seem deceptively similar to another without research and deep thinking about what can reasonably be extrapolated from one to another. Differences in organizational culture can significantly influence the effectiveness of the design of various schools, for example, as can differences in pedagogical techniques preferred. The personalities of residents make the same floor plan a dream come true for some families and a living nightmare for others. Impartial information gathering and analysis increase the probability of successful design.

Among the general public, misunderstandings about optimal place design are plentiful. Misperceptions about how people interact with their physical world move in and out of fashion. For example, there has recently been a widespread belief that the way that humans function in the world around themselves is undergoing a rapid evolution. In reality, this is not the case and human brains regardless of age function in the same way, as David Meyer at the University of Michigan and others have shown.[2] Humans of any age, be they baby boomers or members of generation Y, are distracted in similar ways in open workplace environments, for example. In addition, humans of various ages share a need for privacy (on demand), territory and the ability to personalize that territory to express self-identity, and a space that provide the optimal stimulation level for the task at hand, among other things.

Cultures, particularly national ones, also evolve slowly—hence, the danger of ignoring them when developing spaces. This should put the kibosh on plans for universal, international space plans, which has often been discussed by designers and clients.

These sorts of misunderstandings make research that supports design decisions an important resource, particularly as design specifics are discussed with clients.

## Purpose of Research

The reason why we research is so that we can create the best sorts of places for particular people, at particular times, doing particular things. Even beginning to understand what "the best sorts of places" are can be a formidable challenge, and it's almost impossible to coordinate that without knowledge— real information about the way in which people will experience the spaces that you are developing.

Identifying that intended culmination of a project can be your first challenge. Before you can write a great survey, you need to determine what to cover in those questions. Similarly, there's no sense sitting down for an interview, expert or otherwise, until you have an idea what info you need when you walk away from the session. When a school district hires you to build a school, what is it hoping to accomplish with the new structure, and how will it know if its efforts have been successful? Workplace clients have similar concerns, so before you begin to design an office you need to also know about the client's expectations about whether people will work there or at home, what sort of meetings need to be facilitated, what sort of culture is to be encouraged, and the mix of national cultures that will frequent the place—for starters. For a medical center, you need to learn about not only organizational objectives, but also about health care and employee continuity and planned community outreach, among other things. Will alternative care facilities and a training center and office complex for doctors and research labs to coordinate drug trials be required? These are all relatively traditional programming questions. Moving beyond these queries to understand why particular decisions have been made and to fully explore design alternatives and repercussions in terms of user experiences differentiates great and good design.

This chapter introduces an approach to thinking about design-related information requirements and a little background on the psychology of how people respond to the world around them. In this book we're focusing on research to collect information, not for inspiration, to use the data dichotomy developed by Stephanie Munson and Bruce Tharp.[3] We can't present an exhaustive checklist of "things to learn" here because for each project you need to answer a unique set of design questions, but we can thoroughly explore how you can figure out what you need to know.

The psychology of how people respond to the physical world can't be comprehensively addressed in this chapter, either. Here, you will learn some of the topics to investigate via a literature review or your own primary research. For example, once you realize the psychological importance of territories to human beings, you can investigate the latest research on hospital patients and territories or information workers and territories, as required by a project you are working on.

First, we'll talk about some of the design-based info you need to collect, and then the social science research that can inform the design of spaces that satisfy both stated and implicit client needs.

# DESIGN-PROJECT-BASED INFORMATION GATHERING

A core set of design-project-specific information is needed to move a project forward. The data required can be grouped into two main categories: subjective and objective. *Subjective* here means tightly tied to values, expectations, and opinions, and includes things like the aspirations of a firm. *Objective* information isn't generally open for debate—a certain number of beds are required in an intensive care unit if it can reasonably be expected to break even financially, an office must have a certain number of four-person meeting rooms if the client organization anticipates having the same sort of meeting mix in the future that it does now, and so on.

The design-project-based information required for successful design can be categorized as:

- Subjective criteria

  Aspirations of client leaders in general

  Goals of client leaders for space

- Objective criteria

  Context for project

  Resources available

  Challenges to overcome

  Measures of project success

## Aspirations and Goals

*Aspirations* are often the star of a client's mission statement if it's an organization, or the forces that propel clients forward if they are individuals. Aspirations are the reason that any action is being taken. They are the highest-level objectives for your client, the ones that coordinate their actions, if they are organized. A hospital might aspire to maximize the health of community members, or to serve as a center for learning and research, educating future physicians, and conducting primary research.

Aspirations can guide your design decisions in a general sense. An investment firm that aspires to be a trusted resource for millions of investors wants to use finishes that are not the most expensive that they could technically afford. These lower costs help lock in higher returns on investments and send a "successful but prudent" message to clients. Investment firm clients also might want to place their office in a prominent location to show that they are members of a community and use only fair trade materials to indicate that they are concerned about humankind in general. An investment firm might wish to provide its phone investment counselors with comfortable ergonomic chairs and surround them with high acoustics-enhancing walls so that they always sound pleasant and focused during telephone conversations.

A medical spa that wants to always provide its clients with the most advanced treatments not only needs plumbing, electrical, and structural elements that are easy to change but also needs ready access to a training room for aestheticians and a loading dock for the delivery of bulky new equipment, particularly if it provides hydrotherapy.

*Goals* are also closely tied to the opinions of the leaders of client firms, and they funnel naturally into the measures of success for a space. Like aspirations, they are tightly tied to the values of an organization. Goals are less strategic and comprehensive than aspirations. They directly link a space to aspirations by concretely stating how a space will help an organization achieve those highest-order objectives. They suggest something, behavioral or otherwise, that can be measured. Goals are classified as subjective here, because even a relatively straightforward aspiration can lead to a number of goals, and selecting the specific ones to be pursued in a space is the responsibility of the client organization's leaders.

An oncology facility might have the objective of empathetic support for patients and their families, which would be most likely if caregivers become more comfortable with cancer-care situations. That requires extended employment periods. A goal for an oncology facility project might be increasing nursing staff retention rates; a measure of success could be bringing turnover down to 50 percent of its current level, for example. Design implications of this desire to increase retention rates could be a larger number of restorative spaces for nurses that are clearly separated from areas accessible by patients and their families.

If a high school is being designed, an aspiration could be to graduate students that perform at their highest possible intellectual level and become leaders of society by succeeding in traditional venues, such as Ivy League universities. This aspiration could result in the goal of teaching using pedagogical techniques that are valued in the more-traditional education community and that result in high test-score performance. Space design can support or hinder applying particular teaching techniques. Goal achievement could be assessed via the test scores of graduating students, a doubling of applications to the school itself, or the rate at which accepted students ultimately enroll (yield). A high school whose objective is to mold its students into leaders who will motivate others to more sustainable behaviors could require a different form, depending on the specific goals selected. For example, the goal of educating students on the science behind sustainability could require different laboratory spaces than those in the first school described.

When you are reviewing goals with clients, it's important not to be too deterministic about the implications of specific design decisions. A space can support the achievement of goals and aspirations, but space alone can never guarantee success—that is based on a number of factors. Just as an ill-conceived space might appear to be a good performer because of contextual (e.g., demographic, economic) changes, a brilliantly conceived space could fail due to external factors. That is, regardless of how well-grounded design choices are in research, a number of real-world situations can intervene and prevent a group from reaching its goals. Imagine a plastic surgery clinic in offices that are designed to provide supportive and compassionate care. Repeat business (e.g., botox injections) among its clientele could fall after the practice redesigns its space if the economy hits a rough spot, regardless of the design of the offices. This inability of place to dictate outcomes does not reduce the need for objective performance criteria. It does, however, require that performance on measures of success need to be put in a broader context.

## Measures of Success

*Measures of success* need to be, well, measurable. They are linked to how organizations or individuals want to achieve their aspirations through goals. Determining measures of success can be a real challenge, but clever thought ultimately prevails. Steelcase and its research colleagues, for example, wanted to learn more about how physical design could influence collaboration.[4] They did research at a client design firm and carefully monitored the number of hours spent in each project phase, knowing that some of those project phases were more collaboration intense than others. They compared the number of client hours charged to each project phase before and after the work environments were changed and used that information to assess the effectiveness of a new environment for collaboration.

A restaurant can determine if a redesign is facilitating desired changes by looking at the average receipts per day or week or month. In addition, it can dive in and look at what is being purchased at each meal. An increase in high-margin items that extend time in the space, such as desserts, indicates that patrons feel comfortable enough to want to remain longer. Whether longer stays are desirable or not depends on whether the pricing structure at the restaurant maximizes income (revenue minus expenses) when people buy high-margin desserts or when turn is faster.

An increased number of people gathering/stopping in front of a community feature such as a fountain or sculpture (e.g., Anish Kapoor's Cloud Gate sculpture in Millennium Park, Chicago) indicates a space that resonates with users—people want to be near things that they respect and value. If the goal of a public project is to increase tourist traffic, observing this gathering of potentially local folks is not as useful a measure of success as expert interviews with convention planners or hotel bellhops who give lots of directions to guests.

Perceived quality of care among the local community is something that a hospital might desire, but this can be difficult to measure effectively through surveys or even face-to-face conversations with local citizens. The number of doctors requesting surgical privileges at the hospital reflects perceived quality of care—doctors want to be associated with the places where patients want to have surgery, particularly for highly elective procedures such as plastic surgery. Perceptions of care are also related to requests for interviews by local television stations.

## Resources and Challenges

Resources and challenges focus on the very particular situation in which a project will take place. They ground a project in reality. Resources and challenges can generally be roughly described (financial, human, time), but might also be somewhat difficult to quantify. Examples of the latter condition are the level of access that researchers will have to the ultimate users of a space, a measurement of how easy it is to navigate through a site (important because staff turnover is high), or the importance of a need to keep client separated from others. For example, people leaving appointments with psychologists don't want to run into gossipy passersby. A concert hall faces acoustic challenges and acoustics is a mathematical field generally, but in-office acoustics are difficult to relate directly to worker performance (e.g., if client management has decried an "open" workplace environment).

People with business training can think of the resources/challenges analysis as a project-specific SWOT (strength, weaknesses, opportunities, threats) analysis. The strengths and opportunities of a project are its resources while weaknesses and threats are challenges. Strengths and weaknesses are internal to an organization, while opportunities and threats are external. They include societywide forces such as movement toward sustainability as well as firm-specific considerations such as a superstar R&D team.

The resources and challenges that designers need to recognize can be identified in different ways. Interviews with executives and general employees will reveal some. So will surveys of the client's clients or discussions with them. Talking with suppliers who interact with several organizations similar to the design client can really pay off. Visits to competitors are in order for many sorts of design projects, and undercover missions to current sites, operated by the client and its competitors, can be really productive. This might involve being a "patient" at an emergency room or dining at a café to be redesigned, for example. Content analyzing competitive advertisements can also provide useful information. Never discount the value of applying techniques familiar from literature reviews to market analyses. Any of the research tools profiled in this book can be used to learn about project-related resources and challenges.

## Project Context

Recognizing project context is important for project success and learning about project context informs design at all levels of scale. *Context* is all of the specific information you need about the people who will use a space and the situations under which they will do so. It ranges from employee lunch rituals (e.g., eating at their individual desks or together in a company owned cafeteria) to behaviors that are rewarded (e.g., employees are encouraged to stay late) or censured (e.g., walking by other people's cubicles too often to pick up items from the printer) to whether people need to be able to concentrate while they're in the office, for example. Context is who the users of a space are, what people do (or want to do or should do) in a space, how they do (or want to do or should do) what they do in a space, why they're motivated as they are, what helps them do whatever they're endeavoring to do, and what hinders them from doing what's desired, for starters.

Context is the details of the key questions:

- *Who* (will use the space, their national culture, organizational culture, training, personality, role in the organization or community, etc.)

- *What* (the space will be used for, furnishings need to be reused, relevant building codes, for example)

- *Where* (how climate and culture will come into play, location of sight lines for good views, what is nearby, and other similar information)

- *When* (present and future market conditions for the client firm, preservable history of space, how use of the building varies from day to day or season to season, etc.)

- *Why* (the space should be redesigned, it is important spiritually or culturally, if it is, for example)

- *How* (the use of the space is realistically projected to change during the next five years, technology will be used in the space, the space communicates nonverbally to its users, and other associated information)

When we're discussing design-project-based information needs, we can think of coming to understand the project context as a straightforward person/ place/behavior audit. When we begin to discuss social-science-based information needs, it will be clear that supporting context in design requires attention to additional factors as well.

Information about context is often collected via interviews, surveys, and observations. It can also come from archival research, literature searches (e.g., on industry practices or corporate trends), or other channels.

The research question you are trying to answer does not dictate the research tool you use. Common sense and available resources (financial, manpower, time to project phase completion, etc.) are much more important reasons to choose one research methodology over another. That being said, some situations encourage use of particular tools. If you are trying to identify the aspirations of client executives, it is odd to hand them a survey. In this case, interviews not only permit follow-up questions but also signal appropriate personal attention to issues of great importance to client executives. They are necessary for political reasons. Distributing a survey to all employees is a way for every employee to provide input. This is really important to leaders at some firms—an instance in which culture also influences tool use.

## SOCIAL-SCIENCE-BASED INFORMATION NEEDS

Social scientists of various types—for instance, psychologists, sociologists, anthropologists—study people and their physical environments. Their work specifically augments or complements the information collected in the design-project-based data-gathering process. It ensures that appropriate use is made of that project-specific data. Design-project-based research might indicate that hospital pharmacists need to concentrate as they work, and social science research can then richly inform the designer creating that space for concentrative work. Generally, social-science-based information is gathered through literature reviews after diagnostic information (such as identification on national culture or need to concentrate) is gathered using tools such as surveys and observation.

The material in this section introduces the types of issues that designers need to resolve to move forward with a successful project. Pleasure, which is generally desirable in a space, can be derived in several ways, to start. In addition, culture and personality have an important influence on experience of place, which is discussed in a few pages. Researchers designing a space to be used by members of their own national culture will naturally plan so that the culture is supported through physical form. If they are designing a space that will be used predominantly by another national culture, designers need to learn about how members of the user culture relate to their physical environments. The same goes for personality. Including a member of the culture on the design team is a good idea. Another example: Extensive research has linked in-store smells to purchase behavior. The latest research in this field should influence retail HVAC system design, for example.[5]

The following discussion of social-science-related information needs is cursory but sufficient to indicate the kinds of information that you might need for any project, the range of topics investigated by social scientists, and the importance of reviewing social science research as you begin a project. Any of the topics mentioned here need to be investigated more fully for particular design projects. Since the material discussed here is shared to incite interest and not as a complete exploration of any of the issues raised, references are rare, to encourage review of the literature for each project. All the material provided is drawn from research conducted by people other than the authors, except as noted.

## Fundamental Human Needs and Space Design

There is a movement within design research to increase the pleasure of interacting with places and objects. Whether you are for or against pleasure, it is useful to know potential sources of it as well as displeasure so that you can fine-tune a place design accordingly.

Patrick Jordan has written the definitive book on pleasurable design, and he outlines four types of pleasure (building on the work of Lionel Tiger).[6] *Physio-pleasure* is tied directly to body sensory experiences. Any of the senses can be pleasurably or unpleasurably stimulated by a physical environment. Appropriate and possible physio-pleasure to be provided in a space can be determined through conversations with users, literature reviews, and material research, for example. *Socio-pleasure* comes through relationships with other people, and a product or place can provide this directly or indirectly. Chairs that can be arranged so that it is easy to talk in desired groups can supply socio-pleasure, but so can souvenirs that spur passersby to pause and ask questions. Objects can signal social affiliations, general social situation, and status, all of which are linked to socio-pleasure; this sort of information facilitates social interactions as well as informing them. *Psycho-pleasure* ties directly to cognitive and emotional response to a product or place. Psycho-pleasure can be related to usability of an object or place. *Ideo-pleasure* is the sort associated with green design, among other worthy causes. It ties in to more abstract concepts such as social values and aesthetics, for example.

These descriptions indicate how something can be pleasurable, but not why it is. It is also important to realize that these types of pleasure are perceived and actually derived through the interactions of a person and an object or place; they do not exist independent of that interface. So, designing pleasurable places requires knowledge of the people that will use them as well as how experience is influenced psychologically.

Humans have fundamental psychological needs that must be satisfied in their lives in general. Places can help to satiate them and research such as literature reviews can provide details about how. Maslow outlined a hierarchy of needs that languished, not respected by the mainstream scientific world, for some time. It has recently been substantially revalidated and shown to have a significant influence on human behavior.[7] The official ranking, from most basic (bottom of the pyramid) to higher order needs (at the top of the pyramid) is: immediate physiological needs, safety, love (which includes both affection and group membership), respect, and self-actualization (achieving higher-order, personally meaningful goals). More psychological resources are available to pursue goals further up the pyramid when those of lesser importance are satisfied; the order in these needs can be satiated is not as rigid as the pyramid arrangement may infer.

Maslow's hierarchy can guide design in a basic way. People must feel comfortable enough in a space to lower their self-protective defenses if they are going to socialize or think broadly enough to self-actualize, for example. People are unlikely to want to interact with others in a location in which their backs are exposed or unprotected. More substantive conversations occur in spaces like a high-backed restaurant booth than at a table and chairs thrust into the middle of a corridor (see Figure C.4 in the color insert). A literature review of seating arrangements in which people feel safe would uncover this information.

Reiss has also outlined a collection of basic human desires or drives.[8] Many can be addressed through place design and also influence economic and other decision making. Reiss's list is a lot like Maslow's and can be used in a similar way: to focus a literature review and ensure that a place being created meets as many of these needs as possible. The desires and drives Reiss discusses include:

- *Power*—place has an inherent ability to inspire awe and to indicate power resulting from a social role (such as being a judge).

- *Curiosity*—a space can facilitate your fundamental human need to grow and develop as a person, as outlined by Lawrence and Nohria in 2002.[9]

- *Independence*—spaces help us influence our own destiny, particularly when we have fundamental control over them.

- *Status*—place can communicate social status both directly and through more nuanced, culture-based nonverbal communication.

- *Social contact*—human beings are pack animals, and even introverts shrivel when they are deprived of social contact with others. Spaces design can facilitate or hinder social interaction.

- *Vengeance*—environments that denigrate others, for example, are vengeful.

- *Honor* (meaning tradition in this context)—communicating tradition and the extent to which it is valued is one of the things that places can do well.

- *Idealism*—early examples of green design show how easily places can be used for idealistic purposes.

- *Physical exercise*—exercise is much more feasible in some environments than others

- *Romance*—space design can encourage or discourage romance

- *Family*—through home and playground design, for example, we can interact with our families in ways that we value.

- *Order*—the rise of the closet organizing industry shows how much we crave order in our lives.

- *Eating*—although we can chew and swallow food almost anywhere, it is certainly more comfortable to do so in some environments, such as those that are pleasant temperatures and humidity

- *Acceptance*—following social conventions when we design earns us acceptance from others (well, at least from many of them).

- *Tranquility*—we have a fundamental need to restock our levels of mental energy, and places can help us do just that.

- *Saving*—places are financial investments, and they also stockpile other items of value to us.

## Using Environmental Psychology

Although researchers have been investigating how human beings respond to and interact with the world around themselves for a long time, work in the area was coordinated in the 1960s with the formalization of the field of environmental psychology. Environmental psychologists focus on how human attitudes and behaviors are influenced by the physical world. That means they are experts at answering questions such as what colors will relax people, how wide a dining table should be, and how to arrange furniture in a space. They are also concerned with issues such as ceiling height and how personality and culture (organizational and national) influence our place-based experiences.

In this part of the chapter, you will learn the sorts of things about human experience of place that you should consider when a project begins, how design can influence place experience, and why you should find out about the specific people who will use a space under development. We will discuss fundamental human needs that must be recognized in design. Some needs to be recognized are more project specific and others more universal.

The paragraphs that follow highlight the dangers of extrapolating from your own experiences to those of others when spaces are being designed. It discusses a number of ways in which place-based experiences become customized on the group and individual levels. Generally, you will not be the user of the spaces that you are designing, so it is important to design with an awareness of the types of human-place interactions possible. We all share the same fundamental place-based needs, but don't all satisfy them in the same ways.

The single most important lesson that you should take away from this discussion is the immense number of experiences that different people, all of whom are perfectly "normal," can be having in the same space at exactly the same moment.

## Sensing the World

People generally have the same sets of sensory apparatus, but all those sets of eyes and ears don't work in the same way. Let's use vision as an example. Some people can pick out more details in a scene, at greater distances, than others. Some people, most of whom are men, have a distorted perception of colors—that is, they are color blind. Research also shows that our psychological state influences what we perceive—items more consistent with our current thoughts are more likely to be noted. Even the language that we speak influences distinctions that we see between colors and the information in our physical world that we tend to note. So there are lots of filters between what we believe that we see and what could more objectively be identified in our environment.

All of our sensory experiences are filtered, not just our visual ones. Not all sounds are heard, all scents smelled, or all tactile experiences registered. Some of the experiences that you provide for users of spaces you develop will be lost on them—and it's difficult to predict which ones. What people perceive is what they expect to experience. We form stereotypes of places just as we do of people, and it is those stereotypes that we live through unless material clearly inconsistent with our expectations is extremely obvious. We will "remember" objects and architectural features as being present in a space if those objects and features are consistent with our expectations—even if they weren't actually there. If we expect a friend's stylish mom to live in an apartment with a sophisticated design, we will remember Miro prints on the walls and Mies chairs—even if the prints on the walls really are Kinkades and the chairs are from Ethan Allen.

We build our stereotypes based on our own experiences and those of others that are reported to us. They evolve somewhat as our life experiences accumulate.

### Features of Well-Designed Spaces

All well-designed places satisfy five fundamental performance criteria and having the right information ensures that spaces you design serve their users well:[10]

1. *Comply*—Provide the support required to complete desired activities.

2. *Communicate*—Supply information that the person controlling the space would like to share about who they are, and provide opportunities for speaking with other people.

3. *Challenge*—Facilitate the growth and development of the users of the space.

4. *Continue*—Remain desirable over time.

5. *Comfort*—Relieve tension and prevent potentially stressful situations from developing initially.

Each of these criteria can be addressed in a number of ways. Research stimulates design ideas—but developing design options is what you've been doing through the design process all along. After reviewing these five performance criteria, you will better understand the sorts of issues that you need to probe when researching and the implications of what you learn when you do.

### Comply

People can want to accomplish a lot of different things in a space either one at a time, simultaneously with other goals, or in a clearly anticipatable sequence. Through programming-type research you will learn more about what sorts of functions a space will serve.

Some of the ways that a space can support desired activities are clearer than others. There are certain elements required in a cooking area—an ability to heat food, clean up, and store cooking tools, for example. Different traditions can satisfy these requirements in different ways, however. While a kitchen in the United States does not seem complete without an oven, kitchens in Mexico generally do not have one; there is a tradition of baking in the oven in the United States, but th is not the case in Mexico. Basic functions can be satisfied in different ways in different contexts.

Other ways that a space can support desired actions are less intuitively obvious. Let's work through a detailed example. In workplaces, there are people doing information work as well as people doing knowledge work. We can define *information work* as tasks that, after they are initially learned, don't require a lot of concentration to carry out. *Knowledge work,* by contrast, requires concentration, even after some time in a job—it continuously presents new challenges. Generally, working in a telephone call center is information work, while strategic planning and research/development are knowledge work. If knowledge work is to be done well, the people engaged in it need to be able to concentrate, and the enemy of concentration is distraction.

When we are doing our best to concentrate on knowledge work, the most significant problems arise from audio distractions. Perfect silence is also a problem—it is a very odd experience for humans, and we also find it distracting. Words spoken in languages we understand are most disturbing. The most effective mechanisms currently available to designers to blunt the impact of audio distractions on concentration are walls. People often listen to music on headphones to avoid being distracted, but listening to music on headphones has also been shown to reduce cognitive performance. If designers can't create floor-to-ceiling walls around people who need to concentrate, the only available mechanism to help people do so are fully enclosed (this means floor to ceiling sound-proofed walls) touchdown spaces that can be used on an as-needed basis. These touchdown spaces are not optimal, however, as continuity of physical environments and presence of personalizing items enhances cognitive performance.

Environmental distractions, such as from overheard conversations, create continuing problems for those exposed to them. After being distracted, it takes information/knowledge workers from 15 to 25 minutes to return to whatever they were doing before they were distracted. This happens after each and every distraction, so sitting near a coffee pot or along a central circulation route can be deadly for workplace effectiveness.

Individuals working in an open environment do speak more to each other than people in spaces where they have less visual access to each other—but they spend less time talking about work related issues. It is important that people working together have these non-work-related conversations so that they bond to each other and form a more cohesive workgroup. In an open work environment these bonding conversations can become so extensive that they reduce productivity, however.

Research has shown that regardless of age, no one multitasks very well—humans who want to do well need to stick to the mono-task world, as mentioned earlier in this chapter. In addition, people of various generations move through the same work-life phases, each of which is linked to specific behaviors—and that must be reflected in the design of any work area. When developing a workplace, it is important to consider career and life states and not generations. Instead of designing for particular generations, it is more appropriate to create spaces in which people can do specific tasks well.

When we are doing anything, we perform best if we are at an optimal (moderate) mental energy use level. Unfortunately, there is not a neat equation that can be used to determine whether a person is at this level, but people are fairly good at comparing their performance from one situation to the next. They can accurately report these relative performance levels if they feel safe in divulging this information. Doing a task that requires more focus uses more mental energy than one that requires less focus. In addition, being in a relatively more complex physical environment requires more energy than being in a less complex environment. That's why we can sit on a veranda (a relatively complex environment) and read recreationally (in this case we are at our optimal energy level), but need to move inside into a space without many audio, visual, or other sensory complexities when we are doing technical (textbook style) reading. Figures 3.1 and 3.2 provide examples of a relatively less complex interior environment, as well as a moderately complex one.

Some environments are more energizing and some are more relaxing. Not surprisingly, many of the spatial elements that energize us put us in a more negative mood, while those that are more relaxing put us in a more positive one.

Negative and positive moods are appropriate for different sorts of activities—each is desirable at particular times. Positive moods broaden our thinking, while negative ones narrow it. Positive moods are therefore great if we're doing a task that requires creativity or that people get along well with each other or reach a compromise (e.g., through negotiation). Negative moods are better when it is desirable for people to focus on completing a rigidly defined set of tasks. Unpleasant sounds, flashing lights, and bad smells put us in a negative mood, for example, all else being equal.

In emergency situations, adherence to an established protocol is crucial, just as it is when doing things such as reviewing information provided and looking for deviations from norms or processing data in other very straightforward, specified ways.

**FIGURE 3.1**
This space has low visual complexity.
© iStockphoto.com/ hemul75.

FIGURE 3.2
This place is moderately complex visually.
© iStockphoto.com/
hemul75

Talking with the people who will use a space that you are developing will help you understand their intended use for the space. This will direct you in determining what mood the space should encourage. Place attributes that have been associated with negative moods should be used sparingly, even in areas where a negative mood is desirable, and not at all (if possible) in spaces where positive moods are optimal.

Often, people paying to develop a new space say they want a place in which people are more productive or creative or healthier. Productivity, creativity, and health generally ensue when a space is designed so that it helps people complete desired activities in a positive mood. An integrative review of the social science research reveals that a positive mood in a space is likely to result if, for example:

- Colors used are not very saturated but relatively bright.

- Colors from near each other on the color wheel are used in combination.

- Forms and lines are generally curving.

- Textures are subdued and there is little variety in them.

- Lighting levels are relatively bright and warm.

- People are at desired distances from each other (the appropriate distance varies by situation and by national culture).

- People in the space have views out over nature or a similarly refreshing scene.

- Natural materials, such as wood with relatively light-colored stains and varnishes are used in the area

- Daylight is present in the space.

A positive mood also improves the functioning of our immune system—so the mood of both patients and caregivers is very important and their environments must also be designed to optimize their mood. An extensive body of research has investigated the best artwork for patient, clinical, and staff spaces in a hospital, for example.

The influence of mood on shopping behavior is complex. When people are shopping for fun, it is best for sales if the environment puts them in a positive mood. When people are doing utilitarian, purpose-driven shopping—stopping to buy milk and eggs on their way home from work—that positive mood isn't as important and efficient store layout is highly desirable.

## Communicate

Human beings are communicating all the time—sometimes with words, sometimes without. Many messages sent nonverbally are trusted more than spoken ones. Involuntary nonverbal messages, such as fleeting facial expressions and body movements, gain credibility because they are often revealed involuntarily and then filtered. Nonverbal messages are sent through the items we choose to add to our environments as well as how we modify the spaces themselves. Photos of families or boats, furniture arrangements, and new marble flooring all are introduced to send particular messages.

It's hard to know what's being communicated nonverbally unless you share cultural affiliations with the person transmitting information (see Figure 3.3). As we grow up in a culture we not only learn its spoken language, but also its unspoken one. We come to understand things such as cultural associations to particular colors, how far we should stand from other people in various situations, and how to isolate ourselves politely from other people when we need to mull over recent events and order our thoughts. Many of the place-based rules we learn are tacit knowledge, so we don't really have a mechanism to share them with people from other cultures, except by using them, so it's difficult for people from other cultures to pick them up in any organized way.

Although the specific "words" being used to communicate nonverbally through space vary by cultures (group and national), spaces are used to convey both personal and group identity (See Figure 3.4). The messages we broadcast help us feel comfortable in a space. They also change over time. The skills and mechanisms we use to send those messages evolve, as well. The importance of the messages perseveres throughout our lives and in all of the spaces that we control, whether we are at home, work, in a hospital bed, or visiting the commercial establishments we chose to frequent.

**FIGURE 3.3**
It's difficult to understand what's being communicated nonverbally unless you share cultural affiliations with the person transmitting information.
*Photo: Augustin*

**FIGURE 3.4**
Place is used to communicate information about personal and group identity. *Photo: Augustin*

## Challenge

We all have a personal development plan—one of our fundamental drives as human beings is to grow and develop in a personally meaningful way. Place design can help us achieve this objective. Space can provide the acoustical isolation we need to become a cellist or the chemistry lab we need to develop new pyrotechnics, or spaces to socialize with our children so we can guide them to develop as human beings—as we expand our parenting skills. Our drive to grow and develop as a person is particularly pertinent when designing residential environments.

## Continue

A space that evolves as its users and their needs changes is desirable. Particularly during tough psychological times, people prefer familiar spaces and things. A space that continues to meet user needs can be a significant emotional support. Spaces that support us psychologically over time are also better financial investments and more earth friendly. Flexibility can be provided through architectural elements as well as furnishings that are easy to reconfigure (see Figure C.5 in the color insert).

## Comfort

Several attributes of a space can help us feel comfortable. When people control their experience in a space, they are comfortable in it. *Control* is the ability to make choices as to a space's physical form and attributes. Personalizing a space with family photographs establishes control, which can also be exercised through changing the temperature or turning on a light. Control is at a fundamental level making a choice.[11] (Iynegar's research on choice is discussed in Chapter 2.) Groups need control of their environments, just as people do.

**FIGURE 3.5**
These mall chairs are ultimately unsatisfying to most shoppers, although they do allow passersby to rest. The chairs are bolted to the floor in a configuration that does not allow people shopping together to easily talk with each other while resting, and shopping is often a group activity. The sitters have only limited control of their seating orientations (they can pivot uncomfortably against the chair arms), and cannot make eye contact readily during conversations. The chairs, however, are probably a big hit with solo shoppers who are not required to connect socially with unknown seatmates.
*Photo: Augustin*

When we feel in control of a situation, our stress levels decrease and we are more likely to be in a positive mood than when we're without control. We are also more apt to feel satisfied and comfortable in the space when we feel in control of it (see Figure 3.5).

Feeling in control of our personal space is really important to us psychologically. Personal space is a set of zones that surrounds us and varies from situation to situation. The sizes of the personal spaces that people maintain vary by culture and perceptions of the situation—excellent arguments for providing a range of seating options, some on wheels, so people can maintain their desired distances from each other. Although the exact size of our personal spaces in different contexts varies by culture, each society maintains zones that range from one very close one that we allow only intimates to enter, to spaces used in formal situations that are much larger. We respond negatively when our personal space is broached and become tense. We will also adopt behaviors that help us ignore the troubling situation (see Figure 3.6). We make sure not to catch the space invader's eye, for example, and orient our body so we are not directly facing them—think about what happens in an elevator (even if it only has two people in it), and you get the idea.

**FIGURE 3.6**
Feeling in control of personal space is important psychologically. The design of this bench helps support that control by clearly indicating where people should sit. *Photo: Augustin*

We also control territories. Territories provide us with a home base in which we can decompress, and when we do, we broaden our thought processes. Both individuals and groups have territories and each polices intrusions into their spaces. Some barriers between territories are more traditional, such as walls and doors, and others are more symbolic. An edge of a rug, a change in ceiling height, or the area lit by a particular light can all serve as territorial markers.

Crowding results when we lose control of the number of people nearby. Crowding is an impression and not an objective reality. Crowding by definition is an unwanted collection of people around us—what we're happy to experience with our family is not so pleasant on the subway with strangers, for example. When we feel crowded, we work to escape. Interestingly, architectural features that would, at least theoretically allow us to escape from a situation, such as windows, make us feel less crowded. So do higher ceilings. It's as if when our personal space on the sides is compressed, the lost space can bubble overhead like a balloon and we can still be comfortable.

Human beings are social animals. Even the most introverted introvert needs human companionship from time to time. *Time to time* is key here. We want to socialize as desired and be alone as desired. Being alone has a lot of psychological value—mainly because it helps us reflect on what's happened to us recently and integrate our thoughts and experiences with others that we've had. It also allows us to relax. Privacy is so important that in today's open workplaces employees seem to be taking shelter in bathroom stalls. Being pack animals we are also very attuned to differences in status.

When we're doing the sort of intense thinking that is characterized as knowledge work for a long time, we become mentally exhausted. We can restock our levels of mental energy and reduce stress by looking at scenes we find fascinating and effortless to observe. Fish tanks and fire work well. So do views of outdoor spaces reminiscent of our life on the savanna. The places observed should not be totally wild jungles, but should have sections that look like a gentle meadow bordered by trees, with a few leafy trees in the middle of the space (see Figure 3.9). Best is to look out over this live, and from a higher vantage point onto the scene described, but the image also has benefits when used in two dimensions as artwork.

FIGURE 3.7
A view such as this one, of a meadow ringed by trees, helps people restock their mental energy. *© iStockphoto. com/Auris*

## Sensory Science

Rigorous scientific research has established associations between certain sensory experiences such as colors, scents, sounds, patterns, and psychological responses. Relatively insignificant seeming changes in physical environments can have a dramatic influence on our experience of space. When we are discussing these factors, and space design in general, it's important to keep in mind that space never acts alone in producing a psychological response; it is always one of a collection of inputs that determine an emotional state.

Aromas have a primordial influence on our psychological experience of space, and scents have a direct effect on our emotional well-being. In general, we prefer to be in pleasantly scented spaces, as opposed to unpleasantly scented ones, and being among those pleasing aromas boosts our mood—so we think more broadly and behave more positively to our fellow men. People spending time in a pleasantly scented place feel that they have been there less time there than people in an unscented space—which has repercussions for the design of cashregister stations in stores. Although pleasant aromas differ culturally, generally floral or fruity scents are well received. The olfactory experience in a space needs to be carefully considered, pleasant aromas of baking cookies in a commercial venue can boost mood, but exactly the same smell in a chemotherapy suite at the local hospital can nauseate patients.

Research has shown that certain scents can facilitate particular activities. For example, research by Bryan Raudenbush and his students at West Virginia's Wheeling Jesuit University has determined that smelling peppermint encourages us on to greater physical exertion and keeps us from feeling tired while we're at it, so it is a great smell to use in a gym.[12] Other researchers have found that lemon has roughly the same effect, but on mental activities. Lemon also soothes agitated mental patients and is associated with fewer reports of health problems in doctors' offices, which might reduce hypochondria or cause needed symptoms to be omitted from discussions. Spiced apple scents lower the blood pressure of healthy people three to five points, while green apple decreases feelings of claustrophobia—it's the scent to use in that tiny powder room. The aromas of almond, lavender, marjoram, and vanilla are relaxing. Vanilla is so relaxing that it is used in some MRI suites to calm patients. The scents of marjoram and lavender also reduce anxiety, along with lime and cypress. Rosemary and peppermint smells energize us, so that we put in that little extra effort. These effects continue even after we no longer consciously perceive a smell.

An increasing number of places are being scent-scaped, with scents being wafted into areas throughout the day. Scent-scaping has been used in Japanese offices to beat the 3:00 lull in body rhythms for some time. Muzak now has a division that provides scents for public spaces.

Finding out about these rigorously researched responses to smell is difficult in the general press because of the number of often unsubstantiated aromatherapy claims crowding data sources such as the Internet. Searches on scholar.google.com can reveal some of this information.

Sounds influence us emotionally, just as scents do. Although people from different national cultures may find different sorts of music pleasant, our psychological responses to the sounds we hear is consistent. For example, we all find slow, soft, complex music sad, which makes sense because when we are sad our vocal cords relax, and that muffles our voice. Sad people speak softly, just as angry or happy people do the opposite. Fast, loud, simple music is perceived as joyful, while fast, loud, complex music is seen as angry. Relatively slow, quiet, nonvocal music reduces reactions to stressful situations (such as group meetings) but faster music increases alertness and arousal.

Fast and slow are determined in relation to what is roughly our resting heartbeat, or 50 to 70 beats per minute (bpm). We find things that pulse at that rate relaxing. It's not surprising that sounds with that rhythm calm us, because when we hear a sound our heart starts to beat in time to it, and 50 to 70 bpm is a relatively relaxed pulse rate. Not just *music* with 50 to 70 bpm is calming. Fountains or mobiles that make noise with the same beat have the same effect on us. Music with 30 to 50 bpm is very relaxing.

High-pitched music, and noises in general, are happy and playful, while lower-pitched ones are sad and serious. We find midrange sounds, such as harps and classical chamber music, calming and higher-frequency sounds such as violins and voices, energizing.

Since our ears evolved from our skin, it's not surprising that we have similar responses to patterns of touch (massage) that we do to sounds. We also find touching more textured surfaces more energizing than feeling smoother ones underfoot, for example.

In North America and Europe vision is the most carefully monitored sensory channel, but not all cultures are as focused on information that they receive through their eyes. Regardless of national culture, we have consistent responses to information that we do indeed see. Colors that are less saturated and more bright, generally light and cool colors, are more relaxing and pleasant, while more saturated and less bright colors, generally darker or warm colors, are more invigorating and less pleasant. Colors that are lower in saturation contain more gray. Maroon is a less-saturated red than fire-engine red. Although responses to color saturation and brightness are universal, different national cultures vary in their associations to particular hues.

We feel significantly warmer when we look at warm colors than cool ones, which should influence color palettes for healthcare facilities, for example.

Monochromic color schemes are more relaxing, unless they are done in shades of whites and beiges. White/beige monochromes are upsetting to the general population.

When colors from across the color wheel are combined, the effect is more energizing than when colors near each other on the color wheel are used together. Colors can also be combined in patterns, and we find complex ones more energizing than simple ones.

It's not just the color of walls and surfaces that influences us emotionally; the color of light does so, as well. Warm white light increases our energy level as well as improving our mood (see Figure 3.8). People exposed to warm white light (3000K) reporter a stronger preference for resolving interpersonal conflicts through collaboration than people exposed to cool white light (4200K). People take more risks under warm white light than any other light colors, while cool-white lighting is more stressful to workers than full-spectrum lighting. When the colors of light are varied during the course of the day to mimic the natural light cycle, the well-being and emotional state of workers and patients is improved (see Figure 3.9). Daylight improves worker performance, retail sales, and mood, in general. Patients in day-lit rooms require less pain medicine. When lighting levels are lower, we are less active and speak more softly.

We react to seen objects in predictable ways. Shiny finishes are more invigorating and matte finishes more relaxing. We find pointy shapes less pleasant to be around than curvy ones. Spiky shapes overhead can be particularly unsettling, as can patterns composed of Vs.

Rhythm, symmetry, balance, and harmony in an object or space improve its aesthetic appeal to members of the general public and are generally relaxing. The golden ratio is generally pleasing and is so special that one particular part of the brain is dedicated to perceiving it.

**FIGURE 3.8**
Warm light, as produced by these lanterns, increases our energy level and boosts our mood. *Photo: Augustin*

Usually, we prefer to be in spaces that intrigue us but don't scare us. We like places that we can understand and that we can find our way in easily—they should be moderately complex and novel. We prefer that these pleasant places include elements such as paths that gently curve out of view that lead us forward and through the space. We have many other consistent responses to architectural elements, including ceiling height, wall curvature, room configuration, corner angles, window design, and entryways into a space.

## Biophilic Design

Many of our responses to our sensory experiences can be integrated through biophilic design (see Figure C.6 in the color insert). It involves incorporating natural aesthetic elements into our physical environment—using architecture to evoke the qualities of nature.[13]

We developed on the savanna, and the sorts of environments we found supportive during that early period in our history continue to be valued today. Biophilic designers work to incorporate them into daily spaces in our lives.[14] Natural spaces are sensorily rich, and they vary during the course of a day, for example. They also move—which is an argument for incorporating mobiles into design. Biophilic spaces include special fractal patterns that we find relaxing, such as the ones in fluffy clouds overhead on a pleasant day. Fractals repeat a common shape at different levels of scale throughout an area. Natural scenes include unexpected elements and promote a sense of freeness. Biophilic design also incorporates prospect and refuge into design. We feel very relaxed in a slightly dark space with a lower ceiling looking out over a more brightly lit area with a higher ceiling; this is prospect and refuge (see Figure 3.10).

## Place Design and Personality

For desirable emotional experiences, place should be consistent with the personalities of the people that will most probably use them. In the general population there is such a mix of personality types that it can be difficult to design a communal environment to provide this special support, but spaces being planned for smaller groups can often respond to personality type. People with similar personalities tend to do similar jobs and reference materials can be used to determine personality types likely to be found in a particular profession. For example, both doctors and nurses are more introverted than the population at large, so this should be reflected in their break rooms, for instance, although the personality-tailoring of spaces is not possible in patient areas. There are a number of personality factors that could be discussed, but we will cover just a few here.

Extraverts derive energy from the world around themselves, while introverts draw energy from within themselves. Extraverts enjoy being in areas with high levels of sensory inputs; these are spaces that overwhelm introverts. Extraverts also thrive on interactions with others—if you sit extraverts near the copy machine in an office, they will talk to everyone who visits it, which might not increase productivity. In general, you should plan places where extraverts need to concentrate so that it is difficult for them to make eye contact. Introverts are not as keen on eye contact and gathering spaces that they will use regularly should have some sort of diversion—a window or piece of art, for example—to which they can gracefully divert their eyes from time to time (see Figure C.7 in the color insert) Extraverts like to sit closer to people than introverts, which is another reason to include movable seating in an area. Extraverts when furnishing a home are more apt to use couches in communal areas and introverts are prone to use chairs (see Figure C.8 in the color insert). Introverts, similarly, prefer wider hallways than extraverts. Biologists believe that these differences between introverts and extraverts are due to the fact that introverts do a better job at processing information in their environment than extraverts; a lot of what happens around them is lost on extraverts.

**FIGURE 3.10**
Prospect and refuge, as provided by this canopy bed, are comforting to human beings. *Photo: Augustin*

Some people feel more in control of their own destiny (they are technically known as having an internal locus of control), and other people (externals) feel more strongly that their life events are controlled by forces beyond their control. Internals are more apt to modify an environment in which they find themselves than externals—so if you don't recognize that when developing spaces for groups of them, the places you have designed could get ugly really quickly. Externals are more apt to surround themselves with mementos than internals, which has repercussions for both workplace and home design. Internals also prefer more rectilinear elements in the physical environments that surround them, while externals favor more curvilinear ones.

## Individual Place Experiences

Individual place experience also has a significant impact on how a person or a group of people interacts with the world (see Figure 3.16). Generally, individual experience is reflected in more personal spaces, such as homes, and not in public places since individual place experiences vary dramatically from person to person. Workspaces and other more public environments are developed for simultaneous use by groups of people with a range of experiences. People develop sensory memories that can create associations to particular colors or floor layouts, for example. These associations are very strong and persistent.

## Culture and Environment

The national culture that we learned first continues to influence how we interact with the places around us for the rest of our lives. Scientific research has shown that our national culture, the culture we were raised in until the age of two, has a very important effect on the sorts of spaces in which we thrive as well as how we perceive what surrounds us. Research by Nisbett and his colleagues has shown just how basic these effects can be.[15] When people from a Far Eastern culture experience a scene, they tend to do so holistically, responding to the full range of elements present, while people raised in Western traditions pay attention to the focal elements, often at the expense of all else present. Also, as discussed earlier, North Americans and Europeans live in a very visually oriented world, while the sensory worlds of other cultures are more diverse. For example, the Japanese create multisensory place-based experiences.

Geert Hofstede has identified cultural differences that have direct repercussions for place design.[16] Some cultures value independence more highly and others interdependence, for example. Hofstede's research has determined that independence-minded cultures include the United States, Australia, Great Britain, Canada, Germany, the Netherlands, Belgium, France, Sweden, and Italy, among others. Interdependence-minded cultures include Brazil, Venezuela, Panama, Columbia, Peru, Mexico, Pakistan, the Philippines, South Korea, Hong Kong, China, Indonesia, Russia, and Arab countries.

Independence-minded cultures value representing individuality in spaces,
while interdependence-valuing cultures do the reverse; they prefer to represent group membership. People in independence-valuing cultures are also
more likely to modify their environments to meet their psychological needs
than people from interdependent cultures. People from more interdependent
cultures are more receptive to sharing resources with others than people from
independence-prizing cultures.

Cultures also differ in their desired emotional state, which has implications for the design of both private and communal settings (see Figure 3.12).

FIGURE 3.12
These worship spaces
indicate the significant
influence of national
culture on environmental
design. *Photos: Augustin*

Asians, on the one hand, feel that the ideal mood is a sort of peaceful Zen bliss—they value being relaxed. Americans, on the other hand, think that the ideal state is happy and excited—energized, in other words.

Since national cultures can differ so significantly in how they relate to their physical worlds, it is best to include a person from the users' national culture on any design team.

## Group Cultures and Place Design

We experience cultures on a group level as well as a national one. We all belong to a number of groups—professional, religious, hobby-based, for example. In each of these groups we learn place-based preferences and share them with others. Organizational culture has been extensively studied in workplaces (office and healthcare), and the importance of using place to support group culture is clear in these environments, as well as in retail, residential, and academic settings.

*Prioritizing Design Considerations*

We have identified a number of considerations that should be considered when designing a space: universal responses, personality, national cultures, group cultures, and individual experiences. Our review indicates that universal responses (related to biophilia, etc.) are the most important to recognize when designing a space, followed by personality (if the space type being designed can be personalized in this way). National cultures followed by group cultures are the next most important considerations, with individual experiences generally given least attention, unless a space is being created for a specific person.

## Designing for Particular Space Types

Although people may be people wherever they go, they are not always in the same sort of space. Specific design considerations arise with the creation of each place type.

The following issues are particularly topical as this book goes to press:

- Healthcare design has a significant influence on the immune function of both caregivers and patients through its emotional effect. Aesthetic elements are thus receiving additional attention in healthcare facilities.

- Teleworking/offsite work, need for concentration, psychological experience of working in a green building, personal displays in workplace environments, and appropriate responses to differences in status are often discussed by workplace designers.

- Public spaces are receiving a lot of attention with a particular focus on crowd behavior.

- Residential environments hot topics: more people living alone, issues with increasing mixing of world's populations and flexibility that requires in home environments, merging of work and home environments.

- Changing pedagogical techniques and repercussions for academic place design and increasing knowledge of how children experience environments are of great concern to school/academic designers.

- Retail spaces and their relationship with the seller's online presence are very important topics for store designers.

Design research is currently exploring these hot-button issues. There are some general, and relatively timeless, areas of inquiry for particular place types, however. When this perennially useful information is collected related insights from fields such as environmental psychology and sensory science can be integrated with it to produce important design insights.

Research can provide design researchers with the key information about workplaces and their users needed to design them effectively, such as:

- Jobs people actually do (based on input from workers themselves, not their supervisors) and the resources they need to do those jobs. How success in professional endeavors can be determined.

- How tasks vary from day to day, month to month

- Which tasks add the most value to the firm

- User response to current space and reasons for that response

- Organizational culture—which influences places need and how discussion of place needs will be structured

- Group cultures of particular sets of workers

- National cultures of users

- Meeting types, frequency, and group differences in meetings

- Future form/strategy of company and plans to move the organization from current to future situation

- Image that the leaders wish to project not only to visitors but to employees

It is particularly important to know about users' need to concentrate, as well as adjacencies to maximize value, and place-based tools (such as conference rooms) required for people to work well.

For healthcare designers all the previously mentioned items are pertinent, as well as these issues such as:

- Treatments provided and related strategy (a "destination" hospital for patients from abroad, for example)

- "Usual" patient and their associated friend/family support team

- Average length of stay

- Healing strategy (e.g., use of alternative medicine)

- Image wish to project to community at large, patients, caregivers

Things design researchers need to know about people who will live in a home to design it effectively include:

- Personalities, if designing a single family home

- National culture of residents and neighbors

- Desired activities in the home

- Place-related past experiences—positive and negative

- Possessions that homeowners want to continue to use

- Image wish to project

Things design researchers need to know about a school and its pupils/ teachers before they can design effectively include:

- Educational philosophy and pedagogical techniques used/to be used in the future

- Organizational culture—teachers/staff

- Organizational culture—students

- National cultures of students

- Services provided to what numbers of students and special place related requirements

- Community desired additional uses for building

Things design researchers need to know about a commercial group (store, restaurant, etc.) to effectively design for it include:

- Profit margin in relative items

- Marketing and public relations plans and objectives

- Items use as loss leaders to bring people into establishment

- Target customer attributes

- National culture of shoppers

- Demographics, financial, and social environment in area

- Service-related details (such as type of merchandise or cuisine)

## CORE CONCEPTS

It is important to organize research efforts to collect the material that is most pertinent to design. Design-project-based data requirements and place-related social science research should guide the structuring of a research agenda. Many social science research topics that might be pertinent to particular design projects were not mentioned in the short summary in this chapter, such as the way different segments of the population (e.g., children, elders) experience the environment. Designers need to think broadly when they are determining the research topics that they will investigate in the social science literature.

# ENDNOTES

1.  Jack Nasar and K. Devlin, "Beauty and the Beast: Some Preliminary Comparisons of 'Popular' vs. 'High' Architecture and Public vs. Architect Judgments of Same." *Journal of Environmental Psychology*, vol. 9 (1989), 333–344.

2.  David Meyers J. Rubinstein, D. Meyer, J. Evans. 2001. "Executive Control of Cognitive Processes in Task Switching." *Journal of Experimental Psychology, Human Perception and Performance*, vol. 27, no. 4, pp. 763–797.

3.  Stephanie Munson and Bruce Tharp, "Designerly Research and Problem Definition: Inspiration Versus Information." Presented at the Engineering and Product Design Education Conference (September 7–8, 2006), Salzburg, Austria.

4.  John Peponis, Sonit Bafna, Ritu Bajaj, Joyce Bromberg, Christine Congdon, Mahbub Rashid, Susan Warmels, Yan Zhang, and Craig Zimring, "Designing Space to Support Knowledge Work." *Environment and Behavior*, vol. 39, no. 6 (2007), 815–840.

5.  Joann Peck and Terry Childers, "Effects of Sensory Factors on Consumer Behavior: If It Tastes, Smells, Sounds and Feels Like a Duck, Then It Must Be a…" In *Handbook of Consumer Psychology*, Curtis Haugtvedt, Paul Herr, and Frank Kardes (eds.), pp. 193–219 (New York: Psychology Press, 2008).

6.  Patrick Jordan, *Designing Pleasurable Products: An Introduction to the New Human Factors* (New York: Taylor and Francis, 2000).

7.  Douglas Kendrick, Vladas Griskevicius, Steven Neuberg, and Mark Schaller, "Renovating the Pyramid of Needs: Contemporary Extensions Built Upon Ancient Foundations." *Perspectives on Psychological Science*, vol. 5, no. 3 (2010), 292–314.

8.  S. Reiss, "Multifaceted Nature of Intrinsic Motivation: The Theory of 16 Basic Desires." *Review of General Psychology*, vol. 8, no. 3 (2004), 179–193.

9.  Paul Lawrence and Nitin Nohria, *Driven: How Human Nature Shapes Our Choices* (San Francisco: Jossey-Bass, 2002).

10. Sally Augustin, *Place Advantage: Applied Psychology for Interior Architecture* (Hoboken, NJ: John Wiley and Sons, 2009).

11. Sheena Iyendar, *The Art of Choosing* (New York: Twelve, 2010).

12. B. Raudenbush, N. Corley, W. Eppich, *Augmenting Athletic Performance through the Administration of Peppermint Odor.* Presented at the Conference of the Association for Chemical Reception Science (April 2001), Sarasota, FL.

13. Stephen Kellert, Judith Heerwagen, and Martin Mador, *Biophilic Design: The Theory, Science and Practice of Bringing Buildings to Life* (Hoboken, NJ: John Wiley & Sons, 2008).

14. Judith Heerwagen and Bert Gregory, "Biophilia and Sensory Aesthetics." In *Biophilic Design*. Stephen Kellert, Judith Heerwagen and Martin Mador (eds.), pp. 227–241 (Hoboken, NJ: John Wiley and Sons, 2008).

15. Richard Nisbett, *The Geography of Thought: How Asians and Westerners Think Differently...and Why.* (New York: Free Press, 2003).

16. Geert Hofstede and Gert Jan Hofstede, *Cultures and Organizations: Software of the Mind* (New York: McGraw Hill, 2005).

# CHAPTER 4

# The Goals of Project Initiation

*"The wrong answer is the right answer in search of a different question."*

—Bruce Mau

## RESEARCH FOR COMPETITIVE ADVANTAGE

*Marketing,* also known as seeking and securing work, is a research assignment in and of itself. How a design firm promotes its capabilities has a lot to do with the focus of the design firm's work, employee qualifications, interests, aspirations, resources, and unique competencies. Design firms may either be considered *specialists*—designers that have deep knowledge in a specific project type, or as *generalists*—designers with broad and varied knowledge of multiple project types. Regardless of where on the spectrum a design firm's marketing emphasis resides, a research-based marketing approach supports a design firm in developing and demonstrating competency. This applies to both familiar project types and types that are untried, and it differentiates the design firm from its competition.

A research-based marketing approach supports the design firm in focusing its marketing resources on issues important to a specific audience. Here, research accomplishes two primary goals.

First, through research, the design firm identifies the types of clients, projects, and geographic locations for which it hopes to work. The firm is able to analyze the project type based on understanding the context that surrounds this project area—the business, economic, and/or social drivers, for example, and the motivations that surround the target industry both internally and externally. Additionally, a research approach allows the design firm to compare these contextual issues with the design firm's strengths and interests to assess whether there's an alignment between both.

Second, for both the specialist and generalist, a research-based marketing approach supports the design firm's ability to differentiate from the competition as it demonstrates the design firm's ability to home in on the important aspects of a potential client's area of need. In this scenario, a research-based marketing process shifts the discussion away from what the design firm accomplished in the past to what the design firm is capable of accomplishing in the future—an important distinction that positions the design firm in a proactive and prospective role of seeking and securing new work.

*Example: Since A Design has focused most of its ten years in practice on the design of daycare facilities, to expand the firm's market reach, the designers engage in a research process to investigate the context around other project types that have similar goals and conditions as a daycare center.*

*The design team starts with what it knows. With its extensive body of knowledge on daycare centers that includes demographic changes of communities that have resulted in the growth of the daycare market, the design team explores whether these growth projections apply to other markets. From the research, A Design discovers a corresponding growth in the K–12 school market.*

*As a next step, the team conducts additional research on the K–12 school market—it looks at precedents of the most recent K–12 school projects and assesses some of the unique aspects of each project. It conducts literature searches that provide insights into the leading thinking around education models and how place can influence educational performance.*

*Next, the design team conducts an audit of the design firms being commissioned for the most recent K–12 projects in the region. It examines the core competencies of these practices and maps these competencies with A Design's own practice approach. This serves useful in helping the team identify knowledge sources (like consultants familiar with this project type) and resources that they currently have compared to those they acknowledge are missing.*

*From this research exercise, A Design assesses the risks and rewards in expanding the firm's emphasis to the K–12 market. A Design identifies the firm's strength as having a strong body of knowledge in "play as learning" facilities but lack credentials in executing the formal aspects of education. From the team's earlier research, it knows that the best practices in K–12 education combine both play and formal learning styles.*

*From the results of the research and assessment exercise, A Design decides that the firm's option is to either add this competency by hiring a senior designer with a minimum of five years experience in K–12 education projects or by aligning with consulting firms with a breadth of experience in education facilities.*

A research-based marketing strategy is how a designer or design firm demonstrates competency around a specific project type. Research builds greater understanding around the explicit concerns of the stakeholders and provides the design firm with a source of knowledge that informs the content and direction of the marketing proposal.

Understanding the cultural, regional, economic, and behavioral issues specific to a proposed project type advances the marketing strategy by enabling the design team to frame the proposal and presentations through a filter of the conditions unique to the stakeholders. Here, knowing the sources of knowledge and innovations that surround this project type informs the design team regarding demographic conditions, site context, technological advances, and industry best practices. In addition, how external and internal economics factor into a potential client's considerations when commissioning an architectural project affects how the design team develops a marketing strategy that is distinct and focused on the aspirations and goals of the proposed stakeholders.

*Example: Having only two short weeks to respond to a request for qualifications (RFQ) for a new K–12 school building, the A team assembles to identify the goals for the research to inform the RFQ. First, the team identifies the client and project-specific issues to analyze: who makes up the client team, what are its areas of expertise, what experience (if any) has the client team had on similar building projects, and what were the project costs, schedule, and technologies used in these similar building projects?*

*Next, the team drills down into what is unique to this education facility. It uncovers demographic information for the project location and identifies the key drivers specific to this school board. Through literature reviews, it uncovers how the school board and community are expecting the new facility will address these goals:*

- *Support the district in establishing higher test scores for math and reading.*

- *Build a sense of community through a vital sports facility.*

- *Create an emphasis for the school district as a high-performing school through curricular and extracurricular activities.*

*As a next step, the team identifies the broader cultural, economic, and environmental areas of K–12 research. It explores the current precedents and best practices in K–12 education—what are the objectives for educational facilities today and in the future. The firm also looks to access information on new learning and teaching strategies, as well as innovative uses of technology in primary education.*

*With this information in place, the team is better prepared to shape the content of its proposal on issues that might be of direct concern to these decision makers.*

In today's competitive economy, a research-based marketing approach supports a firm's ability to differentiate among the competition and/or expand into new markets by enhancing a firm's past project experience with insightful new knowledge relevant to a potential client. It establishes a firm's credential based on knowledge, insight, and understanding. It can create new collaborative opportunities with consultants, experts, and colleagues. Finally, a research-based marketing approach supports a firm's ability to achieve an innovative interpretation of a project through understanding the context behind the client's goals.

## SECONDARY INFORMATION

It is always dangerous to discuss stereotypes, but some for information sources are worth noting. Information derived by governments or government-sponsored groups (such as the National Research Council—Canada—Construction, for workplace-design-related information) is rigorously conducted and well-respected in academic circles. Government labs generally work very hard to be impartial and hire well-skilled researchers. Studies conducted in the United States and funded by the National Science Foundation or the National Institutes of Health also are very credible. Statistical information from census bureaus and maps and information about the natural environments provided by geological surveys are also very strong. Additional government agencies that release reliable, design-related information include the General Services Administration (www.gsa.gov), cabinet departments, and special commissions appointed to investigate specific topics. In the European Union, the Community Research and Development Information Service (http://cordis.europa.eu) reports on all EU-sponsored research.

## Sources of Secondary Information

There are a slew of study centers affiliated with reputable, not-for-profit universities that are trusted information providers, including:

- Center for the Built Environment at the University of California, Berkeley (www.cbe.berkeley.edu)

- Lighting Research Center, Rensselaer Polytechnic Institute (www.irc .rpl.edu)

- Advanced Building Systems Integration Consortium, Carnegie Mellon University (www.cmu.edu/architecture/research/centers.html)

- Institute for Social Research, University of Michigan (www.isr.umich.edu)

- MIT Media Lab, Massachusetts Institute of Technology (www.media.mit.edu)

- The PlaceLab, House_n, Massachusetts Institute of Technology (http:// architecture.mit.edu/house_n/placelab.html)

- Center for Assistive Technology and Environmental Access, Georgia Institute of Technology (www.catea.gatech.edu)

- Architecture Research and Design Center, Texas Tech University (http:// arch.ttu.edu/wiki/ARDC)

- Institute on Aging and Environment, University of Wisconsin, Milwaukee (www4.uwm.edu/iae)

- Open University (http:/libeprints.open.ac.uk)

Many schools of architecture and interior design also have strong research programs and share their findings with individuals who contact them.

It can be tricky to determine the value of information from not-for-profit organizations. A good rule of thumb is that the more professors that are on the board of directors of a group, the more likely it is that the information they provide has been thoroughly vetted and is both reliable and valid. It is also a good sign if a paper on a not-for-profit's website can be clearly identified as being authored by a faculty member at a reputable, not-for-profit university or someone who has published books with a commercial publisher (not a vanity press). Some organizations that are good sources of information include:

- American Institute of Architects (AIA) (www.aia.org)

- American Society of Heating, Refrigerating and Air Conditioning Engineers (ASHRAE) (www.ashrae.org)

- American Society of Interior Designers (ASID) (www.asid.org)

- American Society of Landscape Architects (ASLA) (www.asla.org)

- Center for Health Design (www.healthdesign.org)

- Cyburbia (urban planning; www.cyburbia.org)

- Human Centred Design Institute (http://hcdi.brunel.ac.uk)

- International Interior Design Association (IIDA) (www.iida.org)

- Public Library of Science (www.plos.org)

- Rocky Mountain Institute (www.rmi.org)

- Society of College and University Planning (www.scup.org)

Again, this is only a partial list of nonprofit organizations that conduct reputable research and/or share research with their members or the general public.

Association websites are key sources of the information that can be used for competitive advantage—because they show you what your competition will be presenting. To be distinctive, you need to be clever and move beyond these standard precedents and insights to those that will really set you apart—using the techniques presented in this book.

## Cautions When Using Secondary Information

Organizations might have an agenda that they are trying to further, which casts suspicion on the information they are sharing. Sometimes, such a motivation is readily identifiable because of a group's name, logo, or material on its website, for example. If an organization has a reason to potentially distort research findings (it sells a product that is heavily used in an environment being discussed, most generally), it will be clear from text and links on its website. Look for connections to literature published either by academic researchers or by well-respected, commercial publishers. Being an advocacy group does not mean information presented is incorrect; just that it should be verified through another source.

If you cannot determine who originally did research that you find mentioned on websites or other sources that would be useful to you as you answer design questions, it would be best not to use that material. The potential problems that could result from being embarrassed by that data later outweigh potential usefulness to its use.

Reports become more credible when important research is referenced or when information provided about the writers indicates that they have been exposed to, and know how to use, the body of literature in a field. An advanced degree from a reputable university provides that credibility. Reports that are well-reviewed by objective sources are also highly credible.

When groups advance individuals as experts, independently investigate their credibility by doing online searches of a few of their publications and speaking engagements, for example, and by networking with your colleagues. Look for a track record of quality performance and beware of associations to sources that might be motivated to present biased information. More information on vetting an expert is included in the "Expert Interviews" section of Chapter 5.

When reviewing data on a website, also consider the following factors, which influence the credibility of the information reported:

- Are the writers identified? Do they seem professionally qualified? Is there any way to contact the author?

- What is the apparent audience for the website?

- Does the information agree with that from other sources? Always look for more than one data source when working to reach a design solution.

- Are references or a bibliography of some sort available so the sources of the information provided can be assessed? Are the references recent?

- It is generally a good idea to judge a website by its appearance—people who take care to present a good impression on their web pages can usually be counted on to be meticulous about the information they provide as well. Websites that seem to be designed (as opposed to haphazard) are more likely to be good sources of information than those whose owners haven't taken care in their preparation.

- Does the site make a good impression in terms of being organized and free from grammatical and spelling errors? Is the writing clear?

- Who owns the server where the information is found? This can be determined using metatags and Whois tools.

## PEER-REVIEWED STUDIES

Material from peer-reviewed publications is of extremely high quality (see Figure 4.1). You can determine if a source is peer reviewed by looking at the fine print describing a journal or periodical that is included in any hardcopy issues or on webpages describing it. Being peer reviewed is more prestigious than not being peer reviewed, so it is generally mentioned when a publication discusses itself.

**FIGURE 4.1**
Peer-reviewed journals are extremely well-respected sources of information. © *iStock-photo.com/luoman*

*Peer review* means that before the journal agrees to publish a paper, journal editors send the article they have received to people acknowledged as experts by their peers but who have had nothing to do with the article being considered for publication. The authors of the article being scrutinized do not know who is reviewing their paper (reviewers are anonymous), and there are often several rounds of discussions. Critiques are sent to the study authors who deal with a first round of criticisms, as well as future criticisms based on their initial responses. Secondary sources of information—for example, blogs and articles in the professional press such as *Interiors* and *Interior Design* or an AIA publication—often refer to these "gold-standard" peer-reviewed articles, but it is best, if at all possible, to review the original articles yourself, because misquotes or misimpressions are not uncommon.

## LITERATURE REVIEWS

Literature reviews are:

| | | | | | | |
|---|---|---|---|---|---|---|
| Little known | 1 | 2 | 3 | 4 | 5 | Lot known |
| Quick | 1 | 2 | 3 | 4 | 5 | Not quick |
| Info straightforward | 1 | 2 | 3 | 4 | 5 | Info complex |
| Verbal | 1 | 2 | 3 | 4 | 5 | Numeric |
| How | 1 | 2 | 3 | 4 | 5 | Why |
| On-site | 1 | 2 | 3 | 4 | 5 | Off-site OK |
| Well-established | 1 | 2 | 3 | 4 | 5 | Innovative |
| Current | 1 | 2 | 3 | 4 | 5 | Future |
| Special | 1 | 2 | 3 | 4 | 5 | No special |
| Generally considered | 1 | 2 | 3 | 4 | 5 | Potentially considered |

[Score indicated by **bold**ing of number.]

Literature reviews take many forms. You can review the body of knowledge related to a topic, such as the experience of living in a homeless shelter, or design precedents for homeless centers themselves, for example. In the next few paragraphs we will talk about important concepts related to both types of reviews before focusing on design-precedent studies.

Reviewing the research work of others will be extremely useful, particularly as you start to answer a design question. Looking at what others have learned over the years can introduce a mental model that you can apply. For example, research on shopper behavior indicates that there are two major types of people buying things in stores at any one time—those that are utilitarian shoppers and those that are recreational shoppers. Utilitarian shoppers want to quickly accomplish their shopping mission—they have a reason for being in the store, and are working to accomplish it as expeditiously as possible. Hedonistic shoppers, in contrast, are shopping to have a good time. They are the shoppers who, when asked, can truthfully respond that they are "just looking." Store environments for utilitarian shoppers need to be designed in a streamlined way, with aesthetic elements that support efficient shopping, such as relatively bright lighting. The environments for people shopping for pleasure need to encourage exploration and enjoyment. At different times of the day, the same store can have a majority of utilitarian shoppers or hedonistic shoppers, which can complicate the whole design process. A retail space designer armed with this information about shopper types can form some initial ideas about the design issues that must be resolved as a project moves forward. The research can provide a conceptual framework for those thoughts and a catalyst for creativity.

If you have conducted a thorough literature review, you can build on the work of others and establish a unique competitive advantage through your own research (surveys, observations, etc.). There is little value in replicating earlier studies that are available to competitors who have completed a literature review. Well-done completed studies might be difficult to replicate without careful control, anyway—it is possible that the earlier study may turn out to be a stronger project than you could execute with the resources available to you.

## Search Terms

The key to finding previously executed studies and relevant information is knowing the terms that researchers use in reports about them. When you start reading original source materials, give yourself plenty of time, and be sure to check the meanings of new terms you encounter or words used in a different way than you are used to. Being familiar with the meaning of technical terms used in an article ensures that you correctly interpret the information presented.

Remember the first time you saw the word *circulation* in an interior design or architecture text? Did you wonder what the heart and blood had to do with what you were reading? What did you think the first time you saw *wayfinding?* You've already learned about circulation and wayfinding, but there are other terms you'll learn and need to know as you move forward reading research related to place design. For example, if you want to find research related to walls of whatever height, it will be useful to search on the term *enclosure*. If you think that individual differences or personality will come into play and can be reflected in a space design, you need to know the technical terms for aspects of personality that are relevant to search, such as *extraversion, introversion,* or *locus of control*. Whenever you see a term that seems unusual or out of place, check to see if it has a special technical definition in the design world by typing "define: *term*" into the Google search field.

How can you identify the specialized terms you need to know? Buy introductory textbooks in relevant fields such as psychology or biology and skim their indexes, or use wikipedia.org or scholar.google.com to read general papers before doing more detailed searches. Make a mental note of technical terms you encounter so that they are more readily available when you need them. Better yet, work these technical terms learned into the knowledge management system described in Chapter 8 of this book.

Another way to learn technical terms that will be helpful as you read or search for studies is to get access to/go to a local or academic libraries and look at academic design and potentially design-related articles to determine words/terms in use. Academic department (and other) websites can also help identify useful search terms.

Ask reference librarians for help at both local and academic libraries—librarians have training in finding out how to find things out. They can be a useful support to your information objectives—even if they have no formal training in design research,.

A literature review will also introduce you to the terms generally used to discuss the issues being studied, which is always useful, and the research methods frequently used to investigate them, which can also be handy as you begin work. Be creative, however, as you decide what research methods you will use to resolve outstanding issues—although some methods are definitely better for some purposes than others, as outlined in Chapter 2. Creative reinterpretation of established research methodologies breathes new life into what can otherwise be a stodgy field.

Always read reference lists and indexes (particularly in academic texts)—they will introduce you not only to technical terms, but also to the names of researchers that you can search for additional information. They also provide all of the information required to find articles that relate to your research topic—they are preexisting, mini-lit reviews. These lists save you time, but if the person who wrote the article in which they appear did not fully explore all appropriate research avenues, neither will you if you rely on their work.

## Precedent Studies

Designers in all fields learn from and build on the work of previous designers. Often, the design process makes this evolution explicit, in a process that is roughly similar to benchmarking. Just as benchmarking requires comparisons outside the current project, there is an established process for reviewing design *precedents*. The process provides comfort to building funders, who may be risk averse. Precedents also allow designers to make their conversations clearer—a string of adjectives used abstractly can call different images to individual minds, but references to an object/place with a particular form can eliminate confusion. People designing homes often ask future residents about spaces they have found particularly desirable or undesirable — they are probing for the future resident's design precedents.

Reports of previous design solutions to resolve similar issues are a straightforward, pragmatic way to decide on future project directions, and the basis on which to develop innovative design responses. Referenced projects can be built or unbuilt, real world or fantasy. They are important for successful solutions that build on the insights provided by previous efforts.

Through precedent research, designers can also learn from their own previous design work, or that of others. Although individuals may reexamine their own design work casually and sporadically, architectural firms generally review their collective previous design work more formally.

Precedent reviews can be more concrete or more abstract. In their more concrete form, the design attributes of a built environment identified a priori are thoroughly investigated. During a more abstract precedent review, the process moves from criteria of interest to the identification of a collection of particular structures. For example, if the design problem requires knowledge of rest areas built over highways, the Hinsdale rest stop on Interstate 294 in Illinois can be investigated directly, or a more general search for information on structures built over highways may identify the Hinsdale structure, among others. Even if designers start with an investigation of the Hinsdale oasis, that investigation might unearth ideas that can be searched more broadly.

Precedent searches reveal how other designers have resolved design issues similar to those faced by the current project but provide only limited information on the success of the design solution adopted in the precedent projects. Unless a case study or a post-occupancy analysis has been done, it is difficult to determine how well a precedent meets specific user needs, for example, or how well it satisfies economic criteria. Aesthetic success does not require this sort of independent supporting documentation. Through experience, individual designers develop a collection of criteria that they think are appropriate to use to make context-specific aesthetic judgments.

## Precedent-Specific Sources of Information

Design precedents can be identified through a formal literature review and information search, or more casually and personally through a designer's formal or informal file of personally meaningful projects. These projects might be ones they have designed or not. Many of these precedent-related files are collected proactively, before the design project on which they will be applied has been identified. Designers can record their own experiences in places that they visit and use these personal experiences as the basis for future precedent reports. The term *file* here must be expanded to include materials in electronic or paper files, as well as information from books, videos, hand sketches, or any other medium.

If you have access to a library with a strong architecture department, ambling down its aisles can give you a good stock of material to review to find design precedents. These libraries have traditionally had the resources required to purchase review texts on building typologies, such as coffee shops and public libraries. In many states, publicly funded schools allow all citizens of the state into the library building. Getting into the building is usually enough to provide access to books on the shelves, but sometimes libraries do not allow anyone except library personnel to access books. Bound copies of academic and professional magazines may be available on those shelves, and unbound copies of current issues may also be accessible. Many libraries are now purchasing electronic subscriptions to periodicals. The contracts that libraries have with the electronic periodical publishers generally prevent the libraries from letting anyone but students, faculty, and staff members access these materials. These rules are strict—so take a class or teach one.

Information for design precedents that is not stored in personal files can be obtained from online searches. Sometimes these searches will identify particular printed sources that will need to be accessed through a traditional library, but most can be completed entirely online. A good source for precedent-related information online is www.bc.edu/bc_org/avp/cas/fnart/archweb_links.html or www.bc.edu/bc_org/avp/cas/fnart/archweb_noframes.html. The University of Nevada also maintains a similarly useful site (www.library.unlv.edu/arch/rsrce/webresources/). Simply Googling "architecture precedent study" or "architecture precedent studies" also produces valuable material. The online research section that follows describes how to conduct precise, targeted searches for useful material.

If you do have access to a library and its electronic periodical resources, the *Avery Index to Architectural Periodicals* can be a good source of precedent-related information.

There are evolving and existing collections of information that can be useful for online precedent searches. Georgia Tech has also created the Internet site with precedent-related information for Federal Courthouses (www.publicarchitecture.gatech.edu/Research/project/courtsweb.htm). Similar information for healthcare facilities is available at the Center for Healthcare Design site (http://ripple.healthdesign.org). Try a targeted Google search to find active websites with information on the types of structures you are researching. AIA presents multiple building case studies on its website that can be used to discuss precedents. Reports on the ASID, ASLA, and IIDA websites can also be useful for precedent research.

## Precedent Identification Criteria

What criteria should be used to identify comparison buildings and then to determine which of the many possible design attributes should be discussed in a precedent study? Design practitioners and theorists have been thinking about this for a long time, resulting in many lists of ideas that should be addressed in a precedent study.

In 2002, the Art Libraries Society of North America described an easy-to-remember and acceptably comprehensive system for reviewing precedents. It can be summarized using the acronym "BArTLES," which reminds people searching for precedents to review building (name of building), architect, type, location, era, and style. Searches on these parameters are those most likely to turn up useful precedents. The criteria can be searched individually but acquire real power when used in combinations, as described in the following paragraphs. In combination, they can identify completed projects physically or functionally similarity to the one in development.

Any aspect of a space can be featured in a precedent study. Francis Ching lays out fundamental design considerations and the ways in which spaces can vary in his classic *Architecture: Form, Space, and Order, Second Edition*.[1] For example, spaces can differ in form, space, organization, circulation, proportion, and scale. Principles such as symmetry, hierarchy, rhythm, and repetition can be applied to those spaces—or not.

These design factors are reflected in all sorts of spaces, from residential to commercial to public. Ching uses examples from these and other space types liberally as he explains elements of design. For example, when describing how "two points can denote a gateway signifying passage from one place to another. Extended vertically, the two prints define both a plane of entry and an approach perpendicular to it," Ching includes a drawing of the torii gate at the Ise Shrine in the Mie Prefecture, built in Japan in 690.[2] When describing how vertical linear elements can define a space, Ching illustrates the solid defined by minarets on the edges of the Hagia Sophia complex that implicitly form a cubic space that includes it. Dimensional, subtractive, and additive transformation are shown by structures designed by Le Corbusier (Unite d'Habitation), Charles Gwathmey (Gwathmey Residence), and Andrea Palladio (Il Redentore).

A few highlights from Ching's work indicate just how useful his insights can be as you work through a precedent study. Ching writes of architecture experienced through movement—which requires consideration of approach and entry and the sequence of spaces, for example. Sensory elements also define experience, as does enclosure, circulation systems, the site, and culture. Ching exhaustively explores topics ranging from clustered form to rotated grids to corners to the unity of opposites to L-shaped planes to openings in space-defining elements to light to proportioning systems to the depressed base plane (illustrated by the skating rink at Rockefeller Center).

The information that will be useful to you from a precedent search depends on how risk averse the client that you're working with is. If the client is very risk averse, it might want you to essentially recreate another space—a space crated by a well-known and noncontroversial architect. If the client is less risk averse, you can reference designers besides Andrea Palladio and can blend material from a wider range of sources in a precedent search. Always save information that you uncover in your firmwide knowledge management system (see Chapter 8 for details).

## Obtaining Information Online

You can also gain a lot of data by reviewing material online and in print. Often, it can be very useful to analyze materials collected this way using verbal and visual content analysis. Those techniques are reviewed in Chapter 5. The techniques outlined here can be used to source information related to competitive products, marketing and sales strategies, financial conditions, existing literature, and so on.

Determining what you need to research is the hardest part of any research project—and a task that keeps resurfacing as you move forward—a question resolved often brings to mind several previously unconsidered questions that must be answered.

Online searches are streamlined if you use the following rules. The rules are customized for searches using Google because it generally produces more high-quality search results than its competitors. Any of the material presented here could be changed at any time by Google or the other resources noted. Google also allows you to do targeted searches for images (which might or might not be provide without restrictions on their use), books, blogs, maps, and videos. There is also a language translation option through Google that does a pretty good job of translating website content from one language to another. If you type "define:" before a term, the system will produce definitions, and those definitions can contain other potential search terms.

The Google Scholar option (scholar.google.com) links into more academic and technical information by searching an entire posted source for the terms you have typed in, not just the abstract or designated keywords. The material that you can unearth using that site is stupendous, and capabilities are growing on a daily basis. Through Google Scholar, you can search patents and legal opinions and journals, as well as things like books, theses, and articles. Advanced search here is much the same as with Google in general, but it does facilitate searches of specific authors, publications, or particular sets of subject areas.

Google Books, also accessed through google.com, can be a handy source of information. Google Maps and Google Earth provide information that can be particularly useful when you are answering design questions using geographic information systems (GIS). GIS and its role in design research are described in Chapter 6. Google Earth allows you to trace routes and to call out particular geographic areas, which can be handy.

## Speedy Searches

There are several tempting quick sources of information online. Use them with care.

Wikipedia and similar sites can be a good source of information at a basic level and to identify other search terms, but do remember as you access it that its articles are created without peer review and there is no formal mechanism to monitor its content and resolve inaccurate material.

Amazon.com has become an online library that duplicates the local public library—if a vandal with an Exacto knife is cutting pages out of the books at your local library. Not only can you search for books of interest using your own search terms, but also, once you select a book, if the publisher has given permission for within-book searches, you can look for particular terms of interest within the text of a book. The books at Amazon that have been printed by commercial publishers (the opposite of the vanity press) have been vetted by their publishing houses, so you can feel confident in the material that you can quickly access there. To encourage people to purchase the books presented, sections of the books available are not shown online—this is not a problem if those sections are not relevant to the question that you are trying to answer.

Wolfram|Alpha (www.wolframalpha.com) is a go-to site when you need to answer straightforward, factual questions. It allows you to type in your question, written in your own, everyday language and its "computational knowledge engine" valiantly attempts to answer your question—sometimes those answers are absurd, after all even Wolfram|Alpha can only work with the information programmed into it, but generally the answers are very useful. The sections that will be of most interest to designers include the color section, which can provide color swatches, recipes for color mixing, and complimentary colors, for example, and demographic data. The site does, according to its home page, "aim to collect and curate all objective data, implement every known model, method, and algorithm, and make it possible to compute whatever can be computed about anything." With trillions of facts on file, it can go a long way toward reaching its goal.

## Methodical Googling

Google searchers, particularly ones that are a little more sophisticated because they use the tools described here, can be a great source of information. It is generally best to try the most complex search first with all potentially useful wildcards and then, if that is not successful, try a simpler search. Google allows ten terms in the search box, and using all ten options creates a very specialized search—one that can turn out to be too specialized. Although using fewer terms results in more material being retrieved, more material can mean a successful search if a potentially useful search result does not happen to include one of the search terms that would have been included in that potential ten-word set of search terms.

When you are doing a search, it's important to logic check the results you receive, particularly if you receive very few responses or odd responses. Spelling errors are often the culprit in these cases.

Here are some general Internet search tips:

- If there is a distinctive word or phrase that is likely to be used in a discussion of the topic you are investigating, be sure to use it during your search.

- When you put quote marks around a set of words, Google looks for that exact set of words when it is searching. When the words in the quote marks can take on several forms, this can create difficulties. For example, "case study" might well retrieve different sites than "case studies." If you leave off the quote marks, Google will search automatically for all words with the same base or stem as those that you have typed into the search box—it will report results for " case studies" even if you type in "case study."

- Using the ~ symbol (tilde) immediately before a word notifies Google to look for the word following the ~ as well as synonyms for it during the search process.

- Words that are sometimes used joined or sometimes used separately, such as "healthcare" and "health care" don't confuse the Google search formulas; they automatically return phrases with both the single word and the two-word phrase in use. If you are not sure if a single word/word pair you are working with is common enough for Google to recognize, do two separate searches.

- Google also recognizes what it considers common abbreviations and searches both common U.S. and British spellings of the same word (color and colour)—but as with the one-word/two-word phrases noted in the last paragraph, exercise caution.

- Google's advance search options allow you to customize searches in very useful ways. You can search for files of particular types (such as Keynote or PowerPoint) or on one sort of site, such as a government (.gov) or academic one (.edu). This can be useful if you don't want to retrieve information from industry (.com) sites because you fear, for example, that it might be biased. You can also require that returned material be from a particular website or in a specific language. The advanced features on the Google Scholar page allow you to specify a particular author or publication source (a specific journal, for example). You can also require that items returned have been published within a certain range of years. Using the advanced search screen of Google Scholar, you can also require that only certain subject areas on Google be combed for answers to your query. This can be handy when you are searching a term such as "Christopher Alexander" that could retrieve a number of computer science references that wouldn't interest you. An advance search on a Google Image screen permits you to use image usage rights as a search criteria as well as more technical issues such as aspect ratio and coloration.

- If you insert an asterisk (*) in a search phrase, you are using a wildcard. A wildcard is a sort of free pass on using the correct word in a phrase and is helpful when you are unsure of the exact wording you should be searching or you are trying to answer a very straightforward question ("* designed the Guggenheim Museum in New York").

- Google assumes that you want to search all terms in the phrase you type into the search box—if you are into Boolean logic, the technical lingo would be that it assumes an AND. It is also possible to use OR between two search phrases if you are interested in having one term or another used in your search.

- A plus sign (+) in a string of search terms means that the next word must appear in a search result—place a space before the + but not after it.

- There are several ways to ensure that a word does not appear in the search results. Either use a minus sign (–) before it (again, space before the minus sign but not after it) or use the words NOT or AND NOT.

- To identify pages linked to a particular website, type "link:" and the name of the webpage of interest into the search space. To find webpages similar to a page of interest, type "related to:" and the name of that webpage into the same space. You can accomplish the same thing by clicking on the *Similar* or *Cited by* keys that appear on a search results page. Certain sites can be excluded from your search using the phrase –www.*name of site to be excluded.*

- If your search returns more material than you can review, the "search within results" option at the bottom of a results page allows you to search within your previous search results.

- If you returned to a webpage after a while and it seems to have different information than the last time you were there, don't worry that you are losing your mind; it is entirely possible that the content of the page has changed. Look at earlier versions of the page by doing a search and clicking on the cached option beside the website of interest.

- If for some reason you are suspicious that there are materials on the web that your Google search is not uncovering, try searching DogPile at www.dogpile.com. It presents the "best results" that you would have uncovered on searches of Google, Yahoo, Bing, or Ask.

- There are several online, open-access collections of peer-reviewed or quality-controlled articles of interest to designers. The Directory of Open Access Journals (www.doaj.org) contains links to thousands of journals written in several different languages. The linked journals run the gambit from art and architecture to the humanities to the social science to the physical sciences to engineering. OAIster is very similar (http://oaister.worldcat.

org/). The Public Library of Science (www.plosone.org) focuses on material from the physical sciences.

- If your search turns up a paper that has been printed in an academic journal that is not available open source, don't despair. Search the exact title of the paper you would like to read in quotation marks. This is particularly likely to be successful if done from Google Scholar. Regularly, a version of the paper immediately before the one printed is available on the website of one of the article's authors or the website of the organization that sponsored the research. A trip to authors' websites can also turn up related papers that could be useful.

- If your search for a free version of a paper through the authors' websites fails, there is one last step you can take before giving up or breaking down and actually buying the article from the publisher. Go to the publishing journal's website and see if it has a free issue of the journal available online. You may find the exact article that you are looking for is available through that free issue, or that an article in the free issue provides the information you need.

## Other Sources of Information

This chapter has thus far focused on only freely available and searchable materials. However, many others are available for a fee or if you have access to an academic library. Many public libraries will order specific articles for you if those materials are not generally available to the public, but items ordered through interlibrary loan may not be available in time to meet short deadlines.

If you have access to an academic library, or a public library with an extensive collection of academic journals, reviewing the literature has just become much easier. You will end up searching the literature using whatever databases are available, but in general, Avery, Scopus, and PsychLit are good sources of design-relevant information.

Once you identify journals that regularly print the sorts of articles that interest you, such as *Environment and Behavior,* sign up for their issue alert service. Through those alerts, you will likely find out about articles of general value to your firm that you can purchase in advance of any particular relevant project and retain in your firm's design library (see Chapter 8 for additional details on design libraries). If funds allow you to subscribe to these journals, you will have ready access to information of value but also the opportunity to generally boost the knowledge base in the firm. An inviting physical library that not only provides access to journals but also valued texts, including current texts in relevant college courses, can be a good and pleasant way to increase the rate at which research is incorporated into design decisions.

There is so much information available to people who are teaching at schools with good libraries or who are students there that it might well be worth your organization's while to ensure that someone on staff is always teaching or studying at your best local university. Make sure that the number of hours this employee spends teaching/studying is sufficient to qualify for library access—particularly desirable is remote electronic access to the library and its periodicals.

People are an excellent source of information—after all, they are the source of the articles we have been discussing in this chapter. If resources do not allow hiring an expert, there are other ways that you can find someone to beef up your knowledge of a topic. Remember to find and vet your sources using the tools discussed in the Expert Interviews" section in Chapter 5.

You can network to find listservs read by the sort of people who could answer your questions. You can find discussion groups through groups.yahoo. com and groups.google.com. Groups that are likely to have readers with opinions to share include anthrodesign.

Including appropriate images can be very important in precedent and other studies. The Institute for Learning and Research Technology at the University of Bristol maintains a comprehensive guide to sites where images can be obtained (www.tasi.ac.uk/imagesites).

NPR and BBC radio shows are archived at these groups' home pages, and many other radio networks provide a similar service. Podcasts can be found in general online searches by adding the word *podcast* to the search terms used.

## The Value of Literature Reviews

There is a stunning amount of information available to be included in a literature or precedent review. Move boldly forward using the suggestions provided. Always keep track of where you have searched so that you don't waste time inadvertently duplicating a previous search or omitting a planned search because you think you remember doing it. Remember that searches at different times in the design process can serve very different needs. Some can be more exploratory but others need to be very specific to answer precise questions. Literature and precedent reviews expand to fill the time available for them. Set aside as much time as possible—optimally, at least several days to gather data and integrate it into a knowledge base—but realize that when time is up you must move onward with the information you have collected. *Research paralysis*, like analysis paralysis, is fatal in today's speed-obsessed design world. Research often is most palatable to the "research-phobic" when it is introduced through vignettes related to human beings or matrices that present and contrast the information collected.

## Literature Review—Example

For an example of a literature review, you need go no further than the text for your introductory art history text. It comprehensively reviewed written materials on artistic endeavors from the earliest periods of our history to the most recent.

## WITHIN-FIRM ARCHIVAL RESEARCH

Referencing materials previously used by your firm can provide useful information throughout the design process. The information that makes its way into an archive might have been edited by different people with varying objectives. Visual and verbal materials can be content analyzed. Please refer to Chapter 8 for additional information on firm knowledge management and access.

## EXPERIENCE SAMPLING METHOD

The experience sampling method is as follows:

| Little known | 1 | 2 | 3 | 4 | 5 | Lot Known |
|---|---|---|---|---|---|---|
| Quick | 1 | 2 | 3 | 4 | 5 | Not Quick |
| Info straightforward | 1 | 2 | 3 | 4 | 5 | Info complex |
| Verbal | 1 | 2 | 3 | 4 | 5 | Numeric |
| How | 1 | 2 | 3 | 4 | 5 | Why |
| On-site | 1 | 2 | 3 | 4 | 5 | Off-site OK |
| Well-established | 1 | 2 | 3 | 4 | 5 | Innovative |
| Current | 1 | 2 | 3 | 4 | 5 | Future |
| Special | 1 | 2 | 3 | 4 | 5 | No special |
| Generally considered | 1 | 2 | 3 | 4 | 5 | Potentially considered |

[Score indicated by **bold**ing of number.]

The experience sampling method (ESM) provides information about the daily lives of people who will use the spaces you are developing. It eliminates the risk of collecting inaccurate information because people have difficulty remembering situations or their responses to them. This is the advantage of asking people about their experiences while they are having them (see Figure 4.2).

The fundamental components of ESM are very straightforward. Every so often, you interrupt people during their day and ask them questions—both the people you contact and the questions that you ask them are related to the issues you are trying to resolve through research. You might ask people where they are, what they're doing, who they're doing it with, how well they think they're doing what they're doing… The list of things you could ask about is impressively long.

**FIGURE 4.2**
Electronic communication devices make ESM efficient. © *iStockphoto. com/photosbyash*

This is a particularly good way to collect information when the people being asked to supply it spend a lot of time in a space and you are interested in learning about their varied experiences within it. So it is useful with people who work in a store but not the people who shop there, people working in a healthcare facility but not with people visiting it for a single appointment. Patients who are physically capable of participating in a study, who will be in a hospital being treated for a week or more, however, could provide lots of important info using the experience sampling method.

ESM collects a more clearly refined set of information than observation, and unlike observation can begin to get at some of the emotional responses to environments. It can also collect *why* or motivation-type information. It uses surveys, and, because of when they are filled out, those surveys are more likely to collect accurate information than surveys in general. Using the ESM, data can be collected quickly and efficiently.

The ESM is a more sophisticated way to find out how people use space than a time utilization study. The ESM focuses on what the people who will use the space you are working on do during their day, as opposed to inventorying who is in a space that you will be redesigning. An ESM also provides information about people's response to a space and answers to other questions you might ask. A time utilization study is a simple count.

The data collected can be analyzed using Excel or other similar software packages, to uncover patterns in the data.

The technology you will use for ESM will continue to evolve after this book is printed, but you can utilize any tools at your disposal, even if they are a bell and a pad of paper. There are listservs that have been connecting people doing this sort of research for years, and lurking or questioning there can get you started with the technology and data-gathering techniques available when you are planning your ESM study. At the time this book is going to press, useful information is available at www.experience-sampling.org about handy hardware and software—some of it free. Information is also available through online sources about the appropriate incentives to be paid to study participants of various types. We will focus more on generally applicable techniques here than specific data-collection devices.

## Using the ESM

The rudiments of the ESM technique are that some device signals the study participant that you would like the participant to record data. Participants also need to be informed in some way of the questions that they are to answer, and the same set of questions will be asked each time they are contacted. A PDA can alert people via a page or telephone call and a survey can be asked via its screen. Using a PDA has the advantage of allowing all electronic data collected to be funneled together into some sort of database. It is possible to do ESM in a significantly more low-tech way—an old fashioned pager can be used to signal people to complete a survey bound into a paper booklet of surveys they have received. A whistle could, theoretically be blown to let those working in a sea of cubicles know that they need to answer survey questions. Surveys could be distributed once each morning in bound booklets—but that whistle could seem demeaning and would sound odd in telephone calls to the outside world.

Coordinating the required equipment is a significant impediment to using ESM, but the basic tenets of this tool can be adopted by canny researchers.

For example, researchers might just appear in a particular place and request that everyone present complete a brief five-question survey. Similarly, you might employ a silent ESM variation and leave a bound pad of a very brief, five-question or so, survey (in this case about the experience of working in that room) in a conference room where people leaving the room would see it. Completed surveys could be dropped in a nearby physical or virtual (if the survey happens to be electronic and presented via a display screen) box. If you ask people about their experience in a space as they leave it, their memories have already begun to fade, but if resources (human and technological) are not available to do ESM or if information is needed quickly, the in-room surveys described will collect useful information that would otherwise be unavailable.

It is good to have real contact with the participants every day—this helps maintain their commitment to the project and study participants need an easy way to reach you if their equipment malfunctions. Collecting PDAs, pagers, or other survey devices every evening and returning them each morning also prevents these devices from being lost, and data can be downloaded every night. If people are answering questions using bound sets of survey forms, it is also a good idea to collect these each evening and distribute a fresh survey booklet each morning—that keeps them from being lost, as well. In addition, if the previous day's information is collected, participants cannot simply copy their answers from one day onto the information sheets for subsequent days.

Depending on the data collection tool used, it might be necessary to train participants on how to use it. It is a good idea to pretest the survey questions, data collection methodology, and technology in use.

## Participants

Financial considerations will largely determine the number of people that you ask to take part in an ESM project. As with interviewing or other methodologies discussed, you should attempt to sample a group of people that represent the diversity of all potential users (in a workplace design project, this would be people doing the full range of jobs, at all levels [junior, mid-ranked, and senior accountants, marketing managers, logistics coordinators, etc.]). Within these sets of people, actual participants should be randomly selected, perhaps by drawing names out of hats, picking every nth (5th, 8th, etc.) person on a randomly or alphabetically ordered set of names of people who meet the required criteria.

Do not ask for volunteers to participate. Although volunteers can be exemplary study participants, often they have a strong interest in steering the space being created toward a specific form so they intentionally or unintentionally distort the information that they provide.

After a first round of data collection with one group of people, the same tools can be passed along to a second for another round of data collection. If resources are not constrained, you should collect information from 10 percent of the members of groups with more than 100 members, 20 percent of groups from groups with 50 to 99 members, and 30 percent of groups with 49 or fewer members, with always at least 5 members of a group participating.

A group is a set of users who can realistically be estimated to have similar space needs. In the workplace, a group would be a specific classification of accounting clerk. In a hospital, it could be caregivers in various departments of various grades or sets of responsibilities—this might translate to medium-level (pay or responsibility) oncology nurses who admit patients, for instance. Medium-level oncology nurses who administer chemotherapy would be a separate group.

Carefully identify the groups that have different space-related needs and sample from each of their members, if possible. If resources allow you to collect information from only a few sets of individuals, it is best to determine which individuals add most value to an organization and focus on their needs. In a religious setting, that would be the minister; in a commercial setting, the research and development or customer service team might be key (depending on the organization, of course); at an oncology hospital, it might be the doctors who coordinate research regimens or the nurses who administer them or the patients receiving them, depending on how that organization is differentiated from its peers. The people who ultimately participate in the ESM are clearly not the only users with needs but all those who reflect information-collecting priorities. In the hospital example, the place-related needs of doctors and patients would not be ignored if nurses participate in the ESM project.

## When to Conduct the ESM

Generally, good practice is not to page people to complete a survey more than once every 90 minutes if you will be paging them throughout a 24-hour period (which is unlikely to be required for a design project), or every hour if you will only be collecting data during an about 8-hour workday. More paging gets offensive and reduces compliance, whereas less paging, well, collects less information. Participants should not be able to predict when they will be paged because that might distort their behavior and the data collected. So, paging people every 90 minutes really means randomly within each 90-minute period. Theoretically, a person can be paged at minutes 89 and 91 of the study period and still be paged once during each 90-minute period. It's best, however, to make sure pages are at least 20 or so minutes apart. This sort of spacing increases the richness of the data collected and the goodwill of the study participants.

The exact moment at which people are paged during each period can be established in any number of ways—automatically by the tool used to communicate the page to the participant, by you using an online random number generator, or some other means. The times that people are paged should not follow a pattern (e.g., 8 minutes past every hour) and should not be chosen with knowledge of what the participant will be doing at that time; they should truly be random.

Data should be collected from each study participant for at least each activity period and on each day of a week, and, optimally, if time allows, for two weeks. If participants need to be tested in waves and study length is limited, a one-week data collection period is viable. An activity period is a segment of the day when it is reasonable to conclude that people might differ in how they interact with their environment or in which the environment might be physically different. Many spaces to be developed are used in different ways on different days of the week, so when use does vary by day of the week, the same time of day (say, 2 p.m.) would be classified as a separate activity period on Monday and Friday. To continue with the oncology example, there are different times during the day when patients are admitted, treated, and released, and data should separately be gathered during each of those periods and on each day of the week—different sorts of treatments may be administered on different schedules. In an office, Monday morning, Friday afternoon, and Thursday lunch can place different demands on a space, as can Tuesday early morning and Tuesday mid-morning.

Participants need to feel that it is important that they complete a survey at the time that they are asked to do so. People who can be expected to be unable to complete a survey at the designated time (e.g., surgeons while operating) should not be asked to participate in this type of study. People who cannot complete a survey within 10 minutes of when they have been paged should ignore that particular request for information—by then, the participant's memory for the situation at the moment the page was received will be fading, and distortions may be starting to color those memories. During workplace projects (whether those workplaces are offices or schools or somewhere else), participants' bosses should be informed if more than 20 percent of pages are ignored, and they should encourage their employees to participate. If more than 20 percent of requests are not completed, the data collection period for that person should be extended for a week. If the data collection rate does not pick up, that participant should be dropped from the study. To eliminate information collected after the allowed 10-minute lag period, the time that data were entered must be recorded, either electronically in an electronic data collection device or manually entered on a paper form.

## Data Collection Survey

The survey that you will be administering must be short because people will be completing it so often. It does not need to gather material about the person answering the questions because that information will be linked to the code number printed on the data collection booklet or to the data stream incoming from any electronic devices. The date and time that data were collected also must be entered into the database in some way. If this is not done automatically through the data collection software, it must be asked about directly.

There can be at most five questions on an ESM survey—and this means five questions, not a dozen questions within the one-through-five list because each question has more than one part.

The questions should probe topics that will have a significant influence on the design developed, be needed to resolve important design issues, and be multiple choice, so that they can be answered more quickly. Developing those multiple-choice answers may require knowledge that will only be available toward the end of a period of research that has begun using other tools, such as interviews.

The brevity of the surveys requires sacrificing some level of detail. For instance, you might find out that a person is with co-workers in the accounts receivable department but not exactly which ones—unless that is so important to you that you are willing to ask additional questions to get those names. In that case, questions about other topics, such as the functionality of a space or what the study participant was doing when paged, might need to be sacrificed. If you are recording what the participants were doing while paged, they need to be able to record at least two activities.

A specific sort of question that makes the ESM technique particularly valuable asks about users' reactions to experience in a particular space. It's best to ask this question in terms of user experience directly. The basic form of the question is: When you were beeped, were you feeling_____?" Then insert pairs of adjectives (a term and its opposite, for example, productive/unproductive) in random order. Provide 4 to 7 response options between these two extremes from which participants can choose. The form of the answer thus might be:

| Productive | 1 | 2 | 3 | 4 | Unproductive |
|---|---|---|---|---|---|

Select adjectives that are appropriate for the type of place in which people can expect to find themselves. You will have to prioritize the adjectives used; 6 pairs, or 12 adjectives total, are all that the respondent can review quickly enough to allow this question to qualify as a single one—this sort of question is so fast to answer that it does not violate the no-multi-part-question rule mentioned above—but only a single question of this type can be included on a survey. Show your list of adjectives to a few of the sorts of people who will participate in the ESM to ensure that the words to be used have clear, unambiguous meanings in the minds of people who will answer the questions during the data-gathering process.

The issues you have inquired about can be further investigated through interviews or by using other similar tools. For example, if you find out that tax accountants feel productive in conference room A, it would be useful to probe this later, perhaps during discussion groups, to gain insights on specific design elements to be included in rooms for tax accounts.

## Data Analysis

Data collected can be analyzed in terms of particular types of people or for a particular type of place—your choice depends on your research objectives. In general, it is most useful to focus on the people because they will be present in the new space, but the design significance of this distinction might not ultimately be really important. An example makes this distinction clear—you can determine where accountants feel productive (people-based approach) or who feels productive in conference room a (place-based approach). A more detailed example: Using a people-based approach, you can look at where people spend their time, what they do while they are there, who they are with, how being in a particular place makes them feel, and so on. If you analyze the data in a place-based way, you will find out who has been in a particular space, what they were doing there, and how the place makes them feel, for example.

Your data analysis software documentation (SPSS, Excel, etc.) will provide the details you need to set up your database to allow either type of analysis, and electronic data analysis is streamlined (translation: sped up) when data are also collected electronically. Electronic collection also means that error is not introduced into the system by someone keying information in electronically.

Frequency, percent, correlation, and chi square tests, as described in Chapter 5, can be conducted here.

Data collected can also be content analyzed, as described in Chapter 5. First, data are consolidated and content is analyzed on an individual person or space level, and then it is combined for sets of people or spaces who are similar in ways important for the research questions being answered. After data are consolidated, they are again content analyzed.

During data analysis, any individuals whose results are dramatically (which can't be quantified in this case) different than those of the group as a whole should be assessed carefully—sometimes people who deviate from the norm teach important lessons about that norm. Other times, they have just keyed in random, meaningless information.

## Similar Tools

A relative of the ESM is an activity log or experience diary. It is a comprehensive record of people's experiences. People whose daily activities can help answer research questions can be asked to record their actions throughout the day. Because of the time involved in supplying this information over two-week study periods (this study duration is based on the activity period discussion earlier), participants should only be asked to note their actions each hour, for the last hour. They can also be asked one or two questions each hour, similar to the ESM questions described earlier. The data collected with this method are thus subject to memory lapses and distortions, since people are asked about the last hour—but these problems are less severe than with a conventional survey, for example. Also, even with one notation of primary activity, location, and a couple of other pieces of information, a formidable amount of data is collected. This much data cannot realistically be processed if they are not collected electronically, via a PDA or similar device, from a study participant. If any sort of tool is available to contact study participants and collect information about their current activities (including telephone calls), then the experience sampling method is recommended in place of an activity log.

Visual diaries, which contain photos of where people are at particular times of the day, are also similar to ESM. Participants can be contacted at random times during the day or asked to take photos on a schedule. As with the activity log, the less standardized the data collection times, the more likely new information will be collected. Generally, people are also asked to record information to contextualize the images—a few short questions, such as those used with ESM, are utilized here. The answers collected must be linked to the appropriate photograph, which might require that information be collected through two different mediums (e.g., digital camera and separate data collection form). Technology might be available to help link files. The images collected can be valuable if a research question can be answered with a visual content analysis of this material. Since cell phones today generally have cameras, it is not necessary to distribute them to most participants, although if images are not taken with assigned cameras, they must be gathered later in some way. On rare occasions, it is not possible to take photographs at study sites—for security or cultural reasons.

## Experience Sampling Method—Example

Hektner, Schmidt, and Csikszentmihalyi have codified the best practices for ESM surveys and the sample survey that follows uses several of their questions (e.g., those about activities when contacted).[3] A sample survey to be used in a workplace project might take the following form:

What was the main thing you were doing when you were [insert method of contact here, for example, beeped]?—pull-down menu customized for study—about 6–10 options

What else were you doing when you were [insert method of contact here, for example, beeped]?—pull-down menu customized for study—about 6–10 options

Where were you when you were [insert method of contact here, for example, beeped]?—pull-down menu customized for study—6–10 options

How many people were with you when you were [insert method of contact here, for example, beeped]?—pull-down menu customized for study—5 or 6 response options

Describe how you felt when you were [insert method of contact here, for example, beeped]? [Customized to project—but could include]:

| Productive | 1 | 2 | 3 | 4 | 5 | Unproductive |
|---|---|---|---|---|---|---|
| Focused | 1 | 2 | 3 | 4 | 5 | Unfocused |
| Unenthused | 1 | 2 | 3 | 4 | 5 | Enthused |

[. . . .]

# DESIGN CHARETTES

Design charettes are:

| | | | | | | |
|---|---|---|---|---|---|---|
| Little known | 1 | 2 | **3** | 4 | 5 | Lot known |
| Quick | 1 | 2 | 3 | 4 | 5 | not quick |
| Info straightforward | 1 | 2 | 3 | 4 | 5 | Info complex |
| Verbal | 1 | 2 | 3 | 4 | 5 | Numeric |
| How | 1 | 2 | 3 | 4 | 5 | Why |
| On-site | 1 | 2 | 3 | 4 | 5 | Off-site OK |
| Well-established | 1 | 2 | **3** | 4 | 5 | Innovative |
| Current | 1 | 2 | 3 | 4 | 5 | Future |
| Special | 1 | 2 | 3 | 4 | 5 | No special |
| Generally considered | 1 | 2 | 3 | 4 | 5 | Potentially considered |

[Score indicated by **bold**ing of number.]

Design charettes are familiar to most designers. They are working sessions at which information is exchanged and design options are developed. They can be used by a group of designers to hash out design alternatives, or they can be conducted with clients or the ultimate users of a space to resolve outstanding design issues. The first sort of design charette is not so much part of the research process as the second, so we will focus on charettes that involve the ultimate users of a space.

The topics explored need to be pertinent to the specific project-related concerns to be resolved, and participants in the charette must be representative of the user groups for the space being redesigned (see Figure 4.3). Several charettes may need to be held to keep everyone contributing freely—as with discussion groups, conversations in charettes can be warped if they are not carefully organized. A representative sample of the types of users of a space is important, just as it is for discussion groups, but that diversity must be managed so that it facilitates discussion rather than hampers it. That means keeping people of different apparent ranks, social groups, and so on in separate charette sessions. It is best if participants from each of those user groups are selected randomly. For example: You know that to represent the set of people who will ultimately work in a particular hospital area, nurses from intensive-care units and from coronary-care units should both be invited to participate; however, the specific intensive-care nurses should be selected at random (as described in Chapter 5) from all intensive-care nurses.

**FIGURE 4.3**
All stakeholders should participate in design charettes. © iStockphoto.com/Yuri_Arcurs

In many ways, a design charette is just a specific type of discussion group, although its objective is more concrete—to develop a feasible design for a proposed space. The role of the discussion group moderator is similar to that of the charette leader—to get conversation going and to keep it moving on topics of interest, without coloring the outcomes with his/her personal opinions. In each case, the participants must recognize that they have been asked to participate because their experiences/opinions are valued.

Discussion groups and design charettes can be seamlessly combined. The big difference between discussion groups and design charettes is the importance of visuals and the topics of conversation. Visuals are often the focus of attention at a design charette, and information gathered is related more closely to design options; conversation is often more general at a discussion group and visual material is less crucial. The visuals at a charette might be created by the design team, by members of the design team and clients/users jointly, or by clients/users alone. Clients may or may not be the same as users—a retail chain could be a client but its employees and shoppers would be the users, for example. In joint client/design team events, the design team members invariably seem to take on the role of visual historians. In that case, they need to be certain not to use too much of their knowledge of design opportunities to distort user comments.

If all interested parties/stakeholders are able to participate in design charettes, the odds increase that the design decisions that build from them will accurately reflect the needs of the entire community. For example, if a healthcare facility is being built, caregiving staff of all types (doctors, nurses, various types of therapists, etc.) should participate in the charette, as should administrators (including the public relations, research and development, and fundraising teams), facility managers (particularly, teams involved with infection control and food service), and patients (day and overnight).

It is likely that people who participate in the research process will ultimately be advocates for the developed design. They understand the compromises necessary to represent all user needs and meet the needs of a range of different users as well as any resource constraints. Participating leads to advocating.

Although broad thinking during charettes is key, it is also important to have designers of all relevant types present at the charette sessions to ground conversation in basic realities. Attendees may include architects, interior designers, landscape architects, and urban planners, for example, depending on the project. These designers not only can benefit from interacting with the users, but they can gently comment to keep the discussion bounded in reality. To continue with the healthcare example, users at the charette might suggest that overnight patients and their family/friends should be provided with a range of patient-room amenities that effectively create a patient suite. Although it is important for the need for those amenities to be recorded and recognized, it is also true that it might not be a good use of time for users to spend too much of the session discussing a suite. Their thoughts about the priority of each amenity and how several can be provided simultaneously are more valuable to the design team.

People without some sort of design or art training are often concerned about expressing themselves visually in public, and charetting is an interactive process at which most attendees find themselves asked to express themselves visually. Sometimes this apprehension is misguided and people do a great job at drawing and whatever other visual activities they are asked to participate in. In other cases, participants are right; they really can't express any information visually. Because it can be difficult to know in advance which category your participants may fall into—and there can be variations even within one charette session—it is best for people to annotate any drawings with verbal notes to explain major points being expressed and to record discussions of the visual material created—those notes and recordings can be very handy later as attempts are made to incorporate material from users.

In a discussion group, usually everyone in the room participates in the same discussion, but in a design charette people are more likely to work in groups or individually for periods of time and then discuss their individual or small group work with the group as a whole. These discussions are extremely valuable, and compromises can develop as the talk continues on—usually worked out by the representatives of the user groups present. Often, the interplay between participants in these conversations unearths, and suggests solutions for, situations that designers would otherwise not be aware of.

Comments heard by discussion leaders as they circulate between working subgroups can provide valuable information. Leaders should record potentially useful comments as they move about and bring them up for whole group discussion or for further discussion among the design/client team later. Any comments that differ between groups should be discussed during the charette, if possible, so that they can be reconciled. If one set of members of a work team is developing a space that "promotes the activity through which they add most value to the firm" and is trying to create a space where they can concentrate, and another team of people ostensibly doing the same sort of work and doing the same sort of group assignment is creating one that facilitates instantaneous communication to respond to emergency situations, these inconsistencies need to be resolved if everyone is going to be successful in the redesigned space.

Design charettes often last longer than discussion groups. This ensures that individuals and subgroups have sufficient time to not only reach their separate conclusions but also fully discuss them with each other. A charette should not last longer than 2? hours, however. A 2? hour meeting can be difficult to coordinate, and participants often become tired after sessions of that length, so you will start to lose participants after that time period, literally and figuratively. Conversations without representatives of various user groups can reach conclusions that do not represent the best interests of the entire user community.

Design charettes can include site visits. This extends their length, but those visits can be a valuable way for both designers and clients to fully understand a location (see Figure 4.4). Trips need to be planned so that information pertinent to the issues to be resolved via the charette is shared. A visit to any existing site is useful to the design team so that they can gain an understanding of current conditions that will be referred to by users during discussions, as well as some concept of organizational priorities and culture.

The term *design charette* is often used to describe the process of presenting members of the general public with design options and collecting their feedback. These are generally large, formal sessions with individual members of the audience posing questions to the design team. Important information can be collected at these sessions. These meetings can be required on public works projects, and there may be several iterations of this process as the design becomes less conceptual and more concrete.

**FIGURE 4.4**
Site visits help partici-
pants at a design charette
visualize design-related
suggestions. © *iStock-
photo.com/jacus*

The data collected through design charettes should be content analyzed in light of the outstanding design questions that motivated the session in the first place. Verbal and visual analyses will be required to effectively utilize all of the data collected. The analyses should be done simultaneously and using the same set of grouping terms. The final report prepared should include all of the information required for the data to be applied in the correct context. This means reporting not only overall findings, but differences between user groups, for example. In addition, people reading the report must have information about the individuals who participated in the charette (i.e., material that is pertinent to the design project, such as job type and level if developing a workplace) and the design problems that they were asked to resolve.

## ENDNOTES

1. Francis Ching, *Architecture: Form, Space, and Order* (2nd ed.) (New York: John Wiley and Sons, 1996).

2. Ibid. p. 7.

3. Joel Hektner, Jennifer Schmidt, and Mihali Czikszentmihalyi, *Experience Sampling Method: Measuring the Quality of Everyday Life* (Thousand Oaks, CA: Sage Publications, 2007).

# A Story of Practice: A Research-Based Marketing Strategy

Information contributed through interview by Gensler, Chicago, Illinois.

**Contributors:**

Cary Johnson, senior associate

Todd Heiser, senior associate

Leah Ray, communications manager

Project: Panduit, a developer and provider of physical infrastructure solutions to connect, manage and automate communications, computers, and power and security systems

Scope: The marketing strategy that resulted in the firm being awarded the commission to design a five-story, 280,000-square-foot building as a LEED Gold-certified world headquarters

Date: Marketing Phase: 2006 Project Completion: 2010

Location: Tinley Park, Illinois

**FIGURE 4.5**
Panduit is a technology-focused manufacturer of network cabling components for communications, computing, power, and security systems.
© *Christopher Barrett.*

## PROBLEM DEFINITION

Prior to 2006, when Panduit hired the venerable Darrin Norbut as the company's senior manager for workplace resources, they did so to have him lead the organization and its workplace into the twenty-first century. Panduit was looking to build a sustainable headquarters building on a 52-acre site in Tinley Park, Illinois, 25 miles outside of downtown Chicago. Norbut invited Cary Johnson and Todd Heiser of Gensler (along with three other architecture firms) to respond to Panduit's request for proposal (RFP) for predesign, architecture, and interior design services (see Figures 4.5 and 4.6).

Although Panduit's technology-focused core business of manufacturing network cabling components for communications, computing, power, and security systems was highly sophisticated, their 1,000 employees, mostly engineers and administrators were working in a 10,000-square-foot facility that hadn't been updated since its original build-out in the 1950s. Therefore, for the Gensler team, the goal of this marketing assignment went beyond the typical demonstration of design competency by highlighting the firm's experience in similar project types. Instead, the team employed a research-based approach that supported a marketing strategy focused on validating the importance of an effective workplace in meeting organizational goals. Panduit's need to attract a younger workforce to replace employees ready to retire would require Panduit's leadership to first become familiarized with emerging workplace principles. As Johnson notes, this was an area of expertise that Gensler was able leverage to differentiate itself from the competition.

## OBJECTIVE

The objective of this project was to develop a marketing strategy that would demonstrate Gensler's capabilities. The team looked to leverage their experience, bodies of knowledge and specific expertise in both the strategy and the design of effective workplace facilities that can support the attraction and retention of the next-generation workforce. A successful marketing strategy required presenting a clear case to Panduit leadership that the design of the workplace is instrumental in job satisfaction and performance.

**FIGURE 4.6**
Panduit's new head-
quarters in Tinley Park,
Illinois. Project Comple-
tion, 2010. © *Christopher
Barrett.*

## KNOWING THE CLIENT

As a first step in the preparation of the marketing strategy, the project team assembled. The team comprised a project director, a design director, a communications manager, and a sustainable strategist. Through a briefing session, the team established the direction for the research; what sources of knowledge will they look to access, what knowledge sources are available internally within the firm and what type of outside experts or consultants, if any, to draw from.

From this session, the team divided the responsibilities and content areas for research. Each member conducted secondary literature reviews (focused on a specific subject) to become familiar with Panduit's business; its core values, competencies, and business partners.

From this material, Johnson and his team understood Panduit to be a sophisticated and technology-driven organization. With a core business of helping customers with infrastructure solutions to manage and automate their communications, power, and securities systems, this capability established

Panduit as having strong technology relationships with industry leaders on a global scale.

Next, the team scheduled visits to observe work processes and workplace behaviors at Panduit's current headquarters. Here, the team observed first hand how the management philosophy contradicted their forward-thinking business focus and had, in fact, stalled in the mid-twentieth century.

As Heiser jokes, "It was like looking at Frank Lloyd Wright's Johnson Wax installation, but not in a good way." Examples include the use of flashing cherry lights (the emergency light on top of a police car), indicating a worker's receipt of a telephone call, office workers punching in and out of time clocks, plus, as Heiser's reference recalls, a densely packed call center with precise rows of steel desks all forward facing toward the watchful eye of a supervisor's office. Absent were spaces to take a personal call, quiet spaces for focused work, active spaces to encourage collaboration or the sharing of ideas with coworkers, along with access to daylight or acoustic considerations.

Johnson and Heiser recollect an anecdote Panduit's human resource manager described about a young recruit coming to visit the headquarters. As the limousine from the airport arrived at the front door of the facility, rather than enter the building, the recruit instructed the driver to return to the airport.

From this observation, the team understood that framing the marketing strategy around Panduit's need to attract a younger workforce required Panduit leadership to first become familiarized with today's leading thinking around management theory and workplace principles (see Figure 4.7).

**FIGURE 4.7**
The architects demonstrate the connection between the quality of a workplace and improved employee satisfaction.
© *Christopher Barrett.*

## SHARING SOURCES OF KNOWLEDGE

Because Johnson and Heiser had previously worked with Norbut (at different firms), they were well aware that his personal knowledge about workplace performance was unmatched. However, as Johnson explains, "Our job here was to help Darrin get Panduit's leadership up to speed and all speaking the same language."

To start, Johnson and Heiser began culling information from Gensler's Workplace Performance Survey that surveyed more than 2,000 Americans who work in offices (see Figure 4.8). Beyond the survey, the team conducted precedent searches—internal and external—examining workplace projects that helped redefine the culture of legacy organizations. In assembling this information, Heiser and Johnson explain, they were able to assess and analyze the success and failures of these project types based on how these spaces influenced workplace performance.

With the accumulation of the research, and prior to ever presenting the firm's qualifications, the Gensler team sent what it considered the most relevant white papers and articles about workplace performance to Norbut for distribution to Panduit's leadership. Johnson explains that sharing the research with the client team demonstrated the firm's strength in being able to assess, analyze, and quantify how space can influence workplace performance and how a sustainable agenda not only impacts energy efficiency but also employee satisfaction. Whenever possible, the Gensler team aligned design strategies with qualitative information on its impact on worker productivity.

Heiser recalls how the research made Panduit's existing workplace problems more tangible for the client team. One example, notes Heiser, was Panduit's ongoing problem with employees' access to the most up-to-date sourcing information. From the research, the client team understood that the facility's formal structure prevented interaction between employees and therefore the sharing of information, which they ultimately assessed was due to this lack of communication.

## THE PRESENTATION

With the research in place, the Gensler team determined a better strategy for the presentation (rather than the usual "beauty contest" of showing images of previously completed work) to directly address Panduit's business problem was to identify what is different with the next generation employee and what are the qualities of a workplace that will support this difference, enhance performance and act as a vehicle for the organization to attract and retain this workforce?

# What's Going on at the Office?

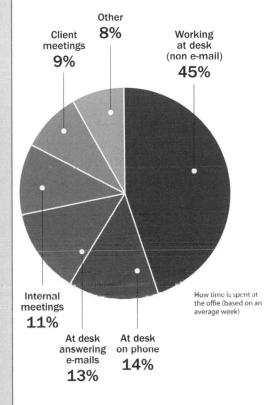

Other
**8%**

Client meetings
**9%**

Working at desk (non e-mail)
**45%**

Internal meetings
**11%**

At desk answering e-mails
**13%**

At desk on phone
**14%**

How time is spent at the offie (based on an average week)

The U.S. Workplace Survey results allow us to paint a picture of the contemporary American office worker.

The average U.S. office worker is 42 years old and has been at her job for 6.3 years. She works in an office with 210 employees for a company with 3,711 total employees. The company's annual revenues are $354 million.

The average office worker feels that he has less time to think than he did five years ago to due to increasing pressure and expectations. About 14.5% of his social time involves work and work colleagues. On a scale from 1 to 5, with five being most satisfied, he would rate his current job satisfaction as 3.6.

Over 80% of workers felt that technology has enhanced their workplace environment. Technologies used include:

Desktop computer 84%
Mobile phone 46%
Laptop computer 38%
Wireless access 28%
Teleconferencing 26%
Video conferencing 17%
Mobile e-mail device (PDA) 13%

**FIGURE 4.8a–4.8e**
Gensler's Workplace Performance Survey and Workplace Performance Index distills the firm's workplace performance research.

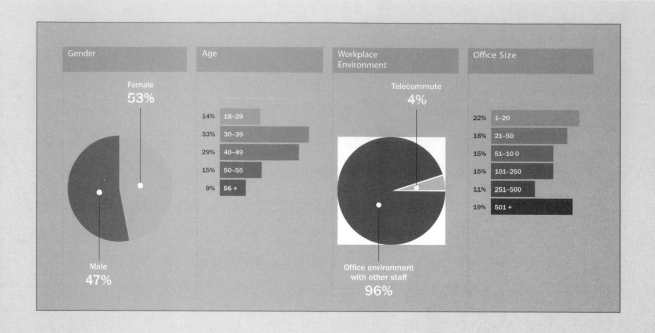

**Gender**

Female
**53%**

Male
**47%**

**Age**

| | |
|---|---|
| 14% | 18–29 |
| 33% | 30–39 |
| 29% | 40–49 |
| 15% | 50–55 |
| 9% | 56 + |

**Workplace Environment**

Telecommute
**4%**

Office environment
with other staff
**96%**

**Office Size**

| | |
|---|---|
| 22% | 1–20 |
| 18% | 21–50 |
| 15% | 51–10 0 |
| 15% | 101–250 |
| 11% | 251–500 |
| 19% | 501 + |

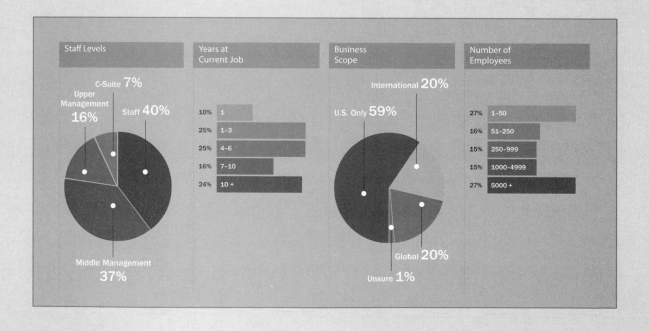

**Staff Levels**

C-Suite **7%**
Upper
Management
**16%**
Staff **40%**
Middle Management
**37%**

**Years at Current Job**

| | |
|---|---|
| 10% | 1 |
| 25% | 1–3 |
| 25% | 4–6 |
| 16% | 7–10 |
| 24% | 10 + |

**Business Scope**

International **20%**
U.S. Only **59%**
Global **20%**
Unsure **1%**

**Number of Employees**

| | |
|---|---|
| 27% | 1–50 |
| 16% | 51–250 |
| 15% | 250–999 |
| 15% | 1000–4999 |
| 27% | 5000 + |

# productivity

Nine of 10 respondents believe that workplace design affects their productivity.

**21%**

Potential for increased performance. Respondents say they could increase the amount of work they perform now by an average of 21% if they had a better-designed working environment.

# collaboration

Only 50% of workers believe that their current workplace design encourages innovation and creativity.

67% 33%

Working better together. 67% of respondents felt they were more efficient when working closely with co-workers. But less than 1/3 of workers believe that creating a productive workplace is a priority at their company.

# competitiveness

88% of C-level/upper management respondents believe that the workplace environment would have a positive impact on their company's bottom line.

**92%**

of respondents agreed that better workplace design can make a company more competitive.

# Key Findings Workplace quality makes a difference.

## In overwhelming numbers, U.S. office workers say that well-designed work settings clearly contribute to individual and organizational performance.

**89%**

When asked to rate the importance of workplace design, 89% of respondents rated it "important" to "very important."

**90%**

90% of respondents indicated that better workplace design and layout result in better overall employee performance.

When asked if the quality of the working environment is very important to their sense of job satisfaction, 88% of respondents agreed.

Asked where they accomplish their best work, 84% of respondents pointed to the office. Twelve percent cited working at home, 2% cited while traveling, and only 1% cited other venues.

When asked where their best ideas are developed, 49% of respondents said at their desk. Sixty-seven percent of respondents felt they were more effi cient when working closely with co-workers.

The survey results indicate that businesses can directly impact worker productivity through workplace design. When asked if they would be willing to work an extra hour per day if they had a better working environment, 49% of respondents said yes.

We asked C-level/upper management to quantify how a better physical working environment could impact the amount of work their company performed. The average estimate was 22.4%. And 88% of upper management/C-level respondents said that the increased productivity would have a positive impact on their company's bottom line.

But the survey also indicates there is a strong disconnect between the value placed on the workplace environment and perceptions of what drove their current workplace design: just 1/3 of respondents believe that creating a productive workplace is a priority at their company.

Only half of the U.S. workforce feel that their environment empowers them to innovate (see graph at right). American businesses may be missing an important opportunity to increase innovation.

As competition for talent continues to increase and as employers are forced to explore more and more ways to attract and retain employees, the workplace can be a key tool to not only keep employees, but to keep them productive and engaged.

The U.S. Workplace Survey

Going back to the research accessed through this marketing process, the team distilled the most relevant material into an easily digestible presentation (see Figure 4.9). The presentation highlighted the emerging research that informs the new drivers of workplace design clustered in four categories:

1. *Diversity*—the way a workplace can be leveraged to create community

2. *Distance*—the way a workplace can mitigate feelings of dislocation due to mobility and technology

3. *Work modes*—the way a workplace can accommodate different, changeable ways of working

4. *Responsibility*—the way a workplace can embrace and communicate the values of social and environmental responsibility

**FIGURE 4.9**
The Gensler team positions workstations to leverage access to daylight. *© Christopher Barrett.*

## LESSONS LEARNED

According to Johnson and Heiser, the success of this marketing strategy was in the team's ability to home in on knowing the client, their vision, goals and future objectives. With that information, they say, getting smart about what matters to the client team helped the Gensler team demonstrate the value of the service it could bring to this assignment. Reflecting back, they acknowledged that the research-based approach helped build a platform for a research-driven design process at each stage of the project.

Johnson and Heiser agree that the focused research was what helped them win this project commission. "I think Panduit's leadership saw us as their partners—able to design a workplace around what matters," adds Johnson.

# CHAPTER 5

# The Goals of Investigation

*"The most important thing in communication is hearing what isn't said."*

—PETER DRUCKER

## RESEARCH AS A PROCESS OF DISCOVERING A CLIENT'S NEEDS

Many factors influence the clarity with which people perceive and communicate their own needs and those of others. As a result, the perceived needs of a single design project can range widely from vague to specific, straightforward to convoluted, and emotional to factual. Programming as a research-based methodology yields insight into stakeholder needs and aspirations, supplying the tools needed to unpack preconceived assumptions.

Implementing a research process in programming allows designers to learn about users and their space-based experiences and cultural goals. Traditional programming is an objective and quantitative process that uses interviews, surveys, and questionnaires to gain perspective from all stakeholders involved. The resulting quantitative data details space requirements and elements within the project that respond to user needs. This information is then compiled to create a checklist of spatial needs for the designer to use when making design decisions regarding space organization. Traditional programming hinges on the knowledge and insight of the project's stakeholders and their ability to clearly communicate what the design team knows.

As a complement to traditional programming, subjective programming employs research to access the unknown or unstated qualitative needs. In this process, open-ended inquiry leads to discovery and redefinition, allowing the team to problem identify, as well as problem solve. The qualitative research establishes the core values of the project by defining performance and cultural goals. These goals are identified through the consideration of various related issues, such as performance issues and user satisfaction, to name a few. Results gathered from subjective programming inform a design brief that supports the client, user, and organization in "knowing the future."

Behavioral observation also reveals unstated opportunities and obstacles, as well as evaluates the validity of established practices. As a part of a research-based programming process, behavioral observation has the potential to yield more information on user-experience and cultural goals than traditional programming methods alone.

*Example: B Architects won a commission for a state-of-the-art performance facility. In order to define the needs and aspirations of the client, the design team begins its research by distributing a web-based survey to targeted stakeholders, including the client's, board of directors, staff, and performing artists. The team also selects a sample group of stakeholders to participate in one-on-one interviews. Literature reviews on new technologies and amenities in performance facilities supplement the team's survey and interview information. The research amasses essential information on the spatial and technical goals of each stakeholder group, resulting in a checklist of the project's spatial and performance requirements.*

*From there, B Architects guides a sample group through a half-day workshop assembled to reimagine the future of the performance facility in response to potential game-changing trends, technologies, or events. This open-ended inquiry generates valuable information regarding the differing performance and cultural goals among the stakeholder groups, as well as which technologies the groups see as changing the performing-arts experience. For example, some saw an increased need for special effects, advanced sound systems, aerial stunts and large marketing and advertising campaigns. Alternatively, some groups emphasized the elements that differentiated the performing arts, such as the intimacy of scale and sensitive acoustics.*

*As a means to reconcile the stated aspirations and goals of the stakeholders with established practices, B Architects conducts behavioral observations. The design team attends rehearsals and performances, observing and mapping the tasks of all groups, including the production crew and ticket sales.*

Effective analysis and synthesis of the multilayered programming information transforms the raw data collected into valuable new knowledge that informs a client-specific design strategy. Analysis involves mapping a space-use strategy based on research that demonstrates the design team's sensitivity to the needs of the stakeholders. The resulting design strategy reaches beyond prescriptive space types to meaningful insights into the aspirations and future needs of the client. The return on the research investment in the programming phase includes developing a greater understanding of the users and stakeholders of the space. Through the effective use of the client's human, financial, and spatial resources as a source of data, the design team is provided with sound information to enable the creation of a project-specific design response that yields greater client satisfaction.

*Example: Through the research process, B Architects has effectively influenced the current human, financial, and spatial resources of its client in order to not only better understand the existing needs of a performing arts center but also anticipate future needs and aspirations. The venue is poised to support technologically advanced performances, while being sensitive to the acoustics and intimacy that theatergoers value from local venues. As a result of the research, the client is confident that the evolution of the design brief responds to its unique position and future.*

# INTERVIEWS

Interviews are:

| | | | | | | |
|---|---|---|---|---|---|---|
| Little known | 1 | 2 | 3 | **4** | 5 | Lot known |
| Quick | 1 | 2 | **3** | 4 | 5 | Not quick |
| Info straightforward | 1 | **2** | 3 | 4 | 5 | Info complex |
| Verbal | **1** | 2 | 3 | 4 | 5 | Numeric |
| How | 1 | 2 | 3 | 4 | **5** | Why |
| On-site | **1** | 2 | 3 | 4 | 5 | Off-site OK |
| Well-established | 1 | 2 | 3 | **4** | 5 | Innovative |
| Current | 1 | 2 | 3 | 4 | **5** | Future |
| Special | 1 | 2 | **3** | 4 | **5** | No special |
| Generally considered | **1** | 2 | 3 | 4 | 5 | Potentially considered |

[Score indicated by **bold**ing of number.]

Interviews are an excellent way for you to collect information from the people who will ultimately use the space that you are designing (and those that control the experiences of those users if you are working on a workplace, healthcare, retail, academic/school, or public space). They gather perceptions from those interviewed. Interviews are particularly useful when you imagine that you may want to probe responses given to questions. A very specialized type of interview, those with a subject matter expert, will also be discussed in this chapter.

## Developing Interview Questions

The first step in creating useful interview questions is to clearly identify the issues that you wish to investigate. This means going beyond the simple ("We need to learn things that will help us design this new school") to detailed and specific questions ("How are pedagogical techniques for elementary school education evolving?" "What aspects of the physical environment increase teacher perceptions that their students are having high-quality educational experiences?"). The interview itself should include a mix of these very specific questions, along with some broad, open-ended questions so a full understanding of the relevant issues results, and so that the person being interviewed has the opportunity to provide relevant information that you may not have known enough about the issues to have planned to discuss. Putting the most open-ended questions early can be handy if you're not that familiar with the issues being researched. They get the interviewee used to speaking at length, and they teach you useful things that you can use to fine-tune future questions.

Have a meeting with your design colleagues, and also potentially with the client, to uncover the issues that need to probed. Determining the issues to be investigated in advance reduces the possibility of *project creep*. A discussion of this sort will also indicate who (within or external to the organization) should be interviewed. This meeting should occur before any expert to be interviewed is hired, to ensure that the person selected has the sorts of expertise required to provide valuable information during the interview.

Interview questions should be written using the same rules used to write survey questions—except the interviewee will generally supply the response options. The rules for writing unbiased survey questions are detailed later in this chapter. For example, ask only one question at a time. Ask the questions using the same terms the interviewee/expert does in conversation. Don't ask a question in a way that steers interviewees to one response option and prevents them from fully considering the issues of interest. That is, don't use questions like, "What do you like about the floor plan of X's innovative nursery school?" but ask, "What components of a physical environment can help nursery-school students develop age-appropriate skills?"

A significant difference between written survey questions and oral interview questions is that spoken questions need to be simpler, with fewer clauses, for example, so that the listeners can really understand the question being asked. Readers find it easier to cast their eyes back over a written question than interviewees find asking that a question be repeated. Similarly, some sorts of questions, such as asking people to rank criteria, can be confusing if they are simply read without some sort of visual aid, such as the list of those criteria to be evaluated.

Another important difference between interview questions and survey questions is that in interview questions, people can be asked to do more complex tasks than they can in a survey. The interviewer is available to answer questions that arise about the task before the participant begins to answer a question, and the participant is more attentive to the task (less likely to simply mark any answer to move on) if the interviewer is nearby.

Sort tasks are an example of this sort of interview-best question. Participants can be asked to sort cards with relevant material samples, words/phrases, design elements, or other images into piles, for example, with the exact task specified based on the research agenda. Images of parts of a space being redesigned could be separated into sets that work well for tasks that require concentration, and those that don't work as well. Another task might be to sort various images into ones that give the interviewee the same sort of feeling as is desired, or not desired, in a place being designed. Photos can also be sorted based on criteria such as the feelings they elicit in the participant or the time of day that they are used, for example. Images, generally mounted on cards, can also be arranged along a continuum—such as from the most to least of something. With these sample tasks, the richest information will come from asking the people participating in the study how come cards were included in particular piles. Frequencies of placement in various piles are used to inform design decisions.

The big advantage of an interview over a survey is that with an oral interview you can ask follow-up questions and pursue topics introduced by the interviewee. Imagine the richness of the data collected by asking people to chose adjectives to describe a real or hypothetical space during an interview when follow-up questions can be asked, compared to asking the same questions on a survey when follow-up probes are impossible. Responses are also not restricted to a set that the researcher feels are likely. People also give more complete answers when they are speaking than they will in response to any written question.

Interviews are an important way to find out about plans that families and organizations have for their future.

Your interviews should be conversations. This is particularly important when you are speaking with an expert who is helping you explore unfamiliar issues.

Some sorts of interview questions are useful for opening up wide-ranging conversations. For example, asking people what happens in a space very generally can be handy; it reveals issues that are top-of-mind, for example. A way to get a comprehensive view of activities is to ask what a bird looking in through a window or a fly on a wall would see. Discussions of a day in a life of a space are also useful. Conversations to prioritize design actions can be asked in terms of allocating a finite number of points or amount of money between alternatives. The number of points or amount of money has to be relatively small (say, a thousand dollars) so that priorities need to be established. If a million dollars is available, users may not prioritize because they feel that any potential changes they can imagine can be made. With any of these prioritization-type questions, it is important to understand why specific choices are made so that underlying important issues can be reflected in design decisions made. Probing performance in a space during extreme situations can be as significant to design decisions as its functionality on an average day.

Some questions are particularly useful for getting useful conversation flowing. These are questions that are so broad that the interviewee naturally leads the discussion toward topics of interest to them. They include:

- *What should never be changed about this space? What's the first thing that should be changed?* These sorts of leading questions, which assume that something should or should not be changed, can be handy ways to open up a conversation with someone who seems to have an agenda to make particular changes in a space or not make any changes in a space. Asking the opposite (talking with people who have stated that *everything* should change about what should never change) can lead to a more nuanced understanding of the situation.

- *Why are you interested in redesigning this space?* This question helps to identify underlying issues and motivations for action.

- *What is the best balance of [one thing] and [another thing] in this space? How come?* The particular issues investigated here should be relevant to the research questions you are trying to answer. You could ask about issues such as abilities to concentrate and collaborate in a workplace, for example, or structured and unstructured learning for a school project.

- *Imagine a world without financial or physical constraints. In that world, what would it be like to be in this space? What would you see? Hear? Smell? What would the experience be like?* These sorts of "anything can happen" questions can lead to discussions that are not grounded in the project context, but can be used as conversation starters.

- *Who would [this concept, or whatever inanimate object/place you are curious about] be if it were a person? What would it do for a living/fun? Where would it like to go out to eat?* The options for these sorts of follow-up questions are endless.

Projective techniques can be really useful during interviews—they can help you overcome obstacles to discussing topics (see Figure C.9a and C.9b in the color insert). These obstacles can arise because interviewees aren't familiar discussing places and don't know quite what to say, or they don't have the vocabulary to have a straightforward, place-specific conversation. Sometimes there are social taboos or rules that make discussions difficult. This technique can short-circuit defense mechanisms, as well.

Whatever the reason they are used, projective questions are really unstructured and ask interviewees to respond to visuals. In a common sort of projective question, interviewees are presented with multiple (say, 50) pictures that are not of the space being designed. They are dewdrops on grass or exterior shots of flying airplanes, for example. The set of images should roughly correspond to the spectrum of human emotions and energy levels. Interviewees can also be asked to bring images/take photographs that meet the stated criteria with them to an interview, but except in the case of individual homeowners working toward the design of a new home, most interviewees will not be motivated to devote a lot of resources to collecting images on their own.

When they are presented, images should all be the same size, all in color or black and white, so that it is not possible to attribute image selection to some aspect of how different visuals were presented. Interviewees pick the images that relate to a particular question asked and the issue that needs to be resolved. Interviewees can be asked to select the images that give them the same feeling as a space being developed or describe being in a current or ideal space, for example. Any discussions of ideal spaces must be tied into the primary planned activities for a space. Interviewees are then asked why the images selected were chosen, what that desired feeling is, and so on. It is this set of follow-up information that provides the most value as design decisions are being made.

Similarly, people being interviewed or completing a survey can be asked to write text in a talk/thought bubble drawn in a cartoon. The scenes pictured should be relevant to the space being developed. Another projective technique has interviewees or survey takers complete sentences whose beginnings are provided to them.

Unless interviewees have design training, do not ask them to respond to a floor plan alone. Most laypeople have difficulty understanding the information presented on them.

Chose a question form based on your resources at hand. Projective data collected should be content analyzed, as described later in this chapter. You may want to analyze the data from different groups of people (set of employees, for example) separately, depending on the research questions posed.

Projective tools you develop should be pretested with people similar on all significant dimensions to the people who will ultimately be interviewed to make sure they work as intended.

You can collect information that is really relevant for your design project with what is known as the *critical incident technique*. It was originally developed to be used after airplane crashes and other similar unpleasant situations, but you can use it to investigate positive situations as well. Ask interviewees to talk about situations that went either very well or very poorly that are related to the research questions you are trying to answer. If you are designing hospital operating rooms, you might ask about a time when the operating team worked particularly well together or particularly poorly, and ultimately lead the conversation around to aspects of the physical environment related to those positive and negative situations.

Critical incident investigations are good to pair with *laddering* interview techniques, although laddering can be used independently as well. It involves asking why answers are provided and continuing to ask the reason for each answer in turn until the information given becomes extremely clear and unequivocal. For example, people might be asked about their desires for a particular design element in their home until it is revealed that the fundamental reason it is coveted is because of the status it will convey. Intermediary answers might have been that the material or whatever in question has been seen in other people's homes or in magazines and that it is unusual. Fundamental motivations, preferences, and so on are revealed as each "why" answer is followed by another "why" question. Data collected are content analyzed.

Gerald Zaltman has developed a form of questioning known as *metaphor elicitation* that can be really handy during interviews.[1] Metaphors are a sort of shorthand we use to simplify thinking about, and discussing, our world. We share them with other members of our culture(s). When Zaltman's ZMET technique is used, participants are asked to bring a collection of images (created or collected or descriptions of images that couldn't be found) to the interview that relate to the research questions to be answered. They might be tied to what it's like to feel relaxed, for example, and each image is taken as a metaphor for the topic being investigated.

The images can be sorted into labeled piles using the card-sorting technique just mentioned or by dividing the images into sets of three, with participants being asked how any two of the images in the three-card sets are different from the third card in the set. This interviewing will reveal issues of interest to participants, and a hierarchy among those issues of interest can be established using question laddering, just described. A single image is then discussed intensely. The image selected is the one that best relates (based on the previous discussion with the interviewee) to the issue being investigated—that's what it is like to feel relaxed in this example. Laddering can then be used specifically to investigate the issue being studied with the discussion focused on this image. Sensory and emotional experience can be reviewed, for example.. The Zaltman technique involves several additional steps, but it is unrealistic to believe that design researchers will have time to complete them. For example, the interviewee can be asked to develop a concept map. Patterns of responses across interviewees can be determined through content analysis.

When you are concluding one segment of the Zaltman-style interview, it's a good idea to very briefly summarize the most important information you have collected from that interviewee that relates to the most significant research questions you are trying to answer. This increases your confidence that you've understood what's been expressed, and it helps the interviewee understand that you value the information he or she shared with you.

Each Zaltman-style interview can take as long as two hours, so only a small number, such as 15 or 20, can be completed, at most, with people similar to those that will ultimately use a space. This style of interviewing can be done with fewer people if a space will have only a small number of users—if a home is being designed, every member of the family who will live there could be interviewed individually, for example.

During interviews, people can do cognitive mapping exercises (described later in this chapter). They can also be asked to arrange scale furnishings and architectural elements on a floor plate template. They can be asked to present current or hypothetical spaces, for example. These sorts of exercises not only collect useful information but also ground discussions in situational realities if the floor plate is consistent with the one that will be present in any future space. Interviewees need to narrate why they are making particular choices; this is the information that is most probably valuable during the design process because a designer can use his or her skills to respond to issues raised in a variety of ways.

## Conducting Interviews

Interviews can be more or less structured. Generally, interviews produce more valuable information when they are more like conversations, which flow naturally from topic to topic. Occasionally, however, you may decide that it is important that information be collected in a rigid order. This might be because you think that talking about one topic will bias discussion of a subsequent one and you want that bias to be minimized.

Always have a few high-fidelity run-throughs of your interview with people like those you will ultimately interview to shake out any potential problems in question forms and to unearth other, similar issues.

People need to feel comfortable when they are being interviewed. Dressing and speaking in a friendly but business-like way communicates you are taking the interview seriously.,

It is important to maintain a pleasant demeanor when interviewing people, but don't seem particularly pleased with answers that you hear. Interviewees are human, and if you seem to like particular information, they will make sure to include more similar material later, even if it is really a stretch to do so—and you won't realize it's a stretch. For example, if you seem to be pleased with information about conflicts between teachers in a particular time/place, more evidence of teacher discord may be presented later, even if a liberal interpretation of a question you are asking is required to make it meaningful. Smiles between questions can be useful, however.

Don't interrupt people who are talking about topics that are even vaguely related to your research topic to march linearly through your list of questions. Interruptions will break their train of thought, which can be time-consuming and difficult to reestablish. Interruptions also devalue the information being presented before the interruption occurs, which decreases the likelihood that similar information will be presented in the course of the rest of the interview. This can prevent pertinent material from being shared. Apparent digressions regularly lead to the collection of information that is relevant to design development, but that researchers did not know to discuss before it was brought up by an interviewee.

Before you begin the interview, you must be very familiar with all of the topics that you need to explore; let the interviewee determine the flow of the conversation through those topics. At logical times in the discussion, ask pertinent questions until all of the issues that you need to investigate are discussed. Memorizing the questions isn't a bad idea; get so familiar with them that it doesn't sound like you've memorized them when they're being asked. At the end of the interview, always make sure to ask if there is anything that should have been asked about that wasn't covered. This makes interviewees feel valued, which encourages them to talk about important issues that might indeed not have been discussed earlier.

Throw the "don't interrupt" rule out the window if the interviewee gets truly off target of the information you need to cover and stays there for more than a few minutes. To move interviewees back on track, validate what they are saying ("That's interesting and later we'll get a chance to talk about this topic again, but right now, let's . . .") and then move on..

Sometimes conversation just seems to die, even if you are an experienced interviewer and the interviewee is both cooperative and knowledgeable. In that case, use simple, direct, but not leading probes such as the following:

- Ask, "What else?"

- Ask the person to tell you a little bit more about X. Say, "Could you tell me a little bit more about X?"

- Throw iut the question "what else?" to encourage the interviewee to supply additional information.Ask "What about X?" referring to something pertinent that the speaker has mentioned earlier.

- If feelings are relevant, ask, "How did that make you feel?"

- Echo what a speaker has just said, or recently said, that is relevant to the objectives of the interview; picking up the words and rearranging them slightly shows that you are attentive and interested. It fills an awkward silence and gets conversation flowing again, and on a desired topic. Repeating without restating can seem derogatory.

- When all else fails, be silent. Humans are social animals; we like to socialize with each other. As a species, we feel compelled to fill silences, and if you hold strong and don't fill the gap, the interviewee will. If the silence lasts for longer than about 30 seconds, probe, using nonconfrontational questions, about why the interviewee does not want to answer a question and determine if it is possible for you to alleviate these concerns.

On some occasions, the people you have arranged to interview will not fully participate in the interview—they might answer questions extremely briefly, for example. It is best to ask these interviewees about their concerns and respond to issues raised truthfully. If they are concerned about confidentiality, for example, tell them how you will ensure confidentiality of responses—if you are going to be able to do so. If people indicate that they don't have time to answer your questions, ask them if they can stay for a set number of minutes (less than the length planned for the entire interview) and speak with you for that period of time—and make sure to ask the most important questions during this period, as well as any demographic questions that you may need to contextualize their answers. Often, once people begin to speak with you, they find the time to stay for the entire interview. It is only fair to let people know when the length of time that they have committed to stay is reached—if they have said they can only speak with you for ten minutes, let them know when ten minutes are up, but ask them at the end of those ten minutes to continue with the interview. Sometimes, reluctant interviewees just need to know that you value their input, and once they do, they become fountains of information.

Be culturally sensitive when asking questions about why something happened, was done, etc. The use of the term "why" is the issue here. Some Far Eastern cultures find being asked "why" aggressive. In those situations it is better to ask people, "How come?"

Always be alert to nonverbal behavior during the interview, both your own and that of the interviewee. Make comfortable eye contact—generally look at the interviewee's eyes, but do look away occasionally. Don't seem aggressive, seem interested. Body language indicating discomfort, such as continually shifting body postures or excessive eye movement, is a sign that you have made the interviewee uncomfortable. Always seem involved and pleasant, empathetic, and understanding, without the leading pleasantness mentioned earlier.

Do not become emotionally upset by the information the interviewee is supplying. Be sure not to be conveying any tension that you are feeling about statements being made with your body language; stay loose and relaxed. If your interviewee seems tense, try to determine why that might be so and alleviate the situation whenever possible. For example, reseat the person in a more comfortable chair, provide acoustical privacy so the person can speak freely, and so on. If the interviewee tension continues to build, it may become necessary to discuss it directly. You can, for example, ask if you have inadvertently caused offense, or if this is no longer a convenient time for the interview.

Try to interviewee people in the precursor to the space being developed. If you are designing a new home, interview people in their existing home—same goes for workplaces, stores, you name it. Interviews in the existing environment put interviewees in the mindset of the place being built, aid them in remembering details about a the space, allow interviewees to point out particular issues (good and bad) in the existing space, and help you understand their most immediate and current reference for the space being developed. This is particularly handy for difficult-to-discuss issues such as noise volume and other sensory experiences. Even if only part of the interview can be held in the research-relevant space, it is desirable to speak with the interviewee in this space.

Interviews should be conducted in places in which everyone is comfortable and feels able to communicate honestly.

Interviews work best when they follow a certain game plan. Each interview session should start with some relatively easy, noncontroversial questions so that both you and the interviewee can get into the flow of the interview. Start the session as you get settled with small talk—talking about the weather at the beginning of each session might get boring to you, but each interviewee will only hear your comments once. The most important questions to be answered should be asked before the interviewee gets tired, approximately 15 to 20 minutes into the interview. Then less important questions should again be asked, because by now everyone involved is getting tired.

Interviews start to become much less productive after they have been in progress for an hour, and with nonexpert interviews it is best to restrict their length to 30–45 minutes. Don't feel required to plan interviews that are this long—sometimes very short interviews are all you need to collect the info needed before the interview starts. Do find out how long an interview will last by asking a couple of people similar to the people you intend to interview to participate in a mock interview. The mock interview should be as realistic as possible so that you get a good idea how long the planned questions really do take to answer.

Always conclude with a question about contacting the interviewee again later if you have any follow up questions. There are two reasons for doing so. First, it gives you permission to do so; second, it indicates to the interviewee that you respect their opinion and that affirmation may encourage additional pertinent comments.

Recording interviews works better than trying to simultaneously take notes and ask questions. It is hard to record all the pertinent information that flows during an interview, and during client sessions it is very useful to have direct quotes available from these sessions. Those direct quotes are hard to write down during the heat of an interview.

Always get permission to tape the interview before you turn on the recording device and again in slightly different words once the recorder is turned on. Audio taping alone generally is less stressful for interviewees. Regularly, people say that they would prefer not to be recorded (audiotaped, videotaped, or both). So always be ready with a pen—if you do need to write down information, do so during the interview; even a few minutes after a session ends your memories will begin to fade. Also, recording devices can malfunction at the moment of truth. Test the placement of the recorder to make sure it is picking up sound before the interview itself begins. Do not hide the recording device, but do not regularly bring it to the interviewee's attention by touching it, for example. The interviewee will become less aware that their comments are being recorded as the interview progresses.

Digital recordings, which can now be made with most laptops as well as with dedicated recording machines, are best because the recordings of the discussions can be electronically transmitted and retained in your design library (see Chapter 8).

Bring a digital camera to interviews to record elements of the environment that are crucial to understand and to follow the flow of the conversation. It is much handier to digitally capture an image of a nursing station currently in use and about which comments are being made than to try to draw or otherwise get a relevant visual later, for example.

Be prepared to take written notes when you turn off the recorder. Many people relax once they know that the conversation is no longer being recorded and that brings pertinent thoughts to mind.

One-on-one interviews (one interviewer and one interviewee) result in the most natural conversations. Two interviewers and one interviewee are acceptable under special circumstances, such as when the client needs to be present. Any more interviewers being present seriously distorts the information being collected. It is important, however, never to be alone with a child that you are interviewing.

## Selecting Interviewees

All of the people interviewed should be randomly selected from the set of all people who could be interviewed that meet specific criteria (more on this later). Random selection decreases the odds that patterns you see in question responses are due to having worked with an unusual segment of users. Ways to randomly select people include drawing names out of a hat or having a computer randomly select participants.

About 50 percent of the people who will use a space being designed should be interviewed if a space has fewer than 10 total users; whenever possible, at least 5 if there are 11 to 20 users. If there are over 20 people who will use a redesigned space, they should be divided into subgroups using the criteria noted in the next paragraph and appropriate numbers from each subgroup interviewed. In subgroups with more than 20 members, a random sample of people should be interviewed, with that number based on resources available and the objective of interviewing 5 to 10 members of each.

If more than 20 people will use a space, it is important to start to think about reasonable subgroups of users and to interview members of those groups. Reasonable sets of users for our purposes are those who can be expected to use a space in the same way and therefore have the same space requirements. For example, all of the copywriters at an advertising agency will probably have the same sorts of space-related needs, while people purchasing advertising time on television stations can be expected to have different ones. To ensure that information collected is not skewed by an extremely small number of interviews, but to also keep the interviewing task manageable, five members of any user groups identified should be interviewed.

## Data Analysis

To formally analyze the information collected during the interview, follow the rules for verbal content analyses provided later in this chapter. Sometimes no formal analyses are required, however, and a simple transcription and sharing of the answers to the questions posed (generally, in summary form) is all that's necessary to move the design project forward.

## Expert Interviews

Expert interviews can be a good introduction to a field. You can quickly gain a wide range of knowledge, possibly about issues that you would not have thought to explore but the expert being interviewed mentions spontaneously. It is particularly useful to use expert interviews to collect information under the following conditions:

- An expert can be identified.

- Time is short and it is possible to conduct the interview within the required time frame.

- The outstanding questions to be resolved do not require extensive knowledge of your design client—this familiarity with a particular client will be missing unless the expert interviewed has worked for your client.

When hiring an expert, consult with your legal department to make sure that the legal requirements of the jurisdictions in which you operate are satisfied.

### Finding an Expert

Finding the expert to be interviewed can be challenging. To identify one:

- *Use your entire social network.* Word-of-mouth recommendation by a trusted, well-informed colleague is the best way to identify someone you can work with to answer outstanding questions. The intermediary recommending the expert is familiar with both you, your organization, and the expert, which increases the likelihood that a mutually desirable and rewarding relationship will result. Word of mouth can help you to identify the "standard" expert on a subject or, if you and your network are very clever, a person with important information on the topic of interest but who brings a fresh approach to the issue at hand.

- *Do a literature review.* An author whose name appears repeatedly can be a good expert. Call or e-mail the names that come up—topic experts are generally quite approachable and often very motivated to pursue consulting opportunities. Sometimes these motivations are financial, but researchers can be motivated by other factors, such as access to real-world sites for future research projects.

- *Contact professional associations.* Groups such as the Society for Environmental Graphic Design (SEGD) and the Society for College and University Planning (SCUP) can be sources of referrals. Some professional societies maintain directories of members who meet minimum training requirements.

- *Drag out the file of people who have contacted your firm in the past.* Experts may have contacted your firm looking for work—now may be the time to talk seriously with them. Finding an outside expert is a good reason to set up a central electronic file of all potential future research partners who contact your company.

- *Contact active, knowledgeable participants at conferences you have attended.* Such individuals could either serve as the needed expert or provide referrals to that expert.

- *Subscribe to listservs.* People with similar interests communicate via listservs or electronic discussion groups, which can be identified through Internet searches, as described earlier. A posting to one of these sites seeking an expert can produce a flurry of names—all of which should be carefully vetted.

- *Follow long shots.* Contact people within your firm as well as outside it who have worked on projects that you think have probed the sorts of issues you are now exploring and interview them either as experts or to find experts whom you should interview.

- *Review the inventory of completed interviews in your firm's design library (see Chapter 8).* If you take a look at this collection of interviews you might find that you do not have to conduct a new interview; you might find a potential interviewee, or identify channels to pursue to find that needed expert.

- *Network internationally and proactively by attending conferences and similar events and talking with other attendees and with speakers.* Do this even before the need for a specific type of consultant has been identified.

- *Develop a request for proposal (RFP).* Posting an RFP is an involved process—one that is usually too cumbersome to employ on the short timeline common for design researchers.

## Making Sure You Have the "Right" Expert

After you have identified a potential expert to interview, it is important to ensure that the person does indeed have the credentials that you require. Legally, it is important that all potential consultants you have identified are treated in the same way, to eliminate the possibility of charges of unfair treatment, particularly if you are seeking experts using an RFP.

Knowledge and experience directly related to your project are key. The expert needs to supply an expertise not currently available to the design team and that is directly relevant to the design project in process and its outstanding issues. The sorts of expertise that the expert must possess should be captured in a written document so that all experts can be evaluated using that same set of criteria and so that *criteria-creep* does not occur. The potential expert interviewee can gain expertise through the following:

- Earning a degree at, or currently being affiliated with in a teaching capacity, a well-respected and relevant department of a college or university.

- Consulting on topics directly related to the issue of interest; five or more years of experience doing this are best. Learn about the expert's direct previous experience using the traditional journalism. questions: [for] whom, what, where, when, how, why, for how much, and how quality of contribution was established. You want to hire someone who has had direct exposure to the topics of interest to you, not supervised people with those areas of expertise.

- Joining professional associations with minimum qualifications criteria.

- Earning professional certification from a not-for-profit organization.

Potential experts can also be assessed with some of the criteria used to evaluate new hires at your firm. These criteria are available through your human resource department. For example, you could contact references to learn about not only the quality of previous work but also what the experience of working with the interviewee was like. It is also interesting to investigate how the interviewee tends to reach conclusions—based on extrapolations from rigorous research, intuition, and so on.

## Project Parameters

When you begin to work with an expert, it is important to establish the criteria that will be used to determine that the project has been successfully completed. You might think that the expert hired will answer questions for an indefinite period of time and respond to any number of post-session follow-up questions, but the expert hired might feel obligated to answer your questions only during one specified two-hour period, for example. Consider having the expert sign a nondisclosure agreement. It must be clear to the expert that your firm owns the project-specific solutions discussed in perpetuity, although the consultant clearly has the freedom to use his or her expertise with other clients, even with firms that compete with you, in the future.

Deciding how much to pay people in any context can be difficult. You and the expert to be interviewed may decide that payment should be on an hourly basis or on a per-project basis, depending on the specific details of the duties required. The traditional rule of thumb for assessing an hourly fee is that if that fee were extrapolated to a yearly salary, it should be two to three times what that person would make as an employee of a firm. Individual experts, often those whose association will add a great deal of prestige to a project, may be paid more than this amount.

### Example of an Expert Interview

Instructions to interviewers are included in square brackets.

Purpose: To inform the design of classrooms for elementary school students

Anticipated Length: 1 hour

Icebreaker: Where did you do your doctoral work? What sorts of topics did you study?

Tell me about your professional work since leaving graduate school. What are the major schools of thought on how primary schoolchildren should be educated? Which do you think is most strongly grounded in research and practical evidence? How come? [Need names so can potentially then independently interview related experts.]

1. Do you think that the ways elementary school students are being taught are changing or staying the same? How come? Do you think they should? Why/ Why not?

2. [If responder thinks they are changing ask this question] In what ways are they changing? How come? What sorts of social environments/physical environments [ask for each separately] support [name of changing technique]? How come? [Probe for general thoughts about social and physical design, such as need for flexibility, general mood to be conveyed, etc.]

3. [If responder thinks they are changing] What sorts of social environments/ physical environments [ask for each separately] do not support [name of technique]? [Use the same set of probes as in question 2.]

4. [If responder thinks they are changing] What would be the ideal classroom for [name of technique]? How come? The worst classroom for [name of technique]? [For both, probe for design-related elements.]

5. [If responder does not think they are changing] [Ask questions 2–4 in terms of existing teaching techniques. Skip "In what ways are they changing?" section of question 2.]

6. Moving beyond classrooms, let's think about the school overall. This means the classrooms as well as the hallways, cafeterias, physical education spaces, playgrounds, and all of the other parts of the school. [Repeat

questions 4 and 5 with appropriate changes in wording. Probe for physical design/floor plate, objects in use, furnishings, lighting, etc.]

7.  [If responder things they are changing] We've been focusing on how things are changing, now let's think about how things are staying the same. [Repeat questions 2 to 44 and 6, with appropriate changes in wording, as above.]

8.  How would you like to change the ways that elementary school students are taught? How come? Stay the same? How come? [Repeat questions 2 to 4 and 6 above, with appropriate changes in wording. Abridge as needed to finish interview in agreed time frame.]

9.  Fifty years from now, what do you think a fly on the wall of an elementary school classroom would see between 8 a.m. and 3 p.m.? How come? What do you think they should see? How come?

10. Add other questions, potentially, dependent on project.

11. Is there anything else that you would like to say about how children learn? Techniques to help them learn? How they are taught within current spaces? With current technology? How should spaces support this? How should technology support this? How space and technology will support future teaching techniques?

12. Is it OK for me to contact you to clarify any points we discussed today? How should I reach you?

## COGNITIVE MAPPING

Cognitive mapping is:

| Little known | 1 | 2 | 3 | 4 | 5 | Lot known |
|---|---|---|---|---|---|---|
| Quick | 1 | 2 | 3 | 4 | 5 | Not quick |
| Info straightforward | 1 | 2 | 3 | 4 | 5 | Info complex |
| Verbal | 1 | 2 | 3 | 4 | 5 | Numeric |
| How | 1 | 2 | 3 | 4 | 5 | Why |
| On-site | 1 | 2 | 3 | 4 | 5 | Off-site OK |
| Well-established | 1 | 2 | **3** | 4 | 5 | Innovative |
| Current | 1 | 2 | **3** | 4 | 5 | Future |
| Special | 1 | 2 | 3 | 4 | 5 | No special |
| Generally considered | 1 | 2 | **3** | 4 | 5 | Potentially considered |

[Score indicated by **bold**ing of number.]

People's mental maps of their worlds are not entirely accurate, and the ways in which those cognitive maps deviate from "reality" provide important clues about how individuals are relating to their physical world. The more effort and attention lavished on a space drawn on a cognitive map, the more important perceptions of that space are to the person who is drawing the map, for example. This is a good research tool when you are interviewing people and interested in their expectations about a space or their individual perceptions of a space or other emotional (i.e., not necessarily rational) space-based experiences. Discussions of both hypothetical and existing spaces can both be structured using this tool.

During a cognitive mapping exercise, you request that the user you are working with draws a map of something. The specific question that you ask to get the map drawing started depends on the research that you are doing and the information you need. It can be broad or very directed. You can ask people to draw a map of the rooms in their home and draw lines on that map to trace out their early-morning activities in their home. You can have them draw that same floor plan of their home and indicate where they feel comfortable and relaxed. Environmental preferences can also be discussed using a cognitive map. A map of a workplace can indicate spaces used for particular purposes during the course of a day or week. Inaccuracies in the drawings can indicate the importance of a region of the floor or another issue with the distorted space. Individuals can be asked to discuss what they're feeling or thinking as they move along a particular path through a structure that is related to the research question being probed or to step through a floor plan drawn—the broad, place-based, open-ended questions that are asked after the drawing is completed are again based on the unanswered research questions.

People are sensitive about drawing anything in front of other people, often because they think they are bad artists. They are usually nervous about their ability to express themselves visually with cause, however. If you are talking with someone as they draw their map, you can ask them questions about it which provide details that will inform your later analysis..

If the basic map has been annotated with additional information, such as those early-morning travel routes, or a general description of spaces used during the course of the day, then all annotations to the map need to be discussed as they are made.

It is a good idea to have users use different-colored pens to record particular types of information—and all users should use the same colors for the same sort of information.

Drawing a cognitive map can take as little or as much time as you allow—time spent will determine the level of detail collected. Data gathered must be organized and analyzed using visual and verbal content analysis, as discussed later in this chapter. The analyses should be simultaneous and integrated, as opposed to entirely separate operations.

## Cognitive Mapping—Example

When you have done a cognitive mapping exercise with several users, you will have a collection of hand-drawn floor plans. Generally, these seem to be an apparently random collection of boxes, if an inside space has been mapped. If an outside space was the focus of the study, there won't be as many rectangles on the page but there will be many more paths and streets shown meeting at right angles than is actually the case (we generally remember paths intersecting at right angles, not obtuse or acute ones). These plans may or may not have any resemblance to the actual design of the areas mapped. They are perceptions or a situation, not photographs of it. Generally, they will also be awash with inks of different colors because you may have asked people to mark sections of the maps to indicate specific sorts of information. ("Please circle in orange/red/yellow/green any places where you can relax/concentrate/that you feel happy when you visit/that you use in at least two different ways during the course of the last 24 hours.") A review of the inks and boxes (and occasional oval or circle) using the visual content analysis tools will unlock the data on the maps. Annotations and explanations should be studied using verbal content analysis.

## REPERTORY GRID

Repertory grids are:

| Little known | 1 | 2 | 3 | 4 | 5 | Lot known |
|---|---|---|---|---|---|---|
| Quick | 1 | 2 | 3 | 4 | 5 | Not quick |
| Info straightforward | 1 | 2 | 3 | 4 | 5 | Info complex |
| Verbal | 1 | 2 | 3 | 4 | 5 | Numeric |
| How | 1 | 2 | 3 | 4 | 5 | Why |
| On-site | 1 | 2 | 3 | 4 | 5 | Off-site OK |
| Well-established | 1 | 2 | 3 | 4 | 5 | Innovative |
| Current | 1 | 2 | 3 | 4 | 5 | Future |
| Special | 1 | 2 | 3 | 4 | 5 | No special |
| Generally considered | 1 | 2 | 3 | 4 | 5 | Potentially considered |

[Score indicated by **bold**ing of number.]

Interviewing is a valuable tool, but sometimes quantitatively oriented clients have difficulty appreciating the richly nuanced information it generates. They think that legitimate information, the sort of data on which important building projects should be based, is unequivocally numeric. When you're working with this sort of client and interview data would be valuable, use a repertory grid to collect information. At the end of a repertory grid project, you will have had the chance to broadly explore the topics of interest to you, often collecting tacit information and preferences. The general information gathered will also be linked to numeric values that suggest and support particular courses of action.

Repertory grid study participants identify the attributes of spaces that are important to them and discuss those attributes in their own terms, so at the beginning of a research project, when you have few ideas about what to discuss and how to talk about whatever you do, working with repertory grids can be the best way to move forward. The grids minimize any concerns that you might have that you are distorting a discussion through the language you are using or the aspects of a space or project you have chosen to discuss during an interview.

Using a repertory grid can be complicated, although all of the related details are laid out clearly in the first few chapters of Devi Jankowicz's book titled *The Easy Guide to Repertory Grids*.[2] The main concepts involved in the repertory grid process will be covered here, but readers who wish to use the technique should read Jankowicz's book.

The first and probably most important step in a repertory grid project is to work with the person you are interviewing to provide lists of descriptors that can be used to categorize whatever sort of place is of particular interest to you. You can collect this information by asking interviewees to state ways in which two members of a random sample of three of the items of interest are similar to each other and the way in which those two are different from the third. Throughout the data-gathering process, assure the person you are speaking with that you are interested in that person's opinions and that there is not a correct set of descriptors or ratings.

For example, if you are interviewing people about the design of places where they might do individual knowledge work, you can provide a list of these sorts of places (private office with walls to the ceiling and a door, seat in a team room, the living room of their home, etc.) and ask the following question: "For each set of three places that we're going to discuss, how are two alike and one different in a way that influences your ability to do individual knowledge work?" For example, two could be places where physical reference materials can be arrayed in a handy way, and the third might not have enough horizontal work area at the correct height to arrange items usefully.

You can also get people to work through sensory comparisons using repertory grids. For example, you could show collections of colors and ask people to work through the same process. Repertory grids can also be used with the experience of sitting in sample chairs or a number of other actual (not theoretical) experiences.

After a while, you will start to see repetitions in the descriptors used to differentiate two items from the third in a set, and you can go on to the next phase of the research process. Try to obtain eight to ten of these descriptor pairs before moving on. It's important to understand the terms that the person being interviewed is using, so don't hesitate to politely seek clarification if any wording is confusing.

To understand how the descriptor information is used, refer to the sample chart in Table 5.1. The way in which the two items are similar is placed on the left end of the rating scale, and the opposite term is placed on the right side of the grid. If, for example, colors A and B are categorized as "happy," place that term to the left of the grid and its opposite, "sad," to the right. These pairs of words need to be opposites for the technique to work well. The item on the left is given a rating of 1, it's opposite a score of 5, with numbers 2 to 4 available as ratings between these end points. Participants select a number between 1 and 5 to indicate their opinion, or rating of an item (such as a color or a place to do knowledge work), and that number is entered on the chart in the square at the intersection of the descriptor (happy/unhappy) and the color name. In this example, red gets a rating on the happy/sad scale, which ranges from 1 (happy) to 5 (sad). It is important to let respondents know that although no rating may exactly represent their opinion, one will come closer than any other, and it is *that* one that should be selected.

**TABLE 5.1**
Sample Chart of
Descriptor Information

|  | Red | Blue | Green | Orange |  |
|---|---|---|---|---|---|
| Happy | 2 | 4 | 3 | 1 | Sad |
| Energizing | 5 | 1 | 2 | 5 | Energy draining |
| Pleasant | 1 | 5 | 4 | 1 | Unpleasant |
| Adultlike | 5 | 2 | 2 | 1 | Childlike (i.e., for children) |

Since each study participant provides his or her own set of descriptors, the data from each stand alone. Although each individual interview produces a quantified table of ratings of items of interest through the descriptors identified by that person, a content analysis of the descriptors chosen is required to combine results from several individuals. It is possible to modify the technique and supply the descriptors to people (it is best to develop the list of these terms with people similar to the interviewees, if possible) and then average individual ratings to develop a single overview diagram. This method is quicker, but it can be very enlightening to have each participant come up with his or her own list of descriptors.

Participants should be chosen that are representative of the ultimate users of a space being designed. It takes at least an hour for each completed repertory grid interview, so it can be difficult to find study participants, unless a significant incentive is being paid. Also, as a researcher your time is limited, so you will probably choose to complete ten or fewer interviews of this type.

## ANNOTATED PLANS

Floor plans or elevations can be reviewed by experts on the human experience of space (see Figure 5.1). Anything planned for a space can be assessed by specialists, although usually just floor plans or elevations get this treatment. These focused discussions are a form of the expert interview discussed in this chapter. The areas of expertise of these experts are pertinent to the research question being resolved and might be psychology, ergonomics, or gerontology, for example. The space-in-use issues that the experts foresee based on the materials presented to them must be fully explored from all reasonable perspectives, both positive and negative, before the design process concludes.

**FIGURE 5.1**
Experts can review plans and models, making notes about their opinions of user experience if spaces are developed as shown and other issues related to their areas of expertise. *© iStockphoto.com/ Franck-Boston*

# CONTENT ANALYSIS—VERBAL MATERIAL

Verbal content analysis is:

| | | | | | | |
|---|---|---|---|---|---|---|
| Little known | 1 | 2 | 3 | 4 | 5 | Lot known |
| Quick | 1 | 2 | 3 | 4 | 5 | Not quick |
| Info straightforward | 1 | 2 | 3 | 4 | 5 | Info complex |
| Verbal | 1 | 2 | 3 | 4 | 5 | Numeric |
| How | 1 | 2 | 3 | 4 | 5 | Why |
| On-site | 1 | 2 | 3 | 4 | 5 | Off-site OK |
| Well-established | 1 | 2 | 3 | 4 | 5 | Innovative |
| Current | 1 | 2 | 3 | 4 | 5 | Future |
| Special | 1 | 2 | 3 | 4 | 5 | No special |
| Generally considered | 1 | 2 | 3 | 4 | 5 | Potentially considered |

[Score indicated by **bold**ing of number.]

Sometimes the research process delivers a collection of words that need to be made sense of in some way—for example, notes from interviews. Other times, you might directly search out texts to be analyzed, such as the statements your client uses to describe itself and its organizational culture or the sales materials of a client firm that might be competing against you for a particular job.

Content analysis allows you to plow through these verbal materials and unearth patterns in both directly communicated information and information more subtly provided between the lines of those overtly stated messages. Content analysis provides the most value when it moves beyond counting objects or the number of times a word appears and discusses underlying issues, such as whether the arrangement of those words can be construed one way or another. The end product of a content analysis is a richer understanding of concepts of interest to the design researcher.

When people learn about content analysis, either written or visual, for the first time it can seem pretty fuzzy. Content analysis can be summarized as categorizing information or looking for patterns in it. That's it. There are many rules that need to be presented in even the most basic text dealing with survey writing, but that's not the case with content analysis. Content analysis does have processes that must be followed, however, to produce respected insights.

Content analysis is a rigorous, valid, and reliable (see Chapter 2 for more on validity and reliability) empirical way to answer questions about words or visual elements. It uncovers the information the people who wrote or spoke the material being analyzed are really presenting. You could think of it as a form of observation, but of inanimate not animate objects.

In both observation and content analysis the design researcher is learning what is present, but not necessarily why a particular situation is present. With both content analysis and observation research, the investigator approaches the project with an analysis plan that can be modified to best reflect that data collected. The proposed analysis plan leads, however, to particular data being collected. What you as the researcher "observe" is based on questions you are trying to answer and the answers you anticipate the observations might be able to provide

The words being content analyzed are carefully studied at both the highest levels (the document as a whole) and the lowest possible level (a single word or a phrase with a few words in it). Overall tone can be noted, which requires reflecting on the entire collection of words or visual elements (if content analysis of visual elements is in process). It is also possible to review the frequency of types of references—for example, hierarchy-related phrases, which would have important implications for resolving design questions.

Content analysis can't establish causal relationships among the data it analyzes, but it does expose underlying patterns in those data. It also has the advantage of not requiring any commitment of time on the part of the group that has prepared the materials being analyzed. This means, however, that the technique can only be used on texts that have been written in the past. If the situations that resulted in those items being written cannot reasonably be expected to continue into the future, content analysis becomes a historical exercise of little interest to practicing design researchers.

Sometimes a content analysis will be based on one document, such as one firm's statement of its organizational culture, and other times it will be based on a number of sources, such as a series of interviews with a corporation's employees about their organization's culture.

Content analysis of written materials guides your review of text crafted by someone else so that you can identify and categorize important themes. What you choose to identify and categorize is based on the questions that you are trying to answer. Often the categorization systems being used evolve over time as the questions the design researchers are exploring develop and become more sophisticated in the course of a project.

At each phase of a project, with each of the sets of categorized data, the same sorts of analyses are completed after data are entered into a spreadsheet, such as those found in Excel. The frequencies of various elements are calculated and the relationships between the data are determined using straightforward relationship matrices based on chi square analyses (for more information on these statistical techniques, visit the survey section of this chapter). The relative number of times something occurs is generally more interesting than absolute frequencies—to know something occurs in 57 percent of the cases is usually more important than realizing that it has occurred 57 total times.

The categories used to organize the data collected should allow all the data present to be placed in one category or another, and each category should be distinct—people categorizing data should never be confused about what being placed in a category means.

The traditional journalism questions (who, what, where, when, why, how) are a good way to begin deciding how to determine issues of interest in the data being read and to categorize the information that's available in written form.

It is very important that the person identifying the major concepts of interest in an item being content analyzed and establishing the categories into which the available information will be placed (coded) be of the same national culture as the people who wrote the material being analyzed. Even people who are expert at speaking a particular language are not truly fluent in that language unless they understand all the nuances communicated through figures of speech—and complete knowledge of those figures of speech only reeliably comes from growing up in the same national culture as the speaker. Sharing, or being very familiar with, the organizational cultures of the speaker also aids in effective data coding.

The patterns in statements related to topics of interest in a written document are revealed to researchers as they read (and reread) the documents being analyzed. Once consistent patterns of discussion are identified in a general sense, it is important to look at how they are manifested in the data available. Text is assigned to (or coded into) categories as written materials available are read and reread. A category that seems appropriate at an earlier stage of a project fades in importance later. For example, the initial analysis of a set of interview questions related to organizational culture might indicate that planning in various forms was important to the organization and various types of planning might be coded. After more of the data are reviewed, it might become apparent that it was not planning that was really the underlying issue but adherence to rules. As the general topic of interest changed from "planning" to "adherence to rules," all previous documents reviewed using the first coding scheme must to be reanalyzed with the second one.

Sometimes data are coded into categories based not only on study objectives but also on the results of a literature review. Literature reviews are recommended before any content analysis begins to identify the sorts of patterns that can be expected to be of importance and relevant to the design project in general.

It can be difficult for even one person to keep straight the reasons that a particular phrase is placed in one category as opposed to another, so a master written directory of the criteria used to sort data into one classification or another needs to be created and updated continuously.

When people begin a content analysis, they have expectations of the data they will uncover—after all, they are only human. When one of the patterns anticipated is not present in the data analyzed, this is also worthy of discussion in a report of findings. Inconsistencies in the data collected should also be noted.

The steps involved in a content analysis thus become:[3]

1. Decide what research question you hope to answer using the content analysis.

2. Select the material to be content analyzed—the material to be analyzed is determined by the research question to be answered.

3. Read repeatedly through the written material available to determine the major concepts being presented in that material.

4. Develop and refine the categories to be used to code the data.

5. Write a guide for the categorization of the data into one group or another (simultaneous with previous step).

6. Determine the cases that fall into each classification category to allow the calculation of frequencies/relative number of occurrences.

7. Code the classification data into a spreadsheet (e.g., Excel), so that chi square tests can be completed to determine the relationships between the data presented (e.g., when the company voices this concern, it is also likely to express this one as well). When there is a significant difference between two sets of materials being content analyzed—for example, their writers are from different national cultures—it is appropriate to analyze information collected from each separately.

8. Attempt to understand and explain the data collected using both patterns in that data and material in the established research literature.

There are software programs available for verbal content analysis (e.g., ATLAS.ti and NUD.IST), but they can be somewhat time consuming to use and expensive to purchase. Particularly for design researchers who will be doing content analyses only occasionally, working with the data manually (except for the Excel statistical analyses mentioned) seems most probable, and that is why it is reported here. The Computer Assisted Qualitative Data Analysis Group at the University of Surrey maintains a data site that supports computerized qualitative analysis tools (caqdas.soc.surrey.ac.uk).

## Example of Written Content Analysis

As a designer, you may already have taken a look at the *World Trade Center Site Memorial Competition Guidelines*. Reviewing that document again now, after reading about written content analysis, you can take a scientific approach to determining what the most important criteria for the memorial among the people writing these competition guidelines. A review of the document indicates that the following themes were used frequently:

Affirmation of life/Life goes on

Exalting New York City

Heroes/heroism

History—American

Martyrs/murdered (not killed)

Rebirth/resurgence/good from bad/optimism and future

Sacred space/serious

Identifying the most frequently used themes and discussing them in the ultimate competition entry cannot guarantee that a submission will be selected, but it does ensure that it will come closer to meshing with the objectives of the people who wrote the guidelines.

## CONTENT ANALYSIS—VISUAL

Content Analysis—Visual is:

| Little known | 1 | 2 | **3** | 4 | 5 | Lot known |
|---|---|---|---|---|---|---|
| Quick | 1 | 2 | **3** | 4 | 5 | Not quick |
| Info straightforward | 1 | 2 | 3 | **4** | 5 | Info complex |
| Verbal | 1 | 2 | 3 | **4** | 5 | Numeric |
| How | 1 | 2 | 3 | **4** | 5 | Why |
| On-site | 1 | 2 | 3 | 4 | **5** | Off-site ok |
| Well-established | 1 | 2 | 3 | 4 | **5** | Innovative |
| Current | 1 | 2 | **3** | 4 | 5 | Future |
| Special | 1 | 2 | 3 | 4 | **5** | No special |
| Generally considered | 1 | 2 | 3 | 4 | **5** | Potentially considered |

[Score indicated by **bold**ing of number.]

Content analysis of verbal data was discussed earlier in this chapter, and we will build on that discussion to introduce the content analysis of visual material. This technique is pertinent to the design process because groups are often asked to select or present images that they feel would serve their needs well, for example. Content analysis of visual information can distill the essence of those images—whether they are of current places in use, photos collected by users, or some other visual element relevant to the research process. It might, for example, reveal that color is an important component of space design for a group and then which colors are most likely to be favored by the population. In this example, it is important to distinguish between spaces favored by a group and those that other evidence indicates might be optimal.

Designers aren't the only professionals who do visual content analysis. People in the U.S. State Department pour over the latest images released by North Korea showing their rulers, also. The people from the State Department are focused on who is standing where, who is looking at what, if anyone's uniform seems a little spiffier than the others—they're looking for any clue about who has the most power at the moment and any indications they can derive about what changes in power mean about policy. Their system is the same as the one we'll lay out in the next few paragraphs, but their motivation is developing the best foreign policy and yours is designing the best space for a particular group of users, at a particular time, with a certain set of resources.

Content analysis of visual information is done for the same reasons that verbal information is studied: to learn more about underlying patterns in it, in the belief that those patterns may increase our understanding of an issue of interest. Visual content analysis may review colors, textures, assortments of "decorative elements," or other parameters to understand issues such as preferred visual form or how a group of people prefer to interact with their physical world. It can be done with images selected for various reasons, as already noted, as well as other materials—basically anything that can be seen. This excludes words, they are verbally content analyzed, unless visual elements, such as they type faces, are of interest.. Any sort of visual can be content analyzed, still or moving, available over the web or in print.

Content analysis of visual material in client advertisements could determine the kind of client that a firm is currently serving, which could be invaluable in the design of a retail space, for example. Visual content analysis can help design researchers develop a greater understanding of the people who will use a space, recognize how a space will be utilized, and collect information that can be used to assess project effectiveness.

The specific image to be content analyzed falls naturally out of the problem statement for the research project. Earlier in this section we discussed analyzing information from collected images and advertisements, for example. Photographs of spaces in use at a range of times of day or on various days of the week can also be content analyzed. This sort of analysis can be enriched if images of the spaces on special occasions are also included. When many images are available, they should be randomly sampled. The number of images to be sampled is dependent on the level of analysis desired, with more vigorous analysis requiring more human resources. Accompanying captions and other written material can be analyzed using written content analysis techniques.

In written content analysis, text is reviewed, and that review is augmented by a related literature review that unearths themes that should be studied in a text. Although themes are also generated in roughly the same way for content analysis of visual material, authorities in the field have identified some visual components that are regularly considered:[4]

- What is shown (pets, fog, no faces just backs of heads, etc.)
- Composition/organization
- Perspective and all other design elements
- Technique used to create image
- Light
- Color (hue, saturation, brightness)
- Form
- Symmetry
- Textures

The components of the images that you focus on must be relevant to the design-related questions that you are answering. . If the focus of a project is learning more about how employees collaborate now, because these same behaviors need to be facilitated in a new environment, users may be asked to supply images of current collaborative sessions. Number of people present, furniture in use, arrangement of furniture in use, and so on would therefore be of interest, while floor coverings need not be noted and analyzed. All of the categories in use must be defined in writing to reduce confusion for the coders themselves, analysts, designers (these last three could be the same individual), and clients.

Each element has an emotional effect while also communicating symbolically. They are considered individually and then an overall emotional and symbolic effect is identified. Although Zaltman[5] presents types of metaphors that research indicates are consistent across cultures (e.g., movement, weather, vision, money), nuanced interpretations of images are only possible by people from the same national culture as the one that created the initial image. In addition, sometimes components not present in an image are as important to code and analyze as those that are. Noting elements not in images that might generally be expected to be included can also lead to useful analyses.

As with the content analysis of written material, coding categories need to be exclusive and exhaustive. Rose, an expert in content analyzing visual material, adds that they should be enlightening.[6] As with the content analysis of verbal material, the themes and coding categories must be flexible to reflect the nature of information uncovered. The coding categories are the verbal information that is pulled from the visuals of interest. As with the analysis of verbal material, software packages are available to assist with data analysis, but those programs are very expensive unless the technique is being used extensively by a firm.

Standard statistical analyses of the data collected can be done with readily available software packages such as Excel and include numbers/percentages of entries in each coding category, and cross tabs and chi square tests to produce association matrices. Patterns in the information can be analyzed for all images or the data collected for individual images can be compared as required by the research questions being answered. Interpretations related to factors such as emotion and symbolism are then made.

## Example of Content Analysis—Visual

Francis Ching, in several texts, has enumerated the visual elements of a space.[7] A visual content analysis can review as many of these elements as feasible. Perusing Ching's list of elements of a space, and then keeping the list in mind while reviewing the contents of a website such as stairporn.org (sorry, just many pictures of staircases, nothing sexual), makes it clear how this tool can be valuable. Each of the stairs can be categorized on the relevant criteria, and then patterns in the categorizations can be found. Are most floating staircases in places with radial balance? Cantilevered stairs made out of translucent materials? Wooden staircases used in symmetrical settings? You get the idea. ·

The visual elements Ching mentions include:

Atmosphere

Axis

Balance

Circulation

Color

Configuration

Definition of space

Degree of enclosure

Edges, corners

Emphasis

Fixtures (lighting, plumbing, etc.)

Flexibility

Forms (subtractive, additive, transformed, centralized, linear, radial, clustered, grid)

Furnishings

Harmony

Hierarchy

Light

Line

Materials/finishes

Pattern

Plan

Plane (overhead, parallel, U-shaped, etc.)

Proportion

Repetition

Rhythm

Scale

Shape

Spatial form

Spatial organization

Style

Surface

Symmetry

Unity and variety

Vertical elements

Volumetric elements

# SURVEYS

Surveys are:

| | | | | | | |
|---|---|---|---|---|---|---|
| Little known | 1 | **2** | 3 | 4 | 5 | Lot known |
| Quick | 1 | 2 | 3 | 4 | 5 | Not quick |
| Info straightforward | 1 | 2 | 3 | 4 | 5 | Info complex |
| Verbal | 1 | 2 | 3 | 4 | 5 | Numeric |
| How | 1 | 2 | 3 | 4 | 5 | Why |
| On-site | 1 | 2 | 3 | 4 | 5 | Off-site OK |
| Well-established | 1 | 2 | 3 | 4 | 5 | Innovative |
| Current | 1 | 2 | 3 | 4 | 5 | Future |
| Special | 1 | 2 | 3 | 4 | 5 | No special |
| Generally considered | 1 | **2** | 3 | 4 | 5 | Potentially considered |

[Score indicated by **bold**ing of number.]

If interviews are a time for a conversation to explore issues in general, surveys are a time for very precise data gathering. Even with the most expertly crafted survey, however, you are only learning about the respondents' perceptions of situations—even when they are answering carefully written questions about "facts." Placebo drugs are effective precisely because our individual realities are very important determinants/reflections of experience.

Writing a survey is an efficient start to collecting information that is useful as a project is being initiated, but certain aspects of good surveys can make them difficult to write. For example, surveys must be written using the same terms that the people completing them use to speak, but sometimes natural sounding language is not very precise. Questions that are not precise, however, can make it hard to analyze the information collected. For example, people often speak about their "office" at work—but if you ask people a question on a survey about their office, how can you be sure whether they are answering that question in terms of the building in which they work, the floor on which they sit, or the area around the chair assigned to them by their employer if you don't clearly defining the term?

Writing effective survey questions is a skill that can be learned—and one that will get better and better with more experience. If you pay attention to details in the questions that you write, they will become more objective and effective. There are lots of details in this section on writing survey questions, particularly when compared to the sections on doing content analysis, for example, but those differences in level of detail are unavoidable.

# Writing Survey Questions

When writing survey questions, follow these guidelines:

- *Plan carefully before you begin to write questions.* Make sure that when you have the information the survey results provide, you will be able to resolve the design issues that prompted the survey to begin with. Write a list of all the things you have to know after the study participants have answered the survey questions that you don't know now. Keep that list in a safe place, and refer to it often. Review the list of things you have to know when the survey is done after you have written the survey questions and selected the response options to make sure that the data collected will move your research project forward.

- *Word the questions carefully.* Sometimes differences in question wording that can appear to be subtle to novices can end up making a big difference here. For example, do you want to know if something has ever happened, or how often it happened, or both? Similarly, if you want to analyze different people's responses to the same question, they do indeed need to be asked exactly the same question—word changes that may seem unimportant to you might not turn out to be benign after all. This is also true if you want to compare responses to the same question when it is asked at different times.

- *Make sure that your survey collects all the information from a single respondent that you will ever want to compare at one time.* It can be tricky to try to link up all the survey responses for a single person at a later date. If you want to know how many people who sit in a cubicle also telework, ask about type of workspace and teleworking on a single survey, not two.

- *Try to collect information at the level at which you will want to analyze it, but when in doubt, collect data at a lower level.* Data can always be consolidated but it can be difficult to split it up later. For example, if you investigate the number of times a teacher takes advantage of a certain physical feature in a classroom during four particular weeks individually, you can always consolidate that information and report it at a monthly level. You cannot, however, divide information collected at a monthly level by four and report it at a weekly level—assuming that feature use during each week is the same could be dangerous to the integrity of the data.

- *Some issues are sensitive and people don't like to answer related questions.* Sensitivity is determined by the person answering the question, not the one asking it. Income is one of those difficult topics. Instead of asking people directly about their income, for example, since you know that they will likely inflate their response to the question, ask about a factor that can reasonably be expected to correlate well with income instead. This correlated factor could be years of completed education or job title, for example. Some people are also reticent to report their age and will lie about it—but will answer a question about the year they were born accurately—so ask about year of birth and not age directly.

## Wording Survey Items

You have many options for the forms of the questions you write. Here are the most common:

- *Ratings by an individual on specific criteria.* There are several different ways that these questions can be answered. People can be asked about agreement or disagreement with a statement (which is a lot like being asked about how true or false it is). They can also be queried about how they would categorize something on a continuum anchored by a pair of adjectives with opposite meanings (hot–cold) and a number of available responses between these extremes. If you use this sort of question, it is important to make an informed decision about whether an odd or even number of response options is provided (see Figure 5.2). An even number of responses prevents people from selecting a neural response. If an odd number of response options are provided, people can end up choosing a middle option. For example:

| Cold | 1 | 2 | 3 | 4 | Hot | |
|------|---|---|---|---|-----|-----|
| Cold | 1 | 2 | 3 | 4 | 5 | Hot |

In the second scenario, 3 means neither hot nor cold. In the first, 1 and 2 are more closely associated with cold, 3 and 4 with hot, and there is no middle option meaning neither hot nor cold.

- *Rankings on a specific criteria.* When rankings are made, categorizations are based on the other items being ranked, which is different from the ratings of a set of items, even on the same criteria. For example, the middle of Grand Central Terminal may be a better place to do knowledge work than the middle of Fifth Avenue, according to the person answering questions, but that person may think that both locations are a lousy place to concentrate. When items are ranked, ties are not possible, which can streamline applying the information collected. As with ratings, rankings on surveys collect information about opinions and not more objective factual information.

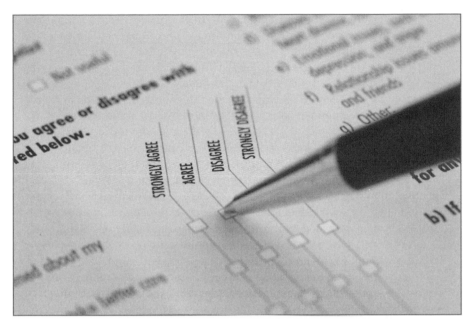

**FIGURE 5.2**
Survey writers must decide if they will provide an odd or even number of responses on ratings type questions. If an odd number of responses are available, survey takers can claim a neutral position; with an even number, that is impossible. © iStockphoto. com/spxChrome

- *Multiple-choice options tailored to the specific issue.* For example, on questions about colors, the responses could be a sample of a red, a blue, or a green, for instance; on a question about ice cream the answer could be chocolate, pistachio, coffee, and butter pecan. With multiple-choice questions, people can only use the categories you supply to answer questions, so those response options must be carefully developed and tested (later in this section we will discuss testing a survey after you have written it). The answers provided must cover the full range of responses that people can reasonably be expected to provide, but it should not be possible for people to select more than one category, unless you direct them to. For example, if the frequency of a certain behavior is of interest, and your response options are 50–100 (A) and 100–150 (B), which option would people wanting to indicate that they did the activity 100 times in the specified time period select? Both factual (accuracy of these facts depends on the respondent) and subjective information can be collected with multiple-choice questions.

- *Open-ended options ask a question but don't provide any sort of ratings, ranking, or multiple-choice options for respondents to choose from.* These queries require that a researcher carefully note the responses written by participants, categorize those responses, and then tally the number of responses assigned to each category—in other words, content analyze them—which can be very time consuming. An example of an open-ended question is, "Tell me about the ways in which you have personalized the desk in the classroom in which you teach" (this also requires several gateway questions, described below ) or, "What one word would you use to describe X? How come?" Use open-ended questions if you can't anticipate which response options people might wish to use or if there are so many possible answers you couldn't include all of them on a reasonably long list—generally no more than ten options is desirable. You might ask an open-ended question if you want q complete report on all of the information that the participant has on a particular topic, but survey takers are not motivated to write long responses to these sorts of questions. Don't anticipate that people will spend a lot of time answering open-ended questions. Their answers may be a lot briefer than you as the researcher would like, leaving out all sorts of details that you would love to know. Also, answers crafted without too much direction can be off-target (not the sort of information you'd hoped to collect) or difficult to understand. Open-ended questions are often more exploratory, so it makes sense to use them on surveys distributed relatively early in the research process, with more close-ended questions being used at later stages when you as a researcher know more about the situation being investigated and can provide a good set of potential response options. Open-ended questions can collect information about facts or opinions.

**FIGURE 5.3**
In order to write useful survey questions about spaces as complex as a nurses' station, it is important to have some knowledge of the environment in use. *© iStockphoto.com/ jsmith*

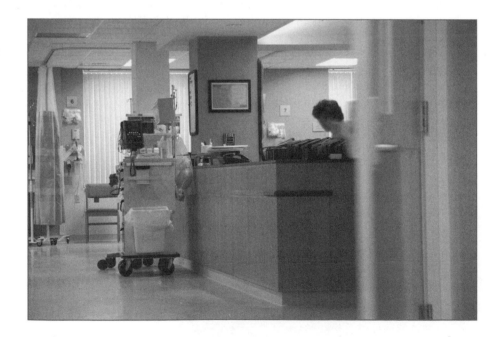

Sometimes people start to answer questions in a pattern—they always chose response 6 for example. You can prevent this from happening by making most of the statements to which individuals are responding positive but a few negative. Those negative statements will break the response patterns—but you have to remember when you are analyzing the data that those questions were asked in a negative form so that the information collected can be properly assessed.

Generally, 5–10 response options are reasonable (although 10 may be pushing the limit) on multiple-choice questions and 5–7 when you are asking people to categorize their responses using a continuum anchored by two opposite adjectives. Use fewer options on a continuum when people are likely to be less personally linked to the response category and more when they are. For example, fewer categories are appropriate when people are assessing a shop they visit to do quick shopping errands and more are appropriate when a boutique at which they purchase clothing they find deeply and personally meaningful is being considered.

Researchers have learned about the appropriate response forms for certain specific types of questions. Fowler and good survey-writing practice suggest the following:[8]

- Frequency questions provide specific numbers of incidents in the specified time period. If this is not possible, the survey writer should ask people to respond using the options always, usually, sometimes, rarely, never, OR almost always, more than half of the time, about half the time, less than half the time, rarely, never.

- Measure of feeling items ask people to respond using the options delighted, pleased, mostly satisfied, mixed, mostly dissatisfied, unhappy, terrible.

- Questions that evaluate use should utilize response options from 0 to 10, where 0 corresponds to as bad as something could possibly be and 10 to as good as it could possibly be.

- Items to measure satisfaction use the options completely satisfied, mostly satisfied, mixed, equally satisfied and dissatisfied, mostly dissatisfied, completely dissatisfied.

- Questions that rate agreement use the response options completely agree, generally agree, generally disagree, completely disagree (the same adjectives can be used to describe categorizations of true/untrue). Fowler also cautions survey writers to remember that there are few situations in which "completely true" and "completely untrue" can be selected.

Russell and Lanius identified a set of adjectives that can be used by both practitioners and academics to describe emotional response to spaces—whether those places currently exist or are imagined.[9] This set of terms is particularly valuable because it can be used to represent the full range of reactions to a place. The adjectives Russell and Lanius introduced to describe emotional response can be arrayed in a circle centered on the intersection of two axes. The horizontal axis can be seen as ranging from unpleasant on the left to pleasant on the right and the vertical axis from energizing on the top to boring at the bottom. The adjectives arrayed around these axes do an excellent job at describing emotional response to a place but are not tied to specific criteria of a place, such as its color.

Adjectives in the energizing and pleasant category are: active, exciting, alive, interesting, exhilarating, arousing, stimulating, sensational pleasing, pretty, and beautiful. Those in the pleasant but boring category include nice, pleasant, serene, restful, peaceful, calm, tranquil, drowsy, and slow. Adjectives in the unpleasant and boring set include lazy, monotonous, idle, inactive, boring, dull, dreary, and unstimulating. Finally, the adjectives in the energizing and unpleasant category are displeasing, unpleasant, dissatisfying, repulsive, uncomfortable, tense, panicky, forceful, frenzied, intense, rushed, and hectic.

Customized sets of adjectives can be used for particular design projects, and survey takers can be asked to select from this list to answer a question. Any time an adjective is added to a survey, its opposite must be added as well, although unless people are being asked to describe a space or experience on a continuum between these opposite pairs, the individual adjectives should be ordered randomly. All adjectives used should be understood by the survey takers and be words that they would actually use in conversation. There are a number of issues that can be probed with a customized adjective list, including how suitable a space is for the activity in question; the emotional, social, physical experience of being in the space; and aesthetics. Forty to fifty total adjectives are an ideal number.

Make sure that each question that you ask is a single question—if you pack two questions into one, it is impossible to fully understand the data provided. For example, do not ask teachers about their response to the lighting and to the overall design of the classroom in which they teach in the same question.

Define all terms in the survey that could be confusing—remember the discussion of "office" earlier? Another example: What does "the past week" mean to you? The person sitting next to you? Check with your client to learn what sorts of place-related terms they use. Read each question that you have written carefully to identify potential "difficult terms" or insider jargon. Define them at the beginning of a question so that a reader transitions right from the actual question to the response options you have provided. Be very conservative when you are evaluating ways in which questions could possibly be misread.

Use gateway questions to prevent people from being exposed to questions that they cannot or should not answer. Ask people if they have an assigned classroom before you ask them how/if they have personalized their desk in their assigned classroom and those questions must proceed more detailed

**FIGURE C.1**
The design of the Seattle
Public Library required
that OMA/LMN think
broadly about cultural,
social, technological, and
functional issues. *Photo:
Augustin*

**FIGURE C.2**
Financial considerations can have unexpected effects on design decisions. For example, cubicles are depreciated (in accounting terms) more quickly than solid-walled offices, which influences decisions about their use. © iStockphoto.com/o6photo

**FIGURE C.3**
Ariely's research shows that not all decisions are entirely rational. © iStockphoto.com/ enot-poloskun

**FIGURE C.4**
Humans feel comfortable and safe in spaces when their backs are protected. Also, feeling safe allows us to devote more mental energy to satisfying other psychological needs identified by Maslow. © iStockphoto.com/ otokimus

**FIGURE C.5**
Introverts prefer environments that are less sensorily rich. Compare this store, which appeals to introverts to Figure 3.15, which appeals to extraverts. © iStockphoto. com/vicnt

**FIGURE C.6**
This space became a green roof as its users' needs changed. *Photo: Augustin*

**FIGURE C.7**
An excellent example
of biophilic design,
this space incorporates
daylight, sensory rich-
ness, and movement
(mobile).  *Photo: Augustin*

**FIGURE C.9A, B**
These are the sorts of images that can be used with projective techniques to help overcome obstacles to discussing topics.
*Fern: © iStockphoto.com/robynmac; Trainyard: © iStockphoto.com/SteveDF*

**FIGURE C.10**
Elevated positions are good spots from which to do behavior mapping.
*Photo: Augustin*

**FIGURE C.11**
Experiences along circu-
lation routes are key in
space syntax analysis.
© iStockphoto.com/
Serp77

**FIGURE C.12**
Observations are regu-
larly one of the method-
ologies used during a
post-occupancy evalua-
tion. *Photo: Augustin*

questions about any personalization that has been done. Gateway questions often probe knowledge of issues before opinion-type questions are asked. They are necessary because people generally answer the questions that you pose to them, and even if they are ill-informed on the related issues, they'll answer the questions anyway because they want to be helpful. When ill-informed people answer your questions, you end up with garbage. Gateway questions can also lead people to describe positive and negative aspects of a place or experience, for example, and direct them on different paths through a questionnaire. They are useful for channeling people with different sorts of life and other experiences into the appropriate stream of questions to answer.

People have bad memories, and they're also not prophets. Don't ask people to project their future behavior or remember their past behavior in a general sense. Instead, ask them about a particular time and place in the recent past—such as yesterday. Get a time-lock on all activities described. Asking respondents about their behavior for yesterday, or some other meaningful but relatively immediate time frame, is fine as long as you have reason to believe that yesterday is representative of usual activity. Asking tax accounts about the number of hours that they were in the office on April 10 does not give you too much idea of how many hours they were in the office on December 1. However, if your design objective is to effectively accommodate all users, even on the busiest of days, the April 10 data are of great interest.

Similarly, people aren't clairvoyant, so answers they provide about why something has happened should not be taken as definitive—merely suggestive.

Make sure that the questions you write do not lead respondents to a particular response. This can happen when the multiple-choice answers provided to a question do not cover the full range of response options but only the positive ones, for example. Question forms can also bias responses—if you ask people how much they like their workspace, you will get a very different set of responses than if you look for feedback on their workspace without using terms such as *like*, for example. Neutral wordings are crucial (see Figure 5.4).

If a question might be difficult for people to answer negatively, provide information in the form of the question that allows them to do so more easily. For example, office etiquette strongly condemns people who listen to other people's telephone conversations intentionally. If you are interested in the occurrence of this sort of activity, mention in the body of the question that this sort of listening can sometimes happen by accident, which will give respondents "permission" to state that they have listened to other people's conversations.

Questions for which society strongly dictates answers can be phrased using a very long time frame ("Have you ever—?"). The most common uses for these types of questions involve participation in illegal activities, which is probably not often directly related to resolving design issues. Using the long time frame prevents you from learning about recent actions.

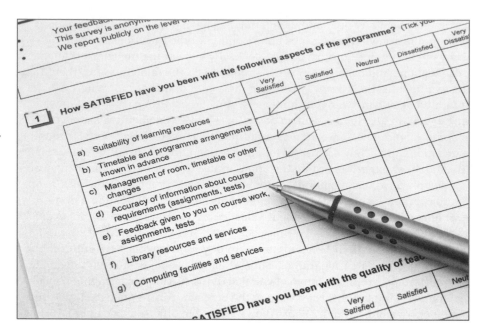

It is often important to ask people indirect questions rather than direct ones because the "correct" answer might be heavily determined by social forces or because people simply wouldn't be able to answer direct questions. For example: In a survey, you can't just ask people which of a set of three, four, or five different organizational cultures matches up with the one at their firm. Instead, it's best to ask questions about specific elements of an organization's culture and combine these responses to learn about culture overall. Asking about others' opinions as a way to overcome this obstacle is discussed in the section of this book covering interviewing.

A topic that is often probed indirectly during workplace design is aligning the physical form of a workplace with the work styles of the users. Questions that ask about activities in a space will help provide this sort of information. In addition, Augustin developed the following questions that can be used to provide work style information:[10] "For you to do your current job well, which of the following should the spaces you work in be more like: Santa's elves' workshop, with places to build and tinker; Bank vault where you get sealed in every morning with your computer and papers and work uninterrupted; Booth at a great restaurant where people drop by to discuss issues throughout the day (unfortunately, this option would have to come without the food); Quaker religious service—at Quaker services people silently ponder religious questions and speak aloud when they have something significant to say; Airline club where amenities are available when you drop in to use them?"

Another topic that comes up frequently when workplaces are being designed is the level of acoustic and visual privacy required because of task complexity. Also in 2009, Augustin presented the following question to inform the design response on this issue:[11] "Which of the following is most like how you spend your day at work: Solving a new puzzle; performing a play that you've acted in before; teaching a class you have taught before to a group of students that occasionally asks thought-provoking questions."

People can relatively accurately describe their relative experiences and performance in a space from one time to another or in a collection of spaces, although they aren't very good at assessing their absolute experience or performance. That means they know whether they work better in one space or another but not the actual level of their performance—whether they are superstars should be uncovered through means other than questions to users. Questions about workplace experiences can collect this relative performance data and look at differences between one space and another for design clues.

If you need to classify people, do so in a way that is meaningful to them. For example, ask the human resource department at your client firm for job titles in use there.

Use a variety of question formats in your survey. Too many questions that look and sound the same get boring, and boredom leads to sloppy question answering and quitting the survey before all questions are answered.

**FIGURE 5.5**
Images of faces can be useful in written surveys, particularly if survey takers are members of populations that may be less verbally adept, such as children. Standardized sets of faces have been developed. © iStock-photo.com/aldomurillo

Sometimes you will need to find out about a topic that requires very specialized or carefully worded questions. For example, you might decide that you need to learn about an organizational culture through a survey, that observational and other tools are not viable options. There are sources for professionally written surveys that will help you learn about organizational culture, job satisfaction, satisfaction with the ambient environment (indoor air quality, ventilation rate, temperature, etc.), organizational commitment, and similar issues. To find these tools, many of which are also available at no charge, do a literature review using the name of what you want to measure and an additional term such as *test, tool, scale,* or *measure.* Use tools prepared by people with academic appointments at respected universities. These are not the only people who can write good surveys, not by a long shot, but looking for these credentials is a quick and almost definitely effective way to vet a survey that you might unearth. Tools that have appeared in a published peer-reviewed article (defined in Chapter 4), are particularly strong candidates for use. Be wary of surveys developed by for-profit firms, such as manufacturers. Even though the people writing the surveys for these organizations often have excellent survey writing skills, it is also possible that survey questions have been developed with commercial objectives in mind or that it has not been financially feasible to completely test the questions developed.

## Administering a Survey

Take a look at the survey responses from each participant if at all possible. If you find surveys completed by people who have clearly not followed directions (e.g., they have selected the second response to each question asked), delete their survey from the analysis. Even with electronic survey tools, such as Survey Monkey or Zoomerang, this is generally possible.

Since rules related to how members of a national culture will use a space are learned as language is learned and are linked to the language being spoken, ask people place-based questions in the same language that they will be speaking when they use a space—even if they are fluent in another one. For example, even if everyone working in your Shanghai office speaks English fluently, if survey takers will be speaking Chinese while working in that office, the survey questions they read and respond to should be written in Chinese.

Write your survey so that respondents do not have to read an introductory block of directions to answer questions correctly—because few will actually read the directions that you agonize over. Do provide those directions, however, and test them by having someone unfamiliar with your project read over them and give you their interpretation of them. Brief versions of the directions can be included in each individual question. Be sure to clearly state what the end points of any numeric scales mean, as well as how to interpret numbers in between those end points. For example, on a scale of 1 to 10, 10 might be the "most positive possible rating," while 1 is the "least positive possible rating."

Numbers 2 to 9 represent intermediary ratings. It is also a good idea in directions to let respondents know that although none of the options provided may exactly represent their opinion [or whatever else is being inquired about], one will come closer than another, and that closer option should be selected.

**FIGURE 5.6**
Repeat directions throughout a survey. © iStockphoto.com/cmcderm1

Technically, any surveys with missing data should not be included in analyses completed, but in practice, this can leave design researchers with tiny data sets. Try to make surveys short so that people answer all of the questions posed, but when it is necessary to include surveys with missing answers in analyses, insert the average answer received for that missing value. This is crucial because some statistical software will not complete analyses if any data fields are empty.

Before you actually distribute a survey, have several people similar to those who will ultimately receive the survey answer the questions. Sit with the first few of these people and have them narrate their experiences and thoughts as they answer the questions aloud, so you can eliminate any problems that might distort questions from their intended purpose. Their monologue might sound like this: "Question 5 is asking about [some topic] and giving me these options to answer the question. A means [paraphrase of response A, followed by similar paraphrasing of all the other responses. For [stated reason], I'll pick response A." Look at the information that you get from a few people that you don't sit with as they answer the questions. Make sure that it makes sense. It is great if you can get at least 10 people to participate in this sort of test. The test will also help you assess the feasibility of any open-ended questions you are asking.

If you require accurate information about the frequency with which something occurs, provide people with some mechanism to keep track of it—even a simple tally sheet that is marked or a straightforward PDA program can do the trick. So can the experience sampling methodology (ESM), which is described in Chapter 4. If you do have people complete tally sheets, make sure that they are turned in each day to prevent them from being lost and to prevent people from stopping their collection of new data and copying data collected on one day onto the forms for all subsequent days in the study.

In the memo that accompanies each survey, do not provide too much information about your data-gathering objectives; be vague. Too much information can lead respondents to particular answers because they may "guess" your objectives. Also in a cover memo do not ask people to be honest or open or straightforward, because that implies that they generally are dishonest. A cover note should tell people that their contribution is valued. Whether information will be kept confidential or anonymous should also be discussed in the cover note. Keep the survey short, and tell participants that it is short—if people have a realistic idea about how long it takes to complete a survey, they will set aside that amount of time (assuming the survey is appropriately short) and answer all of the questions posed. The steps required to complete the survey (e.g., go to this web address, return paper survey to the box marked X in the cafeteria) should also be outlined in the memo. Thank people for spending time answering your questions and make sure the memo is signed by an important person at the client firm.

Here are some additional guidelines:

- A written survey that takes about ten minutes to complete is best.

- Questions should be posed in a certain order, generally.

- Demographic questions should be last, because answering them makes some people self-conscious, which influences subsequent question responses.

- Easy questions should lead off the survey, but the most importantquestions on the survey should immediately follow those first few, easy-to-answer questions so that if people stop answering questions, you have captured that information.

- The space people are in when they answer questions really matters. Answers to questions about a space will be more valuable if they are given in the space being studied.

- Previous questions bring topics to mind that color responses to subsequent questions, so always consider how thinking about a previous topic could influence responses to subsequent questions.

There are a number of very useful online survey tools available, and those tools will inevitably continue to evolve as this book ages. Also, during the course of this book's life entirely new tools will become available. For these reasons, it is recommended that readers research online survey tools using the Google search methodology outlined in Chapter 4. Google Docs/Forms is currently a leader in online surveying, as are Zoomerang and Survey Monkey.

## Who Should Participate

A set of people similar to the larger group of people who will use a space should answer the survey questions posed. Ideally, either all of the people whose opinions you are interested in should be asked to complete a survey or people should be sampled randomly from that set to answer the questions. This is necessary if you want to generalize from your results to the population at large. (Refer to this chapter's section on interviewing for a discussion of defining user types.)

There are a number of ways to select people randomly, but the most straightforward is to chose every $n$th person on any sort of list (e.g., an alphabetized set of employee names). The $n$ in this case is based on the size of the population needed to complete the survey and the size of the population being sampled from. For example, if there are 4,500 people who could be asked to complete a survey, and 150 are needed to complete the survey, 450 people should be asked to answer the survey questions, because it is quite conservative to believe that one in three survey forms will be returned. In this example, every tenth person on the list should be asked to complete as survey ($n = 10$) because 450 out of 4,500 should be invited. After the surveys are completed, it is useful to try to determine if the people who answered your questions are in some way be different from those that did not.

In the real, practical world, it is generally best to distribute a survey to an entire population of people that will use a space. Sending the survey to all users can't work in a situation such as a municipal building where there are potentially millions of total users, but often, projects have a much smaller potential set of users, so it makes sense to contact them all, particularly if the survey is distributed electronically. If the space you are designing will be used by a small number of people, 10 to 15 or less, it is best to have each of them complete a survey. This reduces the likelihood that a single individual with an atypical space experience can distort the design developed from the information collected.

The total number of people required to answer survey questions can be determined by using the tool available at www.surveysystem.com/sscalc.htm or the one available from Zoomerang and include at its website.

The algorithms that calculate appropriate sample size assume that those polled were selected randomly from the group of people you are interested in learning more about. If everyone in the group you are interested in learning more about did not have an equal possibility of being selected to complete a survey, then the estimates of sample size that follow are, strictly speaking, not relevant—but they will provide you with some information on the minimum size sample that you would need. These estimates also apply to the accuracy of the answers to any one survey question, but not to the survey as a whole. According to calculations by Blankenship, Breen, and Dutka, if you want to be 95 percent confident in your findings, are within 5% of the value for a population as whole you should use the sample size of 385, as shown in Table 5.2.[12]

**TABLE 5.2**
**Sample Sizes Needed for Confidence Levels**

| Margin of Error | Sample Size |
| --- | --- |
| Plus or minus 1% | 9,604 |
| 2% | 2,401 |
| 3% | 1,068 |
| 4% | 601 |
| 5% | 385 |
| 7.5% | 171 |
| 10% | 97 |
| 15% | 43 |
| 20% | 25 |
| 50% | 4 |

## Analyzing the Data Collected

When you begin to analyze data, first consider if you should review findings that can be drawn from all of the data collected, and then assess material for each group—with group being defined for our purposes as sets of people who can reasonably be expected to use/be comfortable in different places. This is generally a good idea because individual group differences (for example, those found in different medical units) can have an important influence on a design's success. Group-related differences in needs can be washed out if data are not analyzed for separate groups. Information for all groups combined can usefully be applied to the design of common spaces, however.

Be wary of drawing too many conclusions when less than a third of the members of a user group or ten people, whichever is larger, do not answer the survey questions. Supplement the information from the survey with material gathered using other tools, such as interviews and discussion groups if the number of participants does not meet this standard. If a group is smaller than ten people, every member of that group should return a survey. When only volunteers, or a small number or percentage, of future users answer survey questions, the odds increase that the information you are collecting is not consistent with that to be found in the population of all users. With a very small number of completed surveys it is possible for a single survey to radically change the pattern of responses seen. Surveys whose answers are dramatically different from the rest can be eliminated from the analysis, but the answers on those surveys may be entirely legitimate and correct. This should only be done with one or two "outlying" surveys and after a great deal of consideration. It is always possible, for example, that a person has misread directions.

There are several different ways you can analyze the data you have collected. For questions that collected true numeric data, you can always average the answers given. *True numeric data* is a situation in which pretty much any number could have been chosen in answer to a question—a good example is age. If you have questions that are answered using numbers and those numbers are really labels, then averaging them doesn't make any sense, although noting the frequency with which each response appears does. For example if a person picks 1 to indicate that he is British, 2 to indicate he is French, or 3 to indicate that he is German, averaging the number of 1s, 2s, and 3s provided by all of the people who took your survey is pretty meaningless—what would an average of 2.3 mean here? Instead, ask your statistical software for the frequency with which the answers were supplied. Frequencies can be readily converted into percents of all answers collected.

When you have categorical information, information from ranking items, or numeric data (answers in which numbers stand for quantities of something), you can probe the relationships in your data by asking your statistical software to run chi-square tests. You might, for example, probe differences between the favored working locations of accountants and marketers in this way. Your statistical software—whether it is SPSS, SAS, Excel, or something else—will tell you how to actually set up the analysis.

The software package will also show you where to look in its output to determine if the relationships seen are statistically significant. Statistical significance indicates how likely it is that a given effect would have been seen purely by chance. So a significance level of 5 percent means that there is a 5 percent (also written as .05) chance that the relationship seen in your data does not really exist in the world at large and just appeared by chance in the data you collected.

You can calculate correlations for numeric data. Again, this is data where the numbers are being used to represent real quantities of something and not just for categorization. Correlations tell you what happens to one of the variables you are working with, as the other in the analysis changes. If as one of the variables changes, the other does in the same direction, the correlation is positive, but if they move in opposite directions, the correlation is negative. If there is no relationship in how the sets of information are related, their correlation is 0. Correlations can range from –1 to +1. Again, the software package you are using will tell you where to look to determine whether the relationships observed in the data you have collected are due to chance.

If two items are correlated, that does not mean that one is causing another, it just means that they tend to vary at a particular rate. Ranked data cannot be used in correlations.

When you are reporting the results of a survey, make sure that others cannot identify individual respondents based on the material you provide. If there are a small number of members of a racial, ethnic, or gender group that were polled, make sure to present information in a way so that individual responses cannot be determined. If only one Asian person and one African-American work in the 30-person marketing group and the other 28 people are white, do not report data for Caucasians, Asians, and African-Americans separately.

## Time Frame to Use a Survey

The survey development process can take a month or so, depending on how similar the new survey is to previous surveys that the team has written and the approval process at the client firm. One week after the survey is initially distributed, a reminder should be sent out encouraging returns. Two weeks after the survey is distributed, data collection should end. If an online survey tool is used, the analyses are immediately available, although it might take several weeks to review them and write a final report. This last phase of the project can be condensed as required by the situation.

## Integrative Comments

This section has discussed the mechanics of writing survey questions; Chapter 3 introduced you to some of the tenets behind space design and laid out specific sorts of topics that should be investigated as different sorts of space types are being developed. As you create your own surveys, you will develop a collection of data-gathering tools that differentiate you in the design marketplace and are proprietary. The process of developing these tools is iterative, as is writing an individual survey question—each is continuously in the process of further refinement. Writing your own survey also gives you the opportunity to investigate issues in new ways—for example, asking about what is overvalued as opposed to what is valued.

## Sample Survey—Public Parks

The sample survey illustrates a popular and important survey format, derived from customer satisfaction studies and is closely based on the work of Nigel Gill, John Brierley, and Rob MacDougal.[13] By comparing the satisfaction and importance scores collected using their ten-point response framework, it is possible to determine which aspects of an environment are most in need of modification. When the average importance rating is one or more points higher than the average satisfaction rating, spring into action to change that experience. Prioritizations based on an organization's mission are necessary when resources preclude making changes each time the difference is one or more points.

# Public Parks Survey

We're interested in learning more about your experiences in public parks.

The questions in this survey will take about 10 minutes to answer. After you have answered all of them, please leave the completed survey form in the orange box at the main gate.

Thank you for taking the time to answer our questions.

*Signoff of Park Manager*

Please indicate how important or unimportant each of the following things are to your decision to visit a park, and whether you are satisfied or dissatisfied with those elements at [NAME OF PARK].

When reading the following questions, please circle [change this, based on the survey administration method] the response that comes closest to your opinion.

For each item listed below, how satisfied or dissatisfied are you with that aspect of [NAME OF THIS PARK]? Please select N/A if it is not relevant to you.

| Totally Dissatisfied | 1 | 2 | 3 | 4 | 5 | 6 | 7 | 8 | 9 | 10 | N/A | Totally Satisfied |
|---|---|---|---|---|---|---|---|---|---|---|---|---|
| Grassy lawn | 1 | 2 | 3 | 4 | 5 | 6 | 7 | 8 | 9 | 10 | N/A | |
| Hard surface paths | 1 | 2 | 3 | 4 | 5 | 6 | 7 | 8 | 9 | 10 | N/A | |
| Children's slide | 1 | 2 | 3 | 4 | 5 | 6 | 7 | 8 | 9 | 10 | N/A | |
| Children's swings | 1 | 2 | 3 | 4 | 5 | 6 | 7 | 8 | 9 | 10 | N/A | |
| Children's climbing area | 1 | 2 | 3 | 4 | 5 | 6 | 7 | 8 | 9 | 10 | N/A | |
| Seats along walking paths | 1 | 2 | 3 | 4 | 5 | 6 | 7 | 8 | 9 | 10 | N/A | |
| Seats not along walking paths | 1 | 2 | 3 | 4 | 5 | 6 | 7 | 8 | 9 | 10 | N/A | |
| Paths for runners only | 1 | 2 | 3 | 4 | 5 | 6 | 7 | 8 | 9 | 10 | N/A | |
| Pond | 1 | 2 | 3 | 4 | 5 | 6 | 7 | 8 | 9 | 10 | N/A | |
| Fountain | 1 | 2 | 3 | 4 | 5 | 6 | 7 | 8 | 9 | 10 | N/A | |
| Water cooler for people | 1 | 2 | 3 | 4 | 5 | 6 | 7 | 8 | 9 | 10 | N/A | |
| Ease of parking | 1 | 2 | 3 | 4 | 5 | 6 | 7 | 8 | 9 | 10 | N/A | |
| Accessibility by public transportation | 1 | 2 | 3 | 4 | 5 | 6 | 7 | 8 | 9 | 10 | N/A | |
| Time it takes to travel to park | 1 | 2 | 3 | 4 | 5 | 6 | 7 | 8 | 9 | 10 | N/A | |
| Water cooler for pets | 1 | 2 | 3 | 4 | 5 | 6 | 7 | 8 | 9 | 10 | N/A | |
| Pets allowed in park | 1 | 2 | 3 | 4 | 5 | 6 | 7 | 8 | 9 | 10 | N/A | |

How important or unimportant is each of the following park elements to you when you are deciding to visit a park?

| No Importance at All | 1 | 2 | 3 | 4 | 5 | 6 | 7 | 8 | 9 | 10 | Extremely Important |
|---|---|---|---|---|---|---|---|---|---|---|---|
| Grassy lawn | | 1 | 2 | 3 | 4 | 5 | 6 | 7 | 8 | 9 | 10 |
| Hard surface paths | | 1 | 2 | 3 | 4 | 5 | 6 | 7 | 8 | 9 | 10 |
| Children's slide | | 1 | 2 | 3 | 4 | 5 | 6 | 7 | 8 | 9 | 10 |
| Children's swings | | 1 | 2 | 3 | 4 | 5 | 6 | 7 | 8 | 9 | 10 |
| Children's climbing area | | 1 | 2 | 3 | 4 | 5 | 6 | 7 | 8 | 9 | 10 |
| Seats along walking paths | | 1 | 2 | 3 | 4 | 5 | 6 | 7 | 8 | 9 | 10 |
| Seats not along walking paths | | 1 | 2 | 3 | 4 | 5 | 6 | 7 | 8 | 9 | 10 |
| Paths for runners only | | 1 | 2 | 3 | 4 | 5 | 6 | 7 | 8 | 9 | 10 |
| Pond | | 1 | 2 | 3 | 4 | 5 | 6 | 7 | 8 | 9 | 10 |
| Fountain | | 1 | 2 | 3 | 4 | 5 | 6 | 7 | 8 | 9 | 10 |
| Water cooler for people | | 1 | 2 | 3 | 4 | 5 | 6 | 7 | 8 | 9 | 10 |
| Ease of parking | | 1 | 2 | 3 | 4 | 5 | 6 | 7 | 8 | 9 | 10 |
| Accessibility by public transportation | | 1 | 2 | 3 | 4 | 5 | 6 | 7 | 8 | 9 | 10 |
| Time it takes to travel to park | | 1 | 2 | 3 | 4 | 5 | 6 | 7 | 8 | 9 | 10 |
| Water cooler for pets | | 1 | 2 | 3 | 4 | 5 | 6 | 7 | 8 | 9 | 10 |
| Pets allowed in park | | 1 | 2 | 3 | 4 | 5 | 6 | 7 | 8 | 9 | 10 |

How many minutes does it take for you to travel, on average, to NAME OF PARK? [Select a number from a pull-down list.]

Are you most likely to travel to NAME OF PARK from

_____ Home

_____ Office

_____ Your children's school

_____ Another place. Please specify _____

How do you travel to the park?

    \_\_\_\_ Walk

    \_\_\_\_ Bus

    \_\_\_\_ Drive

    \_\_\_\_ Other. Please specify _____

How many times did you visit NAME OF PARK last week? [Select a number from a pull-down list.]

Did you bring children to the park last week?

\_\_\_\_ Yes

\_\_\_\_ No

\_\_\_\_Can't remember

[If yes] Of the X [software fills in response from previous question] times that you visited the park last week, on how many trips did you bring children to NAME OF PARK? [Select a number from a sliding scale.]

In what year were you born? [Select a year from a sliding scale.]

What is your gender?

\_\_\_\_ Female

    Male

\_\_\_\_ Prefer not to state

Did you graduate from high school?

\_\_\_\_ Yes

\_\_\_\_ No

Did you graduate from a four-year college program?

\_\_\_\_ Yes

\_\_\_\_ No

# ENDNOTES

1. Gerald Zaltman, *How Customers Think: Essential Insights Into the Mind of the Market* (Cambridge, MA: Harvard University Press, 2003).

2. Devi Jankowicz, *The Easy Guide to Repertory Grids* (Hoboken, NJ: John Wiley and Sons, 2004).

3. Bruce Berg, *Qualitative Research Methods for the Social Sciences*, 5th ed. (New York: Pearson, 2004).

4. Gillian Rose, *Visual Methodologies: An Introduction to the Interpretation of Visual Materials,* 2nd ed. (Thousand Oaks, CA: Sage Press, 2007), and Francis Ching, Architecture: Form, Space, and Order (2d ed.) (New York: John Wiley and Sons, 1996).

5. Zaltman, *How Customers Think.*

6. Berg, *Qualitative Research.*

7. Francis Ching, *Interior Design Illustrated* (New York: John Wiley and Sons, 1987); Ching, Architecture.

8. Floyd Fowler, *Improving Survey Questions: Design and Evaluation* (Thousand Oaks, CA: Sage Publications, 1995).

9. J. Russell and U. Lanius, "Adaptation Level and the Affective Appraisal of Environments," *Journal of Environmental Psychology*, vol. 4 (1984) pp. 119–135.

10. Sally Augustin, *Place Advantage: Applied Psychology for Interior Architecture* (Hoboken, NJ: John Wiley and Sons, 2009).

11. Ibid.

12. A. Blankenshio, George Breen, and Alan Dutka, *State of the Art Marketing Research*, 2nd ed. (New York: NTC Business Books, 1998).

13. Nigel Gill, John Brierley, and Rob MacDougal, *How to Measure Customer Satisfaction* (New York: Gower Publishing Group, 2004).

# A Story of Practice: It Starts with Programming

Information contributed through interview by: Workshop Architects, Milwaukee, Wisconsin

**Contributors:**

Jan van den Kieboom, Principal

Peter van den Kieboom, Senior designer

Walter Johnson, Project manager

Maria Ceislik, Interior designer

Project Name: South Campus Union, University of Wisconsin—Madison

Scope: Programming, planning, design, and construction documentation for a new student union with an underground loading and parking facility (with Moody Nolan Architects, Columbus, Ohio, who focused on exterior envelope development).

Date: 2008–2011 (Completed March 2011)

Square Footage: Union: 191,872 GSF, parking facility: 87,792 GSF

Location: Madison, Wisconsin, USA

## PROBLEM DEFINITION

In January 2008, Workshop Architects was commissioned to program and design a new $94.8 million student union for the University of Wisconsin—Madison.

The new South Campus Union building is a five-story structure that includes recreation spaces, restaurants, a coffeehouse, a pub, performance venues, a film cinema, meeting/conference facilities, student and administrative office environments, a 60-room hotel, and a wide variety of lounge spaces. A central feature is the Sun Garden—a major social-gathering space at the crossroads of the building. Outdoor spaces are designed to accommodate a farmers' market and future commuter rail stop. The building's outdoor terraces create an amphitheater for large campus gatherings.

The construction and operation of the South Campus Union building is primarily student-fee funded. Therefore, the student leadership required the project process have robust student involvement. A 15-member design committee, along with the Union Council, Memorial Union Board Association, the University of Wisconsin Design Review Board, the City of Madison's Urban Design Commission, the Railway Commission, and the State of Wisconsin DSF authorities all had oversight and project approval rights. The Design Committee included representation from seven subcommittees, called the design advisory groups.

For this project, Workshop Architects used a participatory research approach that capitalized on the large-scale committee structure as the bench power to access information and identify significant planning principles and criteria for project success.

The participatory research process took a three-part approach, beginning in the qualitative programming phase into the schematic design phase and concluded in the design development phase of the project.

## OBJECTIVE

The University of Wisconsin–Madison South Campus Union project goal was to create a social and vibrant environment that would serve as a people magnet and a socially interactive space. The union's program drove a flexible and adaptable building form. Although the facility is intended to be student focused, it also needed to be welcoming to a broader audience that included the entire university population and the interests of the local community.

As this project was a replacement structure for what was considered a failed late-twentieth-century union building, a primary mission for the substitute building was to complement the existing Memorial Union (located on Lake Mendota and considered the heart and soul of the university) and evoke a similar sense of community, pride of place, and engagement.

A further directive for the project was that the building design, operation, and construction processes were to be sustainable and to meet, at the minimum, a LEED Silver standard.

## CONTEXT DEVELOPMENT

Project kick-off included a campuswide symposium. The design committee invited an international group of experts to work alongside local and student participants to explore the history and the future direction of campus life. "This symposium was an incredibly useful way to begin the project process," says van den Kieboom. "It allowed us to identify the key attributes of a successful campus union building in a broader context." Speakers included Jay Walljasper from Project for Public Spaces, who addressed popular winter-city activities, and Gary Golden, a professional futurist, from Brooklyn, New York, who talked about future technology and its impact on student life. Campus historians provided the history of the Madison campus and the legacy behind the "Wisconsin Idea"—a longstanding principle that fosters the belief that the university should contribute (beyond the classroom) to the state and its people.

## DEVELOPING A FRAMEWORK OF CULTURE

An architectural tour was organized to give the entire project team (students, advisors, and designers) an opportunity to develop a framework or common language for the South Union design criteria. The 35-person group boarded a bus and spent a weekend in Chicago touring campus unions, public spaces, restaurants, and retail environments (see Figure 5.7). In advance of the visit, Workshop Architects gave each participant a workbook that identified evaluation criteria for each building. The group ranked the environments based on level of transparency, legibility of design intent, thick and sticky spaces (spaces that are heavily programmed and highly used), as well as spaces with crossroads and pathways that encourage interaction (see Figure 5.8). "We chose buildings that have some relationship—either historically or functionally—to issues we planned to address in the South Union building to give committee members a shared context and a comparative language to use as we moved forward," recalls van den Kieboom.

**FIGURE 5.7**
The 35-person group boarded a bus and spent a weekend in Chicago touring campus unions, public spaces, restaurants, and retail environments. © *Workshop Architects*

**FIGURE 5.8**
The group ranked the environments based on level of transparency, legibility of design intent, thick and sticky spaces. © *Workshop Architects*

Students reciprocated by touring the design team through the Madison campus with stops at known and little-known favorite places that usually involved a break for food or beverages. Beyond the tours, the design team established a temporary field office on campus to observe and participate in the day-to-day culture.

Concurrent with the tours, seven design advisory groups (DAGs) were formed to represent the broad range of interest groups and student involvement. Each group was made up of students, faculty, administration, and staff to support the qualitative programming research and analysis efforts of the following areas: food service and retail, indoor/outdoor recreation, interior design and art, leadership and involvement, programming and operations, site design, and sustainability.

To reach as many participants as possible, Workshop Architects distributed a campuswide survey that was supplemented with intercept interviews—interviews that take place in situ—as a way to meet and collect just-in-time feedback from the student population. To encourage more dialogs, the Design Committee posted and monitored a student blog and instituted a social program called "Tuesdays After Class." Here, students set up information tables around campus to collect additional input from the University community. "All total, the process touched over 23,000 members of the University Community," notes van den Kieboom.

## DISTILLING THE INFORMATION

To synthesize this research data, a smaller design committee made up of two university-appointed faculty, two Union staff members, two alumni, and nine student representatives was created to distill the research into a usable form. The committee met every other week to review the research data, discuss the qualitative and quantitative implications of the material, and provide feedback to the design team. From this effort, Workshop Architects analyzed the findings to establish South Union's program requirements and create a final program document.

## SCHEMATIC DESIGN: ADJACENCY, STACKING, AND MASSING

With a conceptual program, Workshop Architects again set out to use the power of the Design Committee by instituting a series of design workshops to work through adjacency and stacking options through a process called a Relationship Puzzle.™ Here, the committee members were given a set of precut shapes representing the programmed functions scaled to the required square footage. With the help of the design team, the committee physically moved the program elements horizontally and vertically through the building footprint, noting the advantages and disadvantages of the different spatial relationships (see Figure 5.9).

Afterward, Workshop Architects amalgamated the information from the outcomes of the Relationship Puzzle™ exercises into a series of schematic design sketches. The architects collaborated with a UW-Madison gradu-ate student, Gwen Drury, who, at the time, was developing a program called Socially Ergonomic Environmental Design (SEED™). Using the SEED™ tool, the team was able to rate the design concepts based on how it impacted cer-tain criteria. In this case, it was based on encouraging interaction and user experience. According to van den Kieboom, working with the SEED™ process helped the committee members maintain consistency and a common language when evaluating the different planning strategies and ensured that the design solutions supported the goals set by the Union board.

The SEED™ exercise identified ways to break down the large facility into spaces that would act as what they referred to as *bridge spaces*. One example is inserting a climbing wall inside a bar and lounge to encourage casual con-versations among strangers. The theory is that strangers will be more comfort-able sitting in a lounge if there is an event to watch or discuss. For the South Union, the event is around the climbing wall. Pocket lounges also emanated from the SEED™ exercise as a way to create small, secure, and intimate "bonding" spaces—in this case, a wine bar—that is welcoming and private.

From the amalgamation of the information generated from the multiple Relationship Puzzle™ and SEED™ exercises, Workshop Architects developed nine iterations of adjacency, blocking, stacking and interior massing diagrams for the committee's evaluation. "We had too many iterations for it to be truly effective," notes van den Kieboom, who realized early on that the variations were too subtle for the intended purpose.

## NARROWING DOWN THE OPTIONS

Through a series of meetings and presentations, the nine options were narrowed down to three. From these three, Workshop Architects prepared site plans, drawings, and concept models that they refer to as "rip and tear models" to encourage committee members to physically move and adjust the programmatic elements, while considering the spatial relationships. The committee worked in teams and rotated from station to station, offering feedback from each committee on each concept. "We went from nine concepts to three concepts to the final one," recalls van den Kieboom. "Each committee member had the opportunity to voice his or her opinion and influence the direction of design."

In the spring of 2008, five months after the start of the project, the entire community of project stakeholders reached consensus on the building program, site development, floor plan and a building massing strategy resulting in the completion of the programming and schematic design phase of the project.

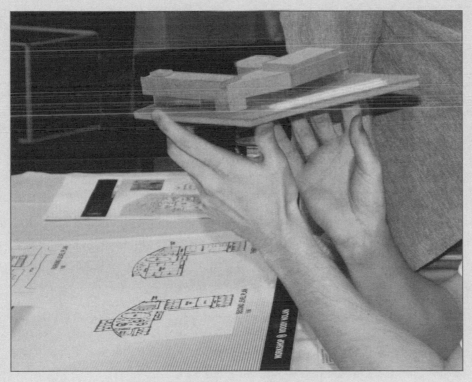

**FIGURE 5.10**
Five months after the start of the project, the entire community of project stakeholders reached consensus on the building program, site development, floor plan, and a building massing strategy. © *Workshop Architects*

## BUILDING IMAGE AND CHARACTER

With the programming and massing strategy in place, the design committee began the design development process by exploring the exterior envelope. "Here is where we reengaged the committee to consider the visual image the building would project," notes van den Kieboom. To accomplish this, the design team hosted a daylong meeting in its Milwaukee office. Using a wide range of historic and contemporary precedents, Van den Kieboom and his staff facilitated a discussion of how architectural form communicates image and values (see Figure 5.11). At the conclusion of the meeting, the committee came away with an agreed visual language for the South Union: *organic*—meaning a building that belongs in its place, has a sustainable aesthetic, and is made of local materials—and *timeless*—a building that gracefully endures the passage of time (see Figure 5.12).

Van den Kieboom and his staff facilitated a discussion of how architectural form communicates image and values.

**FIGURE 5.11**
Van den Kieboom and his staff facilitated a discussion of how architectural form communicates image and values. © *Workshop Architects*

**FIGURE 5.12**
At the conclusion of
the meeting, the com-
mittee came away
with an agreed visual
language for the South
Union. © *Workshop
Architects*

Because the interior spaces also required a visual language to define
the mood and atmosphere of each space, Workshop Architects organized
15 interior-focused user groups to explore preferences for the many types of
interior environments. The groups were asked to collect visual imagery associated with words that evoke a desired emotional response to each group's
designated space. To supplement the effort, an online visual preference survey
was issued to the student population, designed to gather broad-based feedback on the desired look and feel of the Union spaces. Over 3,500 students
responded to the survey.

With words and images in hand, the Design Committee was convened to participate in Workshop Architect's Character Mapping™ process. This interactive exercise, loosely structured like Pandora Radio, collected the user groups' preferred emotive attributes by organizing the words with images, colors, and building materials. For example, the term *comfortable* was paired with images of empty, quiet nature scenes, along with hard and soft surfaces in dark earthy colors. *Cozy*, was paired with images of intimate, contained spaces and warm bright surface materials.

The resulting Character Map™ collage—an assemblage of images, materials, and words—was then used to define and guide the development of the interior spaces, the lighting, the coloration, detail, and the furniture and finish selections of the South Union building (see Figure 5.13).

**FIGURE 5.13**
An assemblage of images, materials, and words were used to define and guide the development of the interior spaces. *© Workshop Architects*

## CONCLUSION

One year after the project kick-off, in the spring of 2009, construction documents were completed, permits were issued, and the groundbreaking ceremony took place—on schedule. The project was officially opened in spring 2011.

"Clients and committees can and should participate in the design process. They fundamentally understand the issues and have so much to contribute," says van den Kieboom. The firm's biggest challenges were bringing a large group of people together who had never participated in a project like this and providing them a common language. Next, the challenge was getting the committee to think beyond the program to imagine how space can influence behavior and performance. "We had an enormous program," adds van den Kieboom, "but it had one single mission: to create a socially interactive space."

## LESSONS LEARNED

A participatory committee-based research approach, when conducted with clear intentions and effective tools, can both facilitate and enhance the design process. Using the credo of being *inspired* by the committee rather than *designed* by committee, throughout the project client and user groups were engaged in the processes of defining and refining spatial relationships and the articulation of values through the built environment. Using the committee as bench power throughout the process explicated the planning and design research and knowledge. In addition, the participatory design process helped validate design decisions and streamlined approval processes.

# CHAPTER 6

# The Goals of Integration in Schematic Design

*"The job of buildings is to improve human relations: architecture must ease them, not make them worse."*

—RALPH ERSKINE

## HOW RESEARCH INFORMS THE SCHEMATIC DESIGN PROCESS

The insights, goals, and challenges articulated in the programming phase serve as key components in the formation of the schematic design. These components can be expressed in countless configurations, each representing different values and beliefs about the project. Schematic design as a research-based approach supports the designers in determining a client-specific *philosophy of use* for the project—a philosophy of use that establishes a lens through which future and refined design decisions will be made.

The philosophy of use is developed using multiple research tactics, including an examination of precedents, context analysis, client/user interaction, environmental impact, material explorations, and literature reviews to establish the goals of how a space will perform. Precedent research can focus on similar buildings or building types, architects, locations, eras, or styles. A context analysis of site and environmental conditions is performed to gain a deeper understanding of the relationship of the design to its surroundings, and how the design will respond to its context. Client/user interaction mapping defines the activities, the circulation, and use patterns of the building occupants. An investigation of the design's potential environmental impact establishes baseline standards for energy efficiency, materials, resources, and LEED ratings. Materiality research surveys a range of materials or substances that support the concept or applied use of the design. Literature reviews are conducted to find published information within a particular subject area relevant to the design project, attempting to aggregate and synthesize existing scholarship.

*Example: C Design is redesigning an international air terminal for an airline looking to transform the flying experience. First, the team analyzes the context of the site, mapping existing traveler arrival and departure movements, lounge and concession use, and queuing behavior. Considering the sustainability goals of the project, the team researches its potential environmental impact with regard to energy, daylighting, and materials. Using the information gathered through the research, the design team conducts a precedent analysis of terminals within the same airport, as well as other design solutions across the globe that respond to comparable context, environmental, number of passengers served, and material concerns. A literature search uncovers progressive thinking in airport terminal design, security issues and mobile-workforce trends.*

Once a philosophy of use is defined, research is used to further inform the spatial development, objectives, and cultural goals of the project both pragmatically and theoretically. The project scope outlines the general aims and goals of the project design. Space adjacency analysis explores the opportunities for linkages between spaces. Adjacencies of design elements are considered in accordance with experience prototypes, which simulate the experience of various users in the space to provide insight into desired spatial relationships, workflow relationships, circulation patterns, furniture, furnishings and art.

*Example: C Design would like to improve the user experience of airport travel in its terminal design. As a means to understand the opportunities and obstacles to dignified air travel, the team constructs a simulation of the air travel experience for a series of different user types. The design team researches the experiences of families, business travelers, and inexperienced fliers as they move through the terminal, communicate, eat, work, wait, and rest. The simulations provide information on desired spatial relationships, including relationships between seating and amenities, furnishings, and technology access.*

Aesthetic design decisions are the most readily perceivable and have the greatest potential to elicit emotional responses. As a subject of research, aesthetics seeks to define the sensory and emotional values of the project. For some organizations, these values may be embedded in the client's brand, while others may require further brand development in order to fully express their unique identity and goals. Schematic design as a research strategy uses space as an asset to communicate an organization's values. Potential benefits include increased sales, differentiation from the competition, improved customer recognition and customer loyalty, as well as a better understanding internally of the project stakeholder's goals and values.

The research conducted in schematic design allows designers and clients to evaluate the design potential in relation to the existing budget and return on their investment. Additionally, research embedded in design decision-making provides a solid basis for communicating the reasoning behind the design intent. Through this process, a body of knowledge is developed that links design objectives to spatial relationships, enhancing client satisfaction by aligning design decisions with client-specific goals.

*Example: As a means to differentiate the air terminal from the competition, C Design conducts brand-strategy research. The design team seeks to communicate the airlines competitive advantage as a generous and refreshing experience in the face of other low-cost high, volume carriers. Using space as an asset, the team embeds the brand in the tangible details of the experience, responding to the needs of different user groups through two- and three-dimensional design responses. As a result, the design communicates the core values of the organization, from the place people place their bags to where they eat a between-flight meal. The research-based approach to schematic design results in increased sales, improved user technology to accommodate work, leisure, and entertainment and an improved positioning and customer recognition for the client. Internally, the design influences employee satisfaction, retention rates, and understanding of the airlines mission. In this process, research supports the design team in effectively communicating to the client how design affects their long-term bottom line.*

# RESEARCH SHAPES REFINING THE DESIGN STRATEGY

*"Where is the wisdom that we have lost in knowledge?*
*Where is the knowledge we have lost in information?"*
T.S. ELLIOT

A critical shift in design occurs when early exploration and discovery transitions to the execution and refinement of a define strategy. Design development refines the design strategy by establishing a research checkpoint that verifies the alignment of design details with project objectives. The research validates design decision making at a greater level of detail, and is strengthened by the knowledge and resources of consultants and experts. As a result, earlier insights are adjusted and refined to reflect the new findings.

As building materials, systems, furnishings, and finishes are selected, research can now be conducted on a variety of interdependent factors that impact the quality and performance of the building or space. The refinement of materials and spaces provides an opportunity for the team to accurately evaluate the design's spatial performance, acoustics, details, and emotive qualities with earlier program objectives. The selection of the building's mechanical systems provides measurable information regarding the thermal comfort of the space. Consultants, coordination meetings, effective team collaborations, and modeling establish research methods for realizing the project as a complex, interdependent system.

Design development as a research methodology tests early design decisions through models, mock-ups, and prototypes to validate performance goals and to establish a more intimate design response through detailing and material expression. Design and object prototypes provide an opportunity for the design team to modify building, space, materials, or object intentions based on the findings. Additionally, the design team is able to determine how spatial experiences, materials, and design details perform in the actual environmental conditions under which they will be used prior to actual construction or fabrication. Detailed computer models are created to analyze the environmental performance of the space or building. The cultural goals and brand strategies can be reproduced in renderings or at full scale to test and evaluate the impact of the communication.

*Example: D Design has been commissioned to design a luxury boutique hotel in a historic building. The firm assembles a coordination meeting to define the research goals of the design development phase. D seeks to push the hotel design to a greater level of detail, allowing the team to investigate exactly how each piece contributes to the performance objectives of the project.*

*The selection of the building's mechanical systems provides an opportunity for the design team to address the types of thermal controls available in each guestroom. Materials, furnishings, and finishes are researched for conformity with established historic reference points, aligning new interventions with the building's historic legacy. In addition, materials experts are tasked with validating manufacturer's claims regarding the performance of commercial materials, furnishings, and finishes. Care and maintenance procedures for all materials, finishes, and specialty details are mocked up to verify compliance with the owner's specific maintenance quality efforts. Acoustic consultants are brought in to ensure that material and spatial decisions support acoustic privacy between guestrooms.*

*Using detailed drawings, the team benchmarks the energy use of the building by creating a prototype in a 3D rendering program capable of complex energy-use calculations. The results are in compliance with the energy benchmarks set for the project. In a coordination meeting, it is realized that specifying materials with a higher recycled content, combined with the energy savings, will push the project to the next level of LEED certification.*

*In order to validate its own performance findings with that of the cladding manufacturers, the team builds full-scale mock-ups of both typical and atypical conditions. Analysis of the digital prototypes and physical mock-ups reveal ways in which the team can improve the performance and appearance of the design, and the drawings are updated accordingly.*

The return on the research investment in design development includes reducing the risk of costly problems that might occur during construction. As the project progresses and research builds, a body of knowledge on source material and performance data is developed to inform future projects. The technical information acquired by the design firm in this process forms the basis of the firm's core competencies, allowing them to differentiate themselves from the competition developing an expertise in this type project and building type.

*Example: At the culmination of the design development phase, D Design presents the clients with detailed architectural drawings, perspective renderings and models. By reconciling each of the drawings and validating the design details in alignment with the performance objectives of the luxury hotel, the design team was able to spot both conflicts and opportunities. Throughout the design process, D Design has accumulated a vast amount of research and knowledge that will be invaluable for future hospitality project pursuits.*

# GEOGRAPHIC INFORMATION SYSTEMS (GIS)

Geographic information systems:

| | | | | | | |
|---|---|---|---|---|---|---|
| Little known | 1 | 2 | **3** | 4 | 5 | Lot known |
| Quick | 1 | **2** | 3 | 4 | 5 | Not quick |
| Info straightforward | 1 | 2 | **3** | 4 | 5 | Info complex |
| Verbal | 1 | 2 | 3 | **4** | 5 | Numeric |
| How | 1 | **2** | 3 | 4 | 5 | Why |
| On-site | 1 | 2 | 3 | 4 | **5** | Off-site OK |
| Well-established | 1 | 2 | 3 | **4** | 5 | Innovative |
| Current | 1 | 2 | 3 | 4 | **5** | Future |
| Special | 1 | 2 | 3 | 4 | **5** | No special |
| Generally considered | 1 | 2 | 3 | 4 | **5** | Potentially considered |

[Score indicated by **bold**ing of number.]

As a way to cull the vast amount of geographic data available to a place, a site, a region, architects and urban planners focus on the information available through geographic information systems (GIS). GIS are computer-based maps prepared by one or several sources, and the information on one map may be valuable information alone to answer a design-related question or it can be superimposed and interrelated with the data on other maps to answer more complex research questions. For example, GIS can be used to apply spatial information at the whole building or site scale, ensuring that physical and/or demographic/social information available about a specific area are used during the design process (see Figure 6.1). GIS maps are helpful resources during programming interviews and focus groups—they can be used to provide context that helps to inform a group discussion.

**FIGURE 6.1**
GIS integrates information from multiple information sources/maps into a single one, and can be used to develop insights for siting and planning designed spaces.
*© iStockphoto.com/ maleapaso*

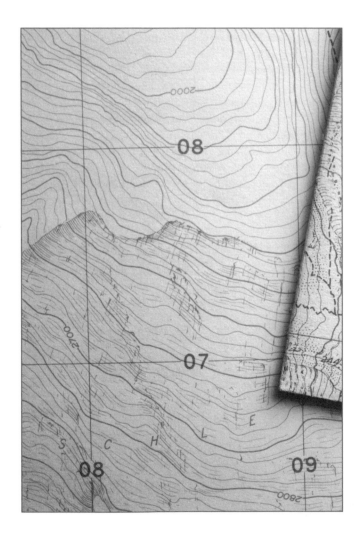

Maps are available of a number of different types of information, from natural phenomena such as the topography of an area to manmade features such as the dispersion of roads, buildings, and other manmade features in an area. Maps can also be information based and not representations of elements that can be seen—maps of demographic data fall into this category, for example. Environmental data available can be used to site buildings to reduce environmental impact or to orient a structure on a site toward views or daylight. It can also be utilized to develop programs for spaces that reflect the demographics of nearby user populations—for example, by providing a community with places to gather if none is currently available. GIS can also inform the design of experiences that are consistent with, or contrast with, those in the current area. This is why utilizing GIS can roughly be seen as using an annotated map of the area surrounding a proposed project to inform design. It is generally done with sophisticated computer software, but many principles can be applied even if that software is not available; at its core is the use of map-based data.

GIS can be used at a variety of different scales, block, neighborhood, city, and so on (see Figure 6.2). It can inform architectural decisions at a very fundamental level and in areas that user interviewees suggest are pertinent to the design project. It can be used to resolve issues of particular concern related to safety or sustainability, for example. It can incorporate trends in geographic features relevant to the design process, such as concentrations of various types of residents or land use or population density changes. Maps created by local teams and incorporated into the analyses can recognize cultural or spiritual information tied to particular geographies that only member of local cultures are familiar with.

**FIGURE 6.2**
Planners can use GIS information about the built environment, such as businesses located nearby, to determine in-building amenities, and the height of other structures to learn more about daylighting in a proposed space. © *iStockphoto. com/4x6*

GIS maps take various forms, depending on the information to be tracked and the level of automation incorporated into the system. It might be drawn from the U.S. Geological Survey database, indicating topography and natural features, or culled from the U.S. Census databases. Alternately, it could be a Google map or Google Earth image of an area, annotated by the local police department with crime statistics or by the local Chamber of Commerce with information about retail or cultural sites in an area. Many layers of data can be incorporated onto the same map. Design researchers can also customize their own maps with information relevant to their current design project, which they obtain themselves by auditing a feature of interest in an area or from reports compiled by others. These design researcher–based maps can be either computer generated, or drawn by hand onto printed street or transportation maps, as resources permit.

The use of GIS inherently increases the sustainability of design. Spaces that mesh with surrounding physical, social, demographic, and other systems are highly valued by the project stakeholders when the information is then integrated into the design response. Maps related to environmental aspects are available from the Environmental Protection Agency (www.epa.gov).

The National Atlas of the United States, which includes social science and other data, is available at nationalatlas.gov. Similar information is also available from some other countries at their national sites. U.S. Census data are regularly available in map form.

GIS technology is evolving rapidly, and a Google search on "geospatial technologies" or "geographic information systems" will produce lists of current software packages. The Center for Spatially Integrated Social Science (www.csiss.org) is funded by the National Science Foundation and is committed to promoting open source access to tools for GIS. Additional information is available at freegis.org, www.pbinsight.com/welcome/mapinfo, www.esri.com, or http://usa.autodesk.com. National geological surveys are also good sources of information. ArcGIS for AutoCAD is available for free download. The Association of American Geographers is an excellent source of information on applying GIS methodologies to real-world issues.

## BEHAVIOR MAPPING

Behavior mapping is:

| Little known | 1 | 2 | 3 | 4 | 5 | Lot known |
|---|---|---|---|---|---|---|
| Quick | 1 | 2 | 3 | 4 | 5 | Not quick |
| Info straightforward | 1 | 2 | 3 | 4 | 5 | Info complex |
| Verbal | 1 | 2 | 3 | 4 | 5 | Numeric |

| How | 1 | 2 | 3 | 4 | 5 | Why |
|---|---|---|---|---|---|---|
| On-site | 1 | 2 | 3 | 4 | 5 | Off-site OK |
| Well-established | 1 | 2 | 3 | 4 | 5 | Innovative |
| Current | 1 | 2 | 3 | 4 | 5 | Future |
| Special | 1 | 2 | 3 | 4 | 5 | No special |
| Generally considered | 1 | 2 | 3 | 4 | 5 | Potentially considered |

[Score indicated by **bold**ing of number.]

Behavior mapping is an effective way to assess how space is used. Design researchers continue to apply it to learn how users of a current space use the space, to provide information that can inform the planning a new or remodeled space for the current users. The technique can briefly be described as keeping track of who is where in a space. Behavior mapping usually focuses on the activities of a set of people, but can also center on activities within a specific space.

Behavior mapping is a specialized form of observation, so observation-specific rules such as making sure that behavior is mapped on all of the days of the week in which the space is used, as well as sampled throughout each of those days apply (see Figure C.10 in the color insert). This sort of sampling is necessary to see a complete picture of how a space is being utilized, and to provide a hypothesis about how future spaces for the same group should be designed (e.g., what behavior capabilities they should facilitate).

Data can be reported overall for an entire set of users, but it is generally of most value to present information by a type of user, such as school administrators or third-grade pupils. The spaces mapped and the individuals observed are determined by the research questions that must be answered to move the design project forward—spaces of various sizes can be studied. The exact behavior recorded is also based on study objectives. Information can be collected "live" with active observers or through review of video images. The sampling of times, people, and places must be sufficient to provide a full understanding of the space in use.

This technique is map-focused observation. It is particularly useful when details about a space's use are required to answer outstanding questions or when user groups (of any age) do not have the expertise, motivation, or capability to discus their interactions with a specific place. The data collection can focus on one of the user groups and their activities or on the use of a particular place of note, depending on the research question. The data itself can be captured with a variety of tools, from annotated maps or floor plans to photographs. Information is classified and studied using content analysis to understand the current use of the space. The amount of data collected, for example, and the number of spaces studied is based on the human resources available to apply the technique. Behavior mapping can be used before and after modifications are made to a space to determine how user actions have been changed (if at all) by changes to the physical environment.

As with all observation research, only readily apparent information can be collected about people being studied. Gender, for example, can be recorded, but motivation for being in a space cannot.

Design researchers using this tool do need to accept the assumption that information collected in the current situation can be applied in future ones. If job tasks will be changing dramatically, for example, then information about space use may not be relevant to the design of new spaces under development.

Behavior mapping differs from observation in general because data are generally marked directly onto maps of the space being studied. Travel paths, for example, can be noted if researchers decide to track the movements of particular users through a space, to determine, for example, future adjacencies or floor plan layouts. In this case, travel maps for specific time segments or sets of individuals are superimposed. Space use at any one time can also be "inventoried" with the number of individuals in specific places at particular times noted—again, this information is recorded on floor plans. This is also known as behavior sampling. The final floor plans prepared at the conclusion of the research process can be annotated with information about users and other information collected that are consistent with the research questions of interest.

Data collection time is dependent on the research question being investigated. Generally, data must be collected over a week to study a space during all possible use situations. Often, design researchers using this technique have time to do other tasks not related to the behavior mapping between action sampling sessions, although travel times to and from the observation areas generally require that they remain at the study site throughout the data collection period. Data collecting over two weeks lessens the possibility that information to be used was collected during a time when a space was used in unusual ways.

Behavior mapping differs from a time utilization study because the research focus is on the floor plate level and on the behavior of user types in a general sense, not the rate at which particular location is used. Time utilization studies, in general, can provide information about the number of people generally in a space, but they don't indicate why users are or are not in a space, the suitability of a space for any activity, and the value to an organization of activities conducted in a space.

Classic behavior-mapping studies have analyzed patient and caregiver travels through healing gardens and movement across workplaces, for example. Workplace researchers found that a set of gathering spaces were not being used through behavior mapping, and subsequent worker interviews indicated those spaces were not used because of their proximity to the offices of company executives. Behavior mapping in hospitals has assessed how nursing staff move through a patient care area, with the objective of ultimately learning how various configurations relate to care staff fatigue.

## OBSERVATION

Observation is:

| | | | | | | |
|---|---|---|---|---|---|---|
| Little known | 1 | 2 | 3 | **4** | 5 | Lot known |
| Quick | 1 | 2 | 3 | 4 | **5** | Not quick |
| Info straightforward | 1 | 2 | **3** | 4 | 5 | Info complex |
| Verbal | 1 | 2 | **3** | 4 | 5 | Numeric |
| How | 1 | 2 | 3 | 4 | **5** | Why |
| On-site | **1** | 2 | 3 | 4 | 5 | Off-site OK |
| Well-established | 1 | **2** | 3 | 4 | 5 | Innovative |
| Current | **1** | 2 | 3 | 4 | 5 | Future |
| Special | 1 | 2 | 3 | **4** | 5 | No special |
| Generally considered | **1** | 2 | 3 | 4 | 5 | Potentially considered |

[Score indicated by **bold**ing of number.]

Observation seems easy, until you set out to do it yourself. Observing is much more than simply hanging out and seeing what happens before you leave. It's a way to learn about how a group of other people interacts with the world. Through observation, you can investigate topics that the people you're studying are unable to discuss because they aren't used to thinking about place-related issues or because they don't know the answers to the questions you need to resolve—such as how often impromptu meetings take place in their cubicles. Observation can be a good tool to choose when the "observees" may know the answers but probably won't want to share them because they fly in the face of the responses they feel are desired. Observing also provides context for information collected using other research methods such as surveys, interviews, and group discussions.

Observation may also be the only access you have to the people who will use the space you are developing. Your client may decide that it does not want its employees to spend time away from work to answer your programming questions about what they do, or your research budget might be so small that it only allows you to spend a few hours of your time collecting data. As a researcher, observation allows you to maximize this time effectively

With observation, you get information about what is happening at the times observations are made in the places they naturally occur. Observing to learn requires an upfront plan so that the information collected can usefully inform the design process. What happens in the break room? Do people sit alone and work during lunch? Have meetings when the group conference room is full? Or, nothing, because no one ever visits it? How do people in the hospital waiting room seem to respond to the television there? Do they change its volume? Turn it off? Position themselves in locations that minimize their interaction with it and read books and magazines? Do they bring those magazines with them, or find them in the waiting room? How long does the average person who visits it spend in the pocket park near the train station? What do they do while they're there? Which benches are used most often for things besides sitting, such as stretching before running?

When information is collected through well-structured observations, it is possible to vigorously support conclusions drawn from the data. You can feel very confident sharing it with colleagues and clients. After you observe, while it is rarely possible to determine why people did one thing or another, the information gathered can be thoroughly reviewed, using the content analysis methodologies discussed in Chapter 5. When observed events are categorized, the number of items in a category and patterns in categorizations can be investigated using the data analysis techniques presented in Chapter 5. Time-utilization studies, which are inventories of people and their locations, produce information that can be analyzed using statistics.

Before we leave the issue of inferring why people are doing something based on observations alone, consider this vignette: Suppose you are doing observations at that pocket park already mentioned. You might find that when the sun falls on a certain bench at the front of the small park (the only one that the sun ever falls on when you're observing), people don't sit there. You might jump to the conclusion that this is because they don't want to get sunburned or they don't want to get too hot and sweaty while they're wearing their work clothes or that the metal in the bench gets too hot to comfortably sit on while the sun hits it, for example. Each of these conclusions has logical repercussions for the design of future spaces—you might make sure all benches in future parks have protection from the sun or install misting machines to keep visitors cool or avoid the use of metal benches. The "true" reason that people might be avoiding that sunny bench, however, which you could learn from follow-up interviews, might be that at the same time that the sun falls on the bench, an odd person sits in a nearby window and glares at whomever is sitting on the bench. You might thus end up depriving people of desired sun if you infer the reasons for people's actions after observations alone. You learn from observations about a matter to be probed during interviews, in this case (see Figure 6.3). Data collected using multiple tools are much richer than those derived using individual ones.

Another example: At a workplace, one of the authors (SA) once observed a collection of battered board games in employee cubicles and on small tables near employee desks. The game boxes looked used, each sported a collection of dings and nicks. Since part of the project mandate was to develop a space in which employees would bond more tightly with each other, the games were of great interest. Employees interviewed revealed that management had brought in the games and placed them in employee cubicles, encouraging people to play with them. The observer never saw the games being played, and none of the employees interviewed could ever remember seeing the games being played, either. The games were not a sign of employee camaraderie, but a signal that employers had already attempted to build team spirit.

**FIGURE 6.3**
Along this street, it is possible to observe the paper in the windows of the house on the right, but why is it there? Is someone keeping track of a major project in process or blocking passersby's view into the space? *Photo: Augustin*

## Doing Observations

### Who to Observe

When you observe, you watch the people who will use a space you are creating (or, in very rare cases, people extremely similar to them) doing something related to your research question. They are in a place that is similar to the one you are developing in terms of primary use or some other important characteristic. You see the roles that people play and get an idea of things around them that support or hinder their activities. Via observation, you have information about what they're up to in their current social and physical environments.

If you plan to modify the current space, if that's what the budget allows, for example, it's better to first develop a concept of what the space you are working on should be like independent of the design of the current space and then create that new environment to the extent possible—if you don't think widely beyond the current space, you may never meet user needs.

It is best to observe the same set of people who will actually use the space that you are developing. This way, your findings will reflect the ways that the actual user group experiences current environments. On occasion, you may need to observe another, but extremely similar, group of people—the current space may be inaccessible, for example, because a security clearance is required to enter it, or there might be no existing space in which to do observations. The designers creating the first industrial clean room had nowhere to do observations—except hospital isolation units, for example. Sometimes the population who will use a space is currently so scattered that efficient observation is impossible or users might be unavailable for some other reason (see the vignette in the next paragraph). Always note when you have observed a non-user group, and when using these findings, take care, particularly when the differences between the people that you observed and the ultimate user group may be relevant.

Say, for example, you are working on a multifamily housing project in China. Although the budget should allow you to travel to China to do some observing, it doesn't, and you're left in New York. You could do observations of Chinese people living in multifamily housing in New York, but all your findings would need to be appropriately interpreted. The structure in which you are observing may be very different than any that can ultimately be built in China because of differences in building codes. People in New York will have had extensive exposure to a more individualistic culture than the people living in China, which influences how they interact with their environments. There could easily be personality differences between the Chinese who have moved to New York and those who have chosen to remain in China (relevant if the people you are observing are recent emigres), and personality influences how we interact with our environments, as well. There are so many issues that need to be recognized in this situation that you could decide not to do the observations—responding to all of the differences would require a really experienced researcher. Moving from the observations in hospital isolation units to industrial clean rooms was much more straightforward.

It is always best to observe the people who will use a space, but if the important differences between how the ultimate users may respond to a space and how the observed group may can be identified and reflected in the ultimate design developed, observations can still be useful.

There are many particularly difficult issues involved in observing children or in healthcare environments. When doing observations at schools, for example, carefully follow all of the rules laid out by administrators and others charged with protecting children. At healthcare facilities, special rules also apply, and administrators will be aware of them. The government is very interested in preventing vulnerable populations from being exploited in any way. For good measure, ask all client firms for written verification that it is legally possible for you to do observations onsite.

## Observing Impartially

As an observer, it's important for you to collect information in an open-minded, nonjudgmental way. It needs to flow unfiltered through you into the final form of the design.

Observe without forming opinions—be a sponge. Simply absorb what's going on around you, remembering and noting as much as possible that's related to your project objectives. Your values and stereotypes can stand in the way of learning what should inform the development a new space, and it is always important to consciously review how they might be distorting your observations.

## Observing with Minimal Impact

To make sure that accurate information is gathered to inform design, be as invisible as possible while you are collecting data. You should dress like the people you are observing and try to be as unobtrusive as possible. For example, if you are sitting in a conference room to observe what is happening there, don't click your pen open and closed. Don't tap your fingers on a PDA into which you will type information when "something" finally happens. (A side note, something is always happening, even if it is not interesting for you personally or related in an obvious way to the project underway.)

If you capture people's attention, you will be what is happening, and if observations you make while you are the center of attention are used to inform the design of new conference rooms or any other space, those rooms may not be very suitable once you leave. It is true that if you are silent and calm, after a few minutes people will stop radically distorting their behavior because of your presence. You have to be realistic, however. If one of the uses of the conference room where you are observing is to take naps after all-night work sessions, you are unlikely to witness any of those naps because people rarely sleep in front of strangers, although it does happen on planes. Or if the purpose of that conference room is to reverse engineer competitive products in a way that is only questionably legal, you won't probably see that, either.

It is best to judiciously record information that could be individually damaging. You might have told any "observees" who ask, and even some who haven't, that you will not use anyone's name in your general report, will not include individually identifying information, and so on. You can be assured, however, that even with some camouflaging, it will generally be relatively easy for clients reading your report to have a good idea who you were observing to reach a particular conclusion. So, there really is no true anonymity in the info collected. Regularly, you will also hear something that might be very damaging to someone's career, such as a lunchtime discussion of someone's mental state. Don't record any of the details of those conversations. You never know when someone else in your organization will try to pressure you to give copies of your field notes to the client, and there are instances in which these notes have been directly transferred in this way, even after assurances have been made that it would never happen. Things that are not written down cannot fall into the wrong hands. Details of personal conversations are none of your business—they aren't why you are there. You want to know who is using the room, the general purpose, for how long, the general sort of conversation underway (personal or job-related), and so on.

Get someone known to the people being observed to introduce you personally or via a message to the observees. The people to be observed should be truthfully told about the amount of anonymity that they will receive in the way that data are recorded and used. Clearly, more is better here in terms of collecting data. Morally, it is necessary to truthfully share with the people being observed how the information collected will be used.

## Being Flexible

Be alert to the need to modify plans for an observation project, particularly if you're observing before you've collected much other information. Observation is often done early in the research process and again later to answer questions that have come to light because of other research activities.

As a project begins, you may not have a good idea exactly what you should be trying to learn more about. As you get started, you might find that there are project-related activities underway in the area being observed that you did not think a priori would need to be considered as you completed a design. By all means, change the observation protocol in response to what you learn as the observations begin, but add criteria only after careful consideration—not everything that's happening can be observed.

Make sure that you do not have any personal ulterior motives for changing the criteria being observed. If before observations began you had a good reason for deciding that some group of people or activity should be observed, it should be hard to cut them from the project once it's underway. If a change would make the situations being observed match closely with your stereotypes about a situation, it is best to verify your decision to make a change by speaking with a colleague.

## When to Observe

You should ideally do observations in each activity period (to be defined in a moment) in each area that you have reason to believe could inform the design of the space you are planning. This may be impossible because of the manpower, financial, and other resources available, but should be attempted and any compromises seriously considered in light of the specific questions you are trying to answer.

An activity period is a segment of the day or week that can be clearly defined, within which behavior can be expected to vary or when conditions in the space are different (sun glare can be present during some parts of the day and not others). Observe, if possible, two or three of each sort of activity period. In a workplace, the activity periods could be early, middle, and later mornings and afternoons and lunch periods Monday through Friday. You need to know about activities during each of these periods—what happens Monday morning and Friday afternoon (or morning, for that matter), can be radically different.

What employees do during lunch periods can increase camaraderie in the group, and since the social environment is important for the success of an organization, you will want to make sure that it is supported. For example, one of us (SA) is familiar with a company where some employees play cards as they eat their lunch. Any space developed for this group should permit them to continue to play cards. There should be an appropriate table located so that it is acoustically isolated from people who need to work through a particular lunch period. If all tables are located in conference rooms in which a no-employee-eating policy is in force to keep the conference rooms clean for client visits, employees will no longer be able to play cards. This will be detrimental to the social climate.

## What to Observe

The answer to the "what to observe" question follows neatly from, "Why is the design project underway?" and, "What questions do you need to answer before moving forward with the design process?" Not everything can be observed, so decide what you will focus on in a space.

You need to observe to increase your knowledge of situations that have the most potential to add value to the organization (a family is an organization if you are designing a home). If you have ever been a reporter, even for a high school paper, you know about the information that reporters try to collect as they work on a story: Who? What? Where? When? How? and Why? The same questions should help you organize your observations. We have discussed the fact that observation can't answer questions about why something happens, but keep "why" in mind anyway as you focus your attention, it may guide you to observations that are ultimately useful..

All behaviors are *observed*. The use of the word *observed* here is very deliberate. You cannot get into people's heads (well, I can't, so I assume you can't), so you won't actually know for sure what they're thinking about or truly planning, but since you are watching them, you will have some idea what they are overtly doing. For example, it is much more likely that a child interacting with another child is trying to play a game with the child than trying to attract the attention of the other child's parent so that s/he can serve as a matchmaker between that parent and his/her own.

You need to decide who you will observe and what their roles are. There are generally a number of different people in a space or moving through a space, and not all of their activities can be studied. If your goal is to create a more productive environment for the research and development team because they add the most value to a firm, observe their actions. Observe the administrators in the department only to the extent that they support the R & D team.

Once the research questions are identified, it is a straightforward process to pick "what" to observe. For example, you might be trying to learn about employee distractions. Within a company, the stated policy might be not to interfere with working colleagues, so on a survey, people will report that they do not do so. Observations might reveal that people talk to each other over or through their cubicle walls all the time. During other projects, other activities will be observed. People may not be used to talking about how they move through a space, so you may observe that. The observees might not be aware consciously that they and their colleagues are quite tense during meetings.

Another example: If you are planning a new playground that will be particularly hospitable to children with disabilities but used by all kids, you could begin by determining if there was a place where you could observe children with and without disabilities playing together, or if you would need to observe each group separately and later integrate the information collected. It is (not surprisingly) best to observe the social environment most similar to the one that will use the space being designed.

Certainly, you'll be keeping track of what the kids (whose ages you need to define) are up to in the space, but generally, they will arrive with some adults or older siblings—the adults could be parents, teachers, or aids. It will be hard for the playground you are developing to be a success if those adults aren't upbeat about bringing their kids by; learning from their experiences in the current space is really important. So, what do the adults do, who with, where do they do it, for how long do they do it, and how do they interact with the environment while doing whatever they do? Now, on to the kids—what do they do, who with, how do they do it, where do they do it, for how long do they do it, and how do they interact with the environment while doing it? How do the behaviors of kids with disabilities differ from those without? *How do they interact with the environment?* means, "How do they use the spaces available to them to accomplish their observed objective?"

Another example: Suppose you are working on the design of a new model store for a chain of drug stores. Spending some time in current drug stores in the chain, of different sizes/physical forms, in different parts of the country, with different primary users is key. The actual number of stores you can visit will be determined by the budget available for this purpose (or that you think is reasonable to have funded. If you cannot visit a sample of the stores of various sizes, in different parts of the country, for example, you might be able to ask colleagues living in cities with the types of stores that you will not be able to visit to take certain specific photos or videos to collect some of the information of interest to you.

All photos and videos should show only the backs of people or no people at all, for legal reasons. If you can see a face or other identifying attributes of a person, even from a distance, you need a signed release form to use that image in any sort of public setting. If someone else is taking photos for you, be clear that it is dangerous for them to be taken in ways that might raise legal issues later. The issue of using a person's image without his or her permission is a serious legal concern, so if there is any chance, an image will be used in a presentation that might be distributed to attendees at any sort of meeting, used in promotional materials or on a website, or any other way, it is best to use images that do not contain people.

When you are doing observations, you should look for signs of wear (called *erosion*) or build-up of something (usually dirt, dust, or lint, called *accretion*). These give you an idea how people move through the space (e.g., store), and what in that space interests them enough so that they reach out and touch it. If that touching experience is consistent with expectations, it increases the chances that a product will be purchased. Erosion and accretion can be valuable cues about how the current environment is used, and how the current environment is used should inform the design of future environments, to the extent that the future environments have the same purpose as the current ones (see Figure 6.4).

Be attentive to ways that users have modified the current environment to meet their needs. Those modifications can give you important insights that can be incorporated into new environments. The harder it was to make a particular modification, the more attention you should pay to it, although none of the ways that environments have been modified should be ignored. For example, rearranging items within a conference room is interesting, but moving furniture from one conference room to another is much more intriguing and potentially important. Changes in a space from one day to the next can give you clues about all of the ways in which the place is used.

The list of things you need to observe can be long, and keeping track of all that you need requires organization—more on that in a moment. While in the store already mentioned, you should observe the following sorts of things if your mandate is to create a retail environment that can be shopped quickly and efficiently while maximizing the income of the store owner: What paths do people generally travel through the store (e.g., right to the back for milk and then straight out the door without passing by any of the high margin products?)? Are there any places in their travels when they seem to slow, as if to change direction, and then continue on their previous path? Are there traffic bottlenecks? How do the behaviors of shoppers who spend different amounts of money on high-margin goods differ (to get this info, you need to observe lots of people in the store, and then monitor what they pick up to purchase—staking out areas with high-margin items can be handy)? Do people use a pushcart or basket or neither while shopping (you will know from your physical inventory of the space where those are placed, for example)? Where do various types of shoppers (age, gender, with children, etc.) seem to spend the most time in the store? Each group can be expected to have certain levels of disposable income. How do people access the items (particularly high margin ones) placed on different store fixtures/display units? (You are looking for matches/mismatches here between ease of access and appropriateness of access.) What products do people ask the locations of? How is the store shopped at different times of day? Days of the week? What's the cash-wrap station experience like for shoppers (what do they see, hear, etc.)? Where do people line up to make purchases? Do you observe people abandoning purchases and leaving the store?

**FIGURE 6.4**
This glass was left on top of a covered water feature in an upscale mall. The mall does not provide a place for shoppers to leave glasses when they are done with them. *Photo: Augustin*

Don't forget to observe employee activities as well: Where are the cash-wrap stations, and how do they influence the travel of store employees and customers? How well do those cash-wrap stations meet employees' needs (have they been modified by the employees, for example)? What's the experience of being in the employee break room like (what happens there, etc.)? What about the functionality and livability of the manager's office? You will have to record specific details about the design of the current break room separately from records of activities in them; for example, via a physical inventory and photo records collected just before the first observations are done. Employees who are rested and in a better mood will be better helpers for shoppers trying to purchase goods efficiently.

Note support functions. How are goods delivered to the store? What influence does that process have on shopper experience?

The behaviors, people, and places observed need to provide information that can help answer outstanding questions and inform the design process.

It is not necessary to observe all aspects of a client's current location, just a sample of the project-relevant ones used by reasonably different groups of individuals during different activity periods, as already defined. Often novice observers set out to observe an entire office building owned by a client, for example, from lobby through every floor to the penthouse suites used by officers. This makes bad use of observation and analysis resources. Discussions with client employees, generally human resource professionals and facility managers at a joint meeting, can identify the places to be observed. This observation sample must align with project objectives and resources. Before you make final selections of places to observe, consider what your helpers' individual objectives might be in steering you to particular spaces to observe (it's a good idea to always keep participant motivation in mind, whether you're observing or using another research method). If accounts receivable clerks in similar groups with similar performance objectives work in similar environments on the twenty-seventh and twenty-eighth floors, it is acceptable to randomly select and observe just one of the teams working on the twenty-seventh floor—a reasonable person could conclude that observations of that group can be assumed to appropriately represent those of all of the accounts receivable clerks.

It is important to focus on the workplaces of the employees that add the most value to the firm or organization. This statement is made in conjunction with a workplace example, but this is true of any space being observed in a general sense. Value may be defined differently outside workplaces, but the concept is always the same—observe in the places whose new form will probably be most important to the perceived success of the new space, and success criteria are identified working with project clients. You might have to sacrifice the observation of various accounts receivable groups altogether if they do not add the most value to the organization. Typically, one could expect value to be added through research and development and customer service or sales teams, for example, which means that the space-related behaviors of those teams must be carefully assessed, through observations and other methods. In a church, the space in which value-adding activity is most likely to occur might be the room in which the minister counsels parishioners, for example.

Often, workplace design client firms want an audit conducted of how much time people spend in the workspaces currently provided to them because they believe that if people are not in those workspaces often, the spaces are not really required. These audits (or time utilization studies) are not observations but a continuous physical inventory of who is where. If your client is insistent that the project be informed by such work, you may find yourself in a difficult situation. Using electronic data recording tools, such as computer tablets, streamlines data collection for time utilization studies, but that does not mean that the information gathered should actually be used. First of all, it ignores the fact that people might not be in their workstations because those workstations are actually so poorly designed that they are just not good places to work. Conscientious employees may have relocated themselves elsewhere. In addition, a time utilization study does not recognize the value to the organization of the work that is completed in a space, how having a territory at the workplace facilitates employee bonding to the organization, or other important psychological issues that need to be considered as spaces are designed.

We have talked about doing observations at typical spaces of a particular type, but it also can be useful to do observations in extreme locations to determine how people experience them and how they modified the environment. During data analyses, separate the extreme location observation data from the usual location data to avoid inappropriate conclusions being drawn from the combination of these two data sets—you don't want to develop a hybrid space that serves neither typical nor atypical situations.

For example, there are nurses' stations in emergency rooms and in obstetrics units. A period of time spent observing those emergency rooms could collect information that could usefully inform design of the obstetrics units, for example, where sudden, life-threatening situations might arise. Transferring insights from one space to another needs to be done with discretion, in light of the fundamental purposes of various spaces.

Another example: Employees at a firm whose cubicles are close to the main reception area sometimes develop culturally appropriate ways to deal with these high-noise situations that could be integrated conceptually or exactly into new offices. The sorts of extreme spaces you chose to observe should be based on the research questions you are trying to resolve.

## The Mechanics of Observing

Certain processes facilitate the data-gathering process. Before you begin the observation process you'll want to record the physical context of where you're observing, using maps, photographs, and videos. All images should be electronic so that they can be easily transmitted and stored, however. These visuals make conversations with clients and colleagues about your findings clearer.

Bring a camera with you when you're observing so you can take pictures of any unusual circumstances. Restrict the number of photos taken, however, to minimize stress among those you are observing.

Sometimes it is better to do observations using video feeds instead of "live." Doing observations of particular customers in a store can be a difficult assignment for people who haven't been trained by the CIA. Customers can easily feel as if they are being followed, which can create unpleasant confrontations or cause them to leave the store immediately without making purchases, which reduces income and distorts the information collected. Surveillance cameras are positioned in most stores so that the entire floor can be filmed (see Figure 6.5). It is often best to do observations as events occur and while watching those monitors from a security observation post hidden in the store. Doing the observations from the control room where feeds are monitored live is easier than trying to gather information from multiple collections of film later as the subject in question moves from the range of one set of cameras to the next. If legally allowed in your area, it can also be better to review film of activities in small spaces such as conference rooms than to actually be physically present in those spaces. If meetings are short, meeting attendees may change just as they are adjusting to your presence. If it is not possible for observers to visit a site (such as a clean room or operating room), using a recording device might be the only way that observation data can be collected. Recording devices on timers can also be useful if observers cannot be present at particular dates/times.

Sometimes you can make all of your observations from one spot and other times you need to move through a space. For example, cubicle walls might be just high enough so that you can't see over them and must walk around them to find out what's happening, even in a relatively small area, square-foot wise.

Generally, the most efficient way to do observations is to study as large an area as possible at any one time and do observations in a collection of spots from which data can reasonably be expected to further inform the design process. If any combination of time, money, and manpower is limited, a collection of spaces that are exemplary on criteria of interest can be observed—with the number of spaces observed based on resources available. For example, you might study the spaces where the three most strategically important employee groups work or a classroom pod from each of three largest-enrollment departments at a university. We will call your observations in each of three work areas or classroom pods *sets of observations.*

During any one set of observations, you can review a space that you can see all of within 15 minutes walking at a reasonable rate if you will be traveling through it. Even if you are staying at one spot to do your observations, it makes sense to change your observation form every 15 minutes—that is a short enough time frame so that it is not necessary to mark specific times of activities. Knowing the times that the form went into use and was replaced is generally sufficient. Sometime it will be necessary to break up a larger area to be observed into smaller, multiple ones, because not all of it can be observed during 15 minutes. Often, this is easy to do, because there are naturally occurring physical dividers.

**FIGURE 6.5**
Recorded images can be the most efficient and effective way to "observe" a space in use.
*Photo: Augustin*

If you are doing observations at the very beginning of a project, when you don't really have a very good idea of what you should be observing, it's best to just take longhand notes on blank sheets of paper (or some higher-tech version of this). After you have been observing for a little while (it's hard to know how long it will take), you will start to see some patterns in what you are observing. Once you get to that point, you can prepare some standardized data-recording aids—the forms already mentioned. These can be on pieces of paper or PDAs, iPads, or whatever is available at the time you're reading this. The technology you use should be portable enough to use as you travel through a space.

An observation form allows you to make hash marks or check off blocks to record activities of research interest in the place you are observing. It allows you to capture all of the details that will be valuable to you later, such as tools in use, people present, position on the floor, and so on. Since the sheets are changed every 15 minutes, you can determine duration of longer events by reviewing on how many consecutive forms they were discussed. Data on the forms will be the basis for your analyses, so make sure to collect all information that will be required to answer the research questions posed. For example, if you will need to know the technology in use, be sure to record it. Generally, it is best to collect the answers to the relevant journalism questions—*who* (job title, etc., as known for people playing active/passive roles in area being observed, with whom), does *what*, *where* (exactly), and *how* (with what tools, etc.). *When* is taken care of by the segment of time during which a form is used, and *why* can't be determined using observation. All forms should have a blank space in which drawings of activities or situations of research interest can be made and other spaces in which information not anticipated when the form is created can be noted. The date, time used, and person collecting data must be recorded on each form.

The form is meant as a data-gathering aid—it can save writing or typing and nothing more; it is not sacred. If you feel better working without one, and simply recording events free form, don't worry about creating one. A form does help you keep track of all of the things that you want to learn in a space. There is nothing worse than getting to the end of an observation project and realizing that you have forgotten to pay attention to something. Forms also increase the consistency of data collected by different people, at different sites, and at different times.

Whatever tools you use, record your notes in written form. Speaking your notes into a tape recorder can be disconcerting for people nearby.

Do take notes and record what you observe right away—our memories can play tricks on us and we can later think that we saw patterns in all of the data collected, not just those that are most recent or top of mind as we begin analysis. You also can just plain forget what you have seen or the necessary details of what has been observed.

There are many particularly difficult issues involved in observing children or in healthcare environments. When doing observations at schools, for example, carefully follow all of the rules laid out by administrators and others charged with protecting children. At healthcare facilities special rules also apply, and administrators will be aware of them. The government is very interested in preventing vulnerable populations from being exploited in any way. For good measure, ask all client firms for written verification that it is legally possible for you to do observations onsite.

## How Long to Do Observations

Observing can be very time intensive. Anthropologists working on a dissertation will observe a space or group of people for a year without batting an eye. It is a safe bet that you don't have a year to observe any group of people. A much more prudent course of action for design researchers is to realistically determine how much time you can spend doing observations and analyzing the collected data. Set aside 25 percent of that time for data analysis. Divide up the remaining 75 percent of your time among all the spaces where you need to collect data—this would be the three university classroom pods mentioned in the previous example. Then try to collect information in each space during each activity period (explained earlier in this chapter). Sometimes, if the spaces where you are doing observations are near to each other, you can visit several of them each day, at different times. Even in a few minutes in a space, it is possible to learn a great deal, so never forgo the opportunity to do observations, even if you don't have much time.

The anthropologist rule of thumb is that there is no need to continue to observe after you can correctly anticipate what everyone in a space will do (be honest about this with yourself). However, if you have committed to a client to be onsite doing observations for a period of time, it can be politically difficult to return home before that time period has elapsed. It is usually sufficient, in any case, to do observations for two one-hour blocks (randomly selected from all of the hours allocated to each activity period) in each of the activity periods in a space. Unfortunately, activity periods are spread throughout an entire week, but times when you don't need to be observing in one space, you can spend doing observations in another.

## Data Analysis

Information you collect through observations can be content analyzed. Content analysis is described in detail in Chapter 5. It is useful to begin the content analysis of the data you have collected just before the end of the observation period, if possible. That way, you can return to do the final observations with an eye toward collecting additional bits of information that might help to resolve outstanding issues, with the caveat that the additional information has not been gathered over the entire time period. When collecting this additional information, it is important for you to remain objective and not allow your perceptions of what you expect to see to influence what you actually do see. If you are continually tough on yourself about this, you can prevent your expectations from coloring your behaviors.

Usually, you will collect information that should be content analyzed verbally, as well as photographs, brochures distributed to people in a space, and similar visual items to be content analyzed as well. Pairing these two techniques results in a particularly rich analysis.

When you're done observing and analyzing the information that's been collected, you know a lot about how a group of people interacts with a space now and have some information about how a space could be used in the future. You will need to corroborate some of what you've learned using other tools to make sure that you were not observing in an anomalous period or that your observations have not too dramatically affected what happens in the space. You will need those additional pieces of information to answer "why" questions.

Computer programs can be used to analyze data collected through observations, and they can be found through Internet searches of the type described in Chapter 4. These programs have traditionally been quite expensive, however, and probably cannot be justified financially unless long periods of observation will regularly be done.

## Example of an Observation—a Wedding

Either vicariously (e.g., on television) or in person, we've all been to a wedding, so working through an example of doing observation in wedding spaces will eliminate the need to discuss what is to be accomplished in the setting. We will assume a rather straightforward set of objectives are satisfied—two people are united in a ceremony that binds them for the rest of their lives and then a celebration ensues. This wedding experience is not the same in every culture, but we will brush over some of those details here. You might actually need to do observations at weddings one day if you become involved with the design of public spaces such as banquet facilities.

Our objective might be to learn to inform the design of a function room with the flexibility to serve the needs of many types of wedding parties—from Indian weddings complete with members of the wedding party riding animals to a more traditional American wedding reception with a DJ and a cake-cutting ceremony.

Without even beginning the observation process, we can anticipate that certain sorts of events will happen at a wedding. Being able to expect these events means we can structure our data collection form early on in the process. Since we are considering the design of a function room, we need only consider weddings in that sort of venue—we are not planning every possible place where a wedding could occur, just a function room and the immediately adjoining areas. We can anticipate that there will be some sort of ceremony (the wedding itself could be at the function hall or other wedding-related ceremonies may take place there), some sort of food, and some sort of celebration separate from the food (this could include people milling around making toasts, people dancing, people displaying gifts, people taking photographs, etc.).

We can collect information about what's going on the banquet hall by moving across the main room and through the adjoining spaces (halls, smaller function spaces also accessible to the wedding party, a nearby outdoor patio, for example), every 15 minutes (at least in our example). Therefore, we will change to a new data-collection sheet every 15 minutes, as we begin each new round of observation. The data-collection sheets will need to be customized to the observation site, so that there are places to record information about each area, spaces to draw maps of the overall place and subsections of the major area, and places to write comments about things that are happening that somehow don't relate to the data-collection options provided. Record the date, time period, place being observed, and name of the observer on the forms as well.

The form must be comprehensive enough to answer the questions about activities in a space (who is involved in, what they are doing, where, when, and how things are being done, and, to the limitedextent possible, why something is happening in a space). In this case, the why would not be psychological but physical—the dancing takes place in the largest room because that is the only space big enough to accommodate the dancers and the band, for example. It is really important that the ambiance of the situation be accurately reported here, since ambiance is such an important part of the wedding celebration. For example, how brightly lit is the space? Changes in the physical form of the space from one visit to the next capture important information about flexibility that must be built into an area. The general atmosphere in the space, the percentage of people present engaged in any activity, and the total number of people in a space are also important pieces of information, in this circumstance.

Observations should continue throughout the weddings attended, because the activity periods are consecutive and relatively brief. By the time you have done an hour of observation in one, well, you're actually into the next activity period anyway. Ideally, several weddings of each type (Indian, traditional, formal Protestant American, extremely informal etc.) at venues designed in a number of different ways (e.g., with/without outdoor courtyards, one large room/a suite of smaller rooms) should be observed. There will almost certainly not be enough time for this, so select events that provide the fullest set of information but that are pertinent to the space being developed—don't travel two hours to go to an Indian wedding if no Indians live in the county where a facility will be built. Also, your activities could be prescribed by the fact that no one in the area will allow you to do observations on site except for your client.

## SPACE SYNTAX

*Space syntax* is extremely complex to do but is regularly discussed in the research world. For our purposes, it can be described as a type of observation that focuses on the most likely behaviors in a space. It can be done in existing spaces to better understand a user group and its responses to environments and via the review of floor plans to determine the most probable behaviors in potential future places.

The most important concept that designers can draw from it is to assess the sight lines, and the possible behavioral implications that can be drawn from those lines, while observing in a space (see Figure 6.6). People bond socially with those that they see.

**FIGURE 6.6**
Sight lines are an important in space syntax research. © *iStockphoto. com/Freezingtime*

Space syntax researchers should also note how people circulate through a place (real or potential) (see Figure C.11 in the color insert). How long are paths, and what are the decision points (intersections) like? What do people moving along them encounter along the way? Travel routes influences who ultimately communicates in person or electronically. Different sorts of circulation are desirable in different contexts. In courthouses, it's best to separate the travels of crime victims and people on trial, while in a newsroom, it seems that the more reporters mix, the better.

Software available to facilitate space syntax analyses includes UCINet. This software package has been rigorously developed and in use for many years.

## SOCIAL NETWORK ANALYSIS

Social network analysis (SNA) may be discussed as a way to develop adjacencies. An SNA reveals who currently interacts with whom, at what frequency, and (sometimes) for what duration. It does not record some very important information, such as the value of particular interactions to the organization. It also only reflects who currently communicates, not interactions that would add value to the organization. Because of the potential to use the SNA information to determine staffing needs, and its inappropriateness for such tasks, its collection by designers is ethically problematic. It is best to use questions on surveys, interviews, and discussion groups, to learn about interactions that add value, or that could add value, to determine floor plate adjacencies.

## DISCUSSION GROUPS

Discussion groups are:

| | | | | | | |
|---|---|---|---|---|---|---|
| Little known | 1 | 2 | **3** | 4 | 5 | Lot known |
| Quick | 1 | 2 | **3** | 4 | 5 | Not quick |
| Info straightforward | 1 | 2 | 3 | 4 | 5 | Info complex |
| Verbal | 1 | 2 | 3 | 4 | 5 | Numeric |
| How | 1 | 2 | 3 | 4 | 5 | Why |
| On-site | 1 | 2 | 3 | 4 | 5 | Off-site OK |
| Well-established | 1 | 2 | 3 | 4 | 5 | Innovative |
| Current | 1 | 2 | **3** | 4 | 5 | Future |
| Special | 1 | 2 | 3 | 4 | 5 | No special |
| Generally considered | 1 | 2 | **3** | 4 | 5 | Potentially considered |

[Score indicated by **bold**ing of number.]

During discussion groups, a set of between 6 and 12 people have conversations that inform design decisions. Participants are never a haphazard collection of people. They are randomly chosen from a population directly related to the design issue being investigated—the participants will work or shop in the new offices or schools or stores, or visit friends and family in new healthcare facilities, for example.

Sometimes these groups are assembled by professionals who have huge electronic databases of particular types of people. You will be working with user (or potential user) groups directly, except on rare occasions, so these recruiters won't be relevant to your project. They are mentioned because if you are ever in need of participants who satisfy very particular criteria (say, you are working on a general floor plan for a home at a particular price point to be mass produced by a developer and you need to find people who could afford to buy the house you're working on) to attend discussion groups or to interview or to observe, it is useful to know that there are professionals who can help you find them.

Poorly run focus groups have tarnished the reputation of discussion groups. A skilled session moderator can use techniques to be outlined in the sections that follow to make sure that conversation flows freely among all discussion group members and that a session does not decay into a series of concurrent interviews. It is this caliber of leadership that distinguishes focus and discussion groups.

Talking with users in groups is a particularly valuable way to collect information. The exchanges between participants can generate important information. Their comments can add details and insights that are otherwise unobtainable. Discussion groups are an important way that you can involve the ultimate users of a space in the design process, and are therefore really popular with participatory design advocates.

## Conducting Discussion Groups

Discussion groups can now be held face to face or electronically. Electronic discussion tools are quickly evolving, and any coverage of them here would be quickly outdated. If you need to conduct electronic discussion groups because you must work with client team members to standardize an interior world-wide (not a good idea because of national culture differences, but sometimes unavoidable), or for some other reason, consider running electronic sessions. A key advantage of discussion groups is the interplay between the participants, and any electronic format that reduces those exchanges should not be used.

## What to Talk About

Certain topics are perfect subjects for discussion group conversations. It is more straightforward to talk about the ones that don't work very well than those that do. The issues that you will want to investigate in other ways are those that, for whatever reason, people don't want to discuss frankly in front of their peers. For example, everyone knows that it is important to wash hands before leaving the restroom, so a discussion of bathroom layouts that facilitate or impede hand washing might not collect too much frank input. Topics that are not so personal, even if they relate to national or organizational culture, can be discussed in groups, however. The culturally prescribed behavior in many offices today is that if people receive or make a telephone call, they should leave their desk and travel to a more isolated area to talk on the phone. People can discuss following this leave-the-desk rule and even each other's behavior on the phone, because failure to follow the prescribed rules does not indicate a lapse in basic personal hygiene or moral behavior.

Conversations that flow really well in discussion groups reflect multiple points of view and sets of information that need to be fused. Groups are also useful for generating—brainstorming—sets of ideas or options to be systematically reviewed later with users via other research tools or by client and design team members.

The rules used to write survey and interview questions should be followed when you are planning a discussion group—no leading questions, for example. Many valuable discussions build from straightforward initial questions about topics that need to be resolved to inform the design process.

Several conversation-generating techniques can be really useful in discussion groups. Attendees can be asked to select from a set of images (none of the sort of place being designed) that give them the same feeling as being in a current space or that they would prefer to have in the new space being development. They can then be asked why they have selected the images chosen. It is this discussion of "why" that provides the most valuable information. The same procedures/questions should be used as when images are shown during individual interviews. It is generally logistically easier to show groups pairs or smaller sets of images (projected on a wall, for example), and to repeat the questioning process several times. A hospice work team could be shown pictures of dewdrops on ferns, train yards, underwater scenes, and so on and be asked which ones gave them the same feelings as they hope to have in the new hospice being designed. You can show people pictures of two random first-aid supplies, for example (such as a Band-Aid and a stretcher), and ask which would be more useful in their current office workspace—always following up with "why" or "how come" to get conversation flowing. You can be creative with these sets of images.

Particularly in larger discussion groups, attendees are often divided into smaller teams of three or so to consider and intensely discuss an issue of importance for five to ten minutes. The smaller groups then report back to the larger group, and those reports can also inspire debates as reasons for conclusions or positions are discussed. Groups can also put together skits or construct models out of foam core, for example, to prevent attendees from getting bored and "tuning out" during a session, as they generate useful information. Similarly, people can work individually for brief period of time on a project, such as a collage that represents what it is like to live in the desired housing development, and then join together again to discuss why they included particular images in their collage, for instance. Separate activities also require people to consider issues raised and then present their own opinions to the group—it is more difficult to slough off the thinking to others or quickly abandon individual positions.

Again, it is the discussion of the logic underlying a decision that is most valuable to the planning process—it can reflect fundamental emotional responses to a place or place design preferences, for example.

People can also be asked to do some individual work before a session begins, for example to take photographs related to the topics to be discussed, and to bring that pre-work to a discussion session. Often, attendees do not spend a lot of time on prework, however, no matter how important they are led to believe that it is.

Discussion groups and design charettes often merge into a very productive hybrid.

When different user groups have legitimately different needs, discussion groups can help you as a designer collect the information that you need to resolve usage inconsistencies. Groups can also develop design compromises together during discussion groups. For example, two sets of people might officially be part of the same work team, but they might have different space needs. An R & D team might include research engineers as well as their assistants. The work of the research engineers might involve periods of intense concentration, meetings, and times when they are doing more routine tasks. The assistants might do those more routine tasks and go to meetings. A discussion among group members about their work activities and the related space needs could result in a department layout acceptable to all; it is more likely to meet their needs because design tradeoffs have been directly discussed in a public forum and compromises have been reached.

Suppose a new workspace, to be used by a group of people with identical space needs, cannot accommodate all of their realistic requirements. During a discussion group, these people could jointly develop a compromise. For example, a group might need to decide between a larger meeting space in their team area where they could all gather together to talk (without heading down the hall to one of the central meeting rooms) or a few much smaller spaces where people could do thoughtful work relatively close to their assigned workplaces. The teammates would probably find value not only in gathering together but also in working effectively alone or in two-person teams—it would be difficult for a designer to determine which need is more important, but the team itself can resolve this issue through discussion.

It is a waste of time to get a collection of people together and ask them questions that can be answered with a simple yes or no. It takes a lot of time to get a discussion group organized; if you need to resolve such clear-cut direct questions, distribute a survey. Also, do not gather people together and serially interview them; that doesn't make the best use of the discussion group format. Systematic questions, for example when people lay out a standardized procedure, are also best documented via interviews or surveys. Those sorts of reviews aren't conversations as much as reports. People should *discuss* during discussion groups.

The information that you get from most discussion groups will be quite exploratory and can be usefully applied to develop a survey that can collect information from more people. From a discussion group you can learn what sorts of things people do in the conference room, and a survey could be useful for finding out more about each of those activities. In a strict, scientific sense, it is hard to extrapolate much from the discussions held with a small percent of the people who do or will use a space. If you choose your participants with care, using the following rules, you can feel more comfortable making generalizations.

## Location of Group

Design discussion groups are generally held in a space readily accessible to all of the participants. For employees of a single firm, this could be the conference room down the hall, while for a session related to the design of homes in a planned multifamily housing complex, this might be at a central site with dedicated session rooms. Some of these session rooms may have one-way glass panels that allow people behind the glass to see what's going on during the discussion, without attendees hearing or seeing them. Being in that space behind the glass can be a handy way for members of the design team to learn nuances in the information shared and to modify the course of a discussion as they feel is necessary. For example, they might pass notes to the person leading the group letting them know that they need more information about this or that issue to move forward. Having discussion groups at a centrally located area reduces travel time and increases the likelihood that all who have been invited will attend.

Discussion groups should be held in spaces that will not themselves become the central topic of discussion—unless that is relevant to the research question being asked. For example, if the session is being held offsite in a conference room, that room should not be so odd or interesting that time is spent discussing it that should be spent on a topic of more central relevance to the research questions being resolved. There should be audiovisual equipment so images can be projected. Participants should be gathered around a central table and seated in comfortable chairs. The table allows people with different personalities to feel comfortable—a ring of chairs without the table makes some people feel too exposed to communicate freely. Also, to encourage free conversation, if the session is being held in a building where colleagues of the participants might pass nearby, the entire discussion area needs to be enclosed with floor-to-ceiling acoustically impermeable walls. Light refreshments are generally served at focus groups, so the meeting space must have a place where they can be arranged.

# Attendees

Who should be at a discussion group? Very few members of the design and client teams. One, or at most two, members of the design team and client organization should be in the room with the discussion group members. No more. The presence of more nonparticipants will distort the social dynamic of participants and the data collected. Having someone from the client management team is particularly undesirable—the pressure on attendees to supply information that the client will want to hear can be intense. Sessions can be recorded and additional members of the design team can later listen to those recordings. People can also watch the session from behind one-way glass, as described earlier. Presession planning may also eliminate at least some of the desire by client management to be in the room while discussions are being held—they can feel comfortable that the information they need will be gathered.

Participants in a focus group are selected because of their relevance to the research question being resolved, often because they are as a group representative of the people who will ultimately use a site as shoppers, workers, or patients, for example. The appropriate participants and the planned discussion guide are developed to resolve the research questions of interest.

In any discussion group, participants should feel free to share their thoughts with the other people present. One of the most common impediments to that is people of different organizational rank being present at the same session. For example, newly hired lawyers are unlikely to speak their minds in front of firm partners, although they may do so in a group of other junior personnel. When people at discussion groups are similar in ways that are relevant to the discussion and share important demographic characteristics such as life stage, more participation generally ensues. Whenever possible, it's best if the group participants do not know each other. That increases the likelihood that tacit information, otherwise unavailable to the group's coordinators, will be shared.

Rank is not the only difference that can impede discussion. Certain issues might be seen as too shocking to discuss outside a professional group or too difficult to explain, for example. You will need to use logic to identify these potential discussion killers. To make this point clearer: At a discussion to collect information for the design of a new obstetrics wing, nursing staff and first-time mothers might not work together well in a discussion group. The mothers would not necessarily be aware of their needs during the birthing process, and nurses in the same group with those mothers might not want to stress them. Those soon-to-be mothers can easily discuss attributes of birthing centers that favorably and unfavorably influence their decisions about where to have their babies. If we return to the discussion of the hospice care center mentioned earlier, it's pretty easy to see that very productive conversations can be held when caregiver and family members are in separate groups.

You want to hear from people with more than one perspective, however, so different group sessions need to have different sorts of members—this follows neatly from the examples in the last paragraph. People of similar ranks should be in one group, and you should hold groups with all of the ranks of people who will use the space you are developing, if it is at all possible. People with different relationships with a space—such as the nurses and first-time mothers in the earlier example—need to be separated, with (hopefully) group discussions held with each such user group. At each rank and for each user group type, it is good to conduct three discussion groups. Sometimes there will not be enough of a particular group of people at a client organization to have three discussion groups, but it is important to have multiple groups in case the members of one have had unusual experiences or are just plain odd themselves.

Sometimes the participants in discussion groups will be recruited from lists (such as employee rosters) supplied by the client. In those case, the lists of people provided should be divided into the sets of people that are relevant to the discussion groups. This would be employees of a similar rank, or patients and nurses, to continue on with the examples mentioned already. Then, people in each group need to be asked to participate. The potential participants should be randomly chosen.

Making random selections is very straightforward. If you have a list of potential participants—people who satisfy your selection criteria—alphabetical or otherwise mixed together, you could write each name on a piece of paper and pull the required number of names from a hat (physically or electronically) or do a little math, for example. If you will need 10 participants and you have a list of 30 people, every third person on that list could be asked to take part.

Unfortunately, people often do not show up for discussion groups they have agreed to attend, even after reminders to them; you will need to ask twice as many people to attend as you ultimately want to participate. So, if you want 9 people to attend, ask 18. If all 18 (or close to that) do show up, you have a couple of options. You might be able to hold an additional, simultaneous session if the facilities and discussion leaders are available to do so. You can send the extras home, making sure that a good mix of people remain. Don't send home all of the more experienced nurses, for example, or all of those that work with a sort of patient or doing a certain sort of task with the patient. This means you need to have all participants supply pertinent information about themselves as they arrive or in advance. Any people who show up whose presence is not needed to retain the desired mix of people in the discussion session can be excused. They should receive the same sort of compensation that they would have gotten if they'd actually been in the group. Do not ask for volunteers to leave the session; the people who volunteer may be different in some pertinent way from the people who choose to remain.

On occasion, you will need to use a professional discussion group management firm to help you recruit participants to your sessions. Participant recruiting firms maintain lists of potential participants (they will have the names of all the thoracic surgeons in town) and can quickly identify and invite anyone you might want to speak with—parents of young children, recent immigrants from Laos, people shopping for new homes in a particular price range). In this case, you will need to provide them with the exact parameters of the people that you would like to participate, and the sorts of people you would like excluded—this might be people working for competitors of your client, as an example. Recruiters are easily identified through an Internet search.

## Compensation for Attendees

If you have recruited participants from a list supplied to you by the client, compensation for attendees is usually a token payment—for example, a modest gift certificate to the employee cafeteria. Some clients will object, in principle, to their employees and similar groups being paid even a token sum to participate in a discussion group, and in this case, no compensation can be paid. If attending the discussion group requires extra effort on the part of participants (they need to stay after work, travel to a distant site), some sort of sign of appreciation is appropriate, however.

The group management firms can let you know what the prevailing rate is for payments to particular sorts of participants. The rarer the sort of participant required, the more the participants will cost—thoracic surgeons will require more compensation than accounts payable clerks, for example.

## Being the Discussion Group Moderator

The reason that focus groups got a bad name was because some discussion leaders did not ensure that everyone present participated and was engaged.

There are useful techniques for keeping the talk flowing, however. First, at the beginning of the session, have everyone in the room state his or her name and supply a piece of relevant information, such the units they have worked on at the hospital being redesigned. Since each person speaks, this helps people analyzing audio recordings later link statements to particular people and the profiles they have filled out (they learn that the woman with the squeaky voice is Lynn, and from the form used to collect relevant info from Lynn, they find that Lynn has a particular type of job, or some other info pertinent to the project). Second, having spoken once, people are much more likely to speak again, later in the session. Third, intros help set everyone in the room at ease; they find it comforting to know who is present. Also, this can be a handy way to collect some useful type of information that might have been hard to get through a closed-ended survey question. This might be how often the session attendees get to spend time with immediate family members at home (if a home is being designed, for example) and what the family members tend to do during that shared time.

If you are the moderator, keep yourself out of the discussion. Don't interject your own opinions; remain objective. Also, make sure that you are very familiar with the goals of the session so that you can pick up on relevant comments made by participants and so that you can maintain a naturally flowing conversation that addresses all issues of interest. The best discussion group leaders are similar to the participants in ways relevant to the discussion, to help establish rapport. If a maternity suite is being discussed with women who have recently given birth, the moderator should be a woman, for example—but that woman must maintain an objective viewpoint, even if she has had children.

Sessions should lead off with a brief, broad statement of the issues to be discussed. This statement must be extremely high level. Something such as, "We're here to talk about your workplace experiences," is sufficient. Too many details can distort discussion later. All present should be encouraged to participate and the rules of the session need to be laid out—such as "No conversations between two people that are separate from the group discussion" and "Cell phones should be turned off."

Discussion should flow from broader to more specific issues. Any sensitive questions—and sensitivity here is to be judged from the perspective of the participants—should be introduced after the participants have become comfortable with each other, after approximately a minimum of ten minutes of conversation. As with one-on-one interviews, it's important that discussion-group conversations flow naturally, which will happen if the moderator is very familiar with all of the topics to be discussed.

Sharing findings from one group with participants at another session will distort the discussions in the second group—to coincide with those of the first group if it is respected. If comments on findings from a previous group are required for some reason, which is unlikely, the previous group's discussion should be brought up at the end of the session so that distortion of subsequent statements in the second group is minimized.

Asking people to clarify comments locks attention onto a topic and is a good way to guide discussion toward issues of interest. It can also consolidate the entire group on a discussion of a single topic—subdiscussions can distort the group dynamic and prevent coverage of all topics of interest. Echoing or paraphrasing a comment made in slightly different words has a similar effect and can also get a discussion restarted if it seems to have collapsed. Echoing and paraphrasing are also a good way to get a stalled discussion restarted.

If no one present speaks after you ask a question in a session or if conversation stops, just wait. A silence is socially awkward, and someone will ensure that it is filled. You can effectively keep conversation on a desired topic going by repeating phrases related to the desired topics of conversation. If you use these techniques and the silence continues, it is probably time to move on to another topic. At this time, summarizing the conversation to date on an issue will conclude a segment of the conversation and draw out any remaining comments. You'll find many of the tools you use to keep conversation flowing in interviews useful here (see Chapter 5 for additional details).

If there is a particular person who never seems to speak, looking at him or her generally does the trick of bringing that person into the discussion. If not, direct a question by name: "Bill, what do you think about what Jim is saying?" Sometimes, people simply will not participate, and repeated attempts to include them just ruin the flow of the session.

Some people (a single one or a small group) will occasionally try to dominate a session. If they are treated in the correct way, this behavior can be curtailed. Stop looking at them, for starters. Tell them that you respect their opinion but that you need to hear from others. ("Matt, thank you for sharing that information [or, now, we're familiar with your position on X, etc.], let's hear from someone else. John, [rephrase of question most recently posed to the group].")

The session must not disintegrate into a number of simultaneous discussions among subsets of the attendees. When this happens, productive discussion often fades away and it is difficult to understand recorded conversations.

Discussion groups should be scheduled to last about 1.5 hours, with a half-hour transition time between groups. After 90 minutes, participants are tired and the sessions become unproductive. Adhere to the schedule—the participants will, and any discussions that occur after people begin to leave the group will be different than it might have been if all participants had remained. During the half hour transition, the moderator can take a break and needed modifications can be made to the topics to be discussed. The discussion guide may need to be modified for a number of reasons—participants may not feel comfortable discussing a particular topic, a not-so-important part of the discussion may be taking such a long time that information more relevant to resolving outstanding design issues cannot be fully discussed, and so on.

## Data Analysis

After the discussion group ends, you will need to analyze the data collected using verbal (and visual if images were created) content analysis techniques.

## Example of Discussion Groups

A well-planned meeting at which the people in the room participate and the topics that brought the group together are discussed is an example of a well-functioning discussion group. The defining factor is that the meeting leader effectively integrated all of the people present into the conversation, which collected material useful for moving projects forward. As the number of bad meetings that we have all been to attests, being an effective discussion leader is a rare skill.

# SPACE SIMULATION

Space simulation is:

| | | | | | | |
|---|---|---|---|---|---|---|
| Little known | 1 | 2 | 3 | 4 | **5** | Lot known |
| Quick | 1 | 2 | 3 | 4 | **5** | Not quick |
| Info straightforward | 1 | 2 | **3** | 4 | 5 | Info complex |
| Verbal | 1 | 2 | **3** | 4 | 5 | Numeric |
| How | 1 | 2 | 3 | 4 | **5** | Why |
| On-site | 1 | 2 | **3** | 4 | 5 | Off-site OK |
| Well-established | 1 | **2** | 3 | 4 | 5 | Innovative |
| Current | 1 | **2** | 3 | 4 | 5 | Future |
| Special | 1 | **2** | 3 | 4 | 5 | No special |
| Generally considered | 1 | 2 | 3 | 4 | **5** | Potentially considered |

[Score indicated by **bold**ing of number.]

Simulating a space being developed, whether virtually or in physical form is a lot of effort—but the value of the information collected from simulations is justified. Simulations help you understand real-life experiences before spaces are built and those real-life experiences are complicated (see Figure 6.7).

The more true-to-life a simulation is, the more confident you can be that what you learn through it will be consistent with situations in the space in actual use. Psychological measures such as satisfaction with the environment are more useful as the space becomes more realistic, and so do tests of the functionality of a space. A segment of a place can be simulated—for instance, a doorway or an oncology bay in a new hospital. A mock-up of a part of a space may be useful to answer ergonomic and other more mechanical questions, such as whether a gurney will fit comfortably through the doorway in a room.

Additional real-world-type details come at additional cost, and so you need to develop a space simulation weighing the poorly defined criteria of needed attention to detail and the easy-to-measure criteria of cost. If you have limited time and budget to create a simulation, concentrate on the elements of the environment most closely related to the research question that you need to resolve most urgently. If you are working on a problem related to handedness in a hospital patient room, don't spend a lot of time laying out a patient bathroom, but do take a careful look at the route the patient will travel from the bed to the toilet. If you are interested in making dramatic changes to the cash-wrap stations at a retailer client, make sure that the new stations that you have developed are carefully modeled in the test environment—the product display areas are not so important—although they must be constructed to a level of detail that does not distort the responses to the criteria being tested (see Figure 6.8).

**FIGURE 6.7**
Space simulations can be incredibly detailed and realistic, such as this sales center mock-up of a kitchen in a condominium for sale. *Photo: Augustin*

**FIGURE 6.8**
Even rough approximations of spaces can collect useful information to inform design. *Photo Augustin*

Flight simulators can serve as a model here. They are used to train pilots to fly particular aircraft, so all the "flying-the-plane" details exactly match those out of the simulator in the real world. In those elements, the simulated space is the same as the true cockpit—dials are in place, displays come up on the screens, lights flash on the control panel, and so on. In some simulators, the situation is made more realistic as the pilot's chair tilts or vibrates to recreate aspects of the flying experience. However, it's just the elements needed to learn to fly a plane are present. That's it. It is important that pilots have a very good idea what will happen in particular situations, so the developers of flight simulators have made sure that they will be able to move seamlessly from the teaching environment to an actual airplane.

Other places where split-second decision making may also mean life and death, or at least serious consequences, are regularly simulated before construction. This includes spaces such as air traffic stations and control rooms of all sorts—from nuclear reactors to train systems.

In cases where post-construction modifications to the environment may be difficult or impossible, simulations are a very important part of the design process. This is the case with laboratories, clean rooms, other similar technologically sophisticated workplaces, and often kitchens in homes.

Spaces that will be replicated hundreds or thousands of times are also often simulated so various sets of users can visit them. The prime example of this sort of simulation is usually known as a *mock-up,* and it is done before the design of a new office cubicle or other workspace (including patient rooms in hospitals) is locked down. Ideally, people even work in these mocked-up areas (when they're offices) before a space design is finalized.

Spaces that are being developed to generate an association to a particular brand or a feeling can benefit from being simulated—a lot of sensory elements are debated in this circumstance, as well as organizational ones. Often, a prototype of a store is a completely functional simulation of a store concept, built to inform the design of future stores. Prototype stores often evolve over time, as designers test a variety of different concepts.

Space simulations should also "learn" over time. As users interact with one simulation, it should be reconfigurable, so that as new information is collected with the space—with this process of learning and redesigning continuing until developers run out of time, money, or staff hours. It is unlikely that there will be any shortage of ideas for tweaks to the space.

Space simulations are useful research tools toward the end of the design/learning process. Their form needs to reflect what has been learned in earlier research. Projects using a simulation put the activity and experience scenarios formally or informally recognized earlier in the research process to work and to the test.

The sorts of data-gathering techniques used earlier in the research processes can be reapplied here. In store prototypes and other space mock-ups, where people move through their usual activities, individuals can be interviewed, fill out surveys, and be observed, for example. The exact form of the survey or interview schedule or observation plan should be determined by the research question being resolved through the simulation. If the simulation was built to judge visitor emotional response, then the surveys, interviews, and observation plan should focus on that emotional response, for example.

Even if the form of the space simulation created is not as complete and functional as an operating prototype store or an in-use office space, study participants can be observed using traditional observation tools, or asked to walk through certain activities in the space (to the extent that its scale allows)—with the activities recreated being dictated by the questions that research must answer before the design process can move forward. Subjects can also be left alone in the space and queried at the end of their visit using a survey. The way that the simulation is used should be based on the data that must be collected from it, the resources available to collect information, and the favored research techniques of the designers and clients. (Hey, when all else is the same, why not use the tools you enjoy most applying?)

Information can also be collected in various ways during the simultaneous visits of several users to the simulation. People can be involved in a simulation-situated discussion group that first probes what a space looks like, for example, and then, after people have been in the space for some time, moves on to questions about the space in use—for example, the experience of actually ringing up a customer there, or wheeling the patient to an out-of-room procedure. Visitors to the simulation can then be surveyed and various prototypical activities observed as they're recreated in the simulation.

A space simulation can take several forms, from a display that looks like it belongs in a dollhouse, to a recreation of a room that would seem comfortable in a high-end condominium staged to sell via a virtual-reality walkthrough.

Computer simulations of spaces are becoming more true-to-life and therefore more effective research tools. This technology will continue to evolve. Research in these virtual environments is fundamentally the same as that in real-world ones. Recent research has shown that computer simulations can linger too long in an environment to effectively simulate the experience of being there, so make sure virtual walkthroughs proceed at a true walking pace.

## Example of Space Simulation

Simulations can be entirely electronic. The National Research Council Canada provides software that can simulate several sorts of workplace conditions. Visit its website to use these tools (www.nrc-cnrc.gc.ca).

# EXPERIMENTS

Experiments are:

| Little known | 1 | 2 | 3 | 4 | 5 | Lot known |
|---|---|---|---|---|---|---|
| Quick | 1 | 2 | 3 | 4 | 5 | Not quick |
| Info straightforward | 1 | 2 | 3 | 4 | 5 | Info complex |
| Verbal | 1 | 2 | 3 | 4 | 5 | Numeric |
| How | 1 | 2 | 3 | 4 | 5 | Why |
| On-site | 1 | 2 | 3 | 4 | 5 | Off-site ok |
| Well-established | 1 | 2 | 3 | 4 | 5 | Innovative |
| Current | 1 | 2 | 3 | 4 | 5 | Future |
| Special | 1 | 2 | 3 | 4 | 5 | No special |
| Generally considered | 1 | 2 | 3 | 4 | 5 | Potentially considered |

[Score indicated by **bold**ing of number.]

Rigorous experiments are the standard against which all other research is compared. They come closest to unequivocally identifying what is responsible for any changes in whatever is being measured—but conducting an experiment outside a laboratory is difficult. Nonetheless, sometimes, you will be able to run true experiments to collect information. You might need to know more about a sensory experience's influence (such as a set of lighting level effects) on users of a space, or how a particular floor plan alters within cubicle collaboration.

Since it is difficult to conduct an unimpeachable experiment, even if you are an academic, always make doubly sure that one is even necessary. A really thorough literature review might unearth experiments done by others that supply the information that is needed.

For our purposes, we will define an experiment as research in which you can vary one aspect of a situation of interest to you and see the effects generated. While that one factor changes, everything else in an experiment stays the same (more on this later). When only one thing in an environment is modified, you can attribute all changes in performance or other variables to the changed factor.

First, we should define *one thing:* It is a single design element. It is a floor covering, or providing control of the lights to the users. It is clear-cut. If you vary more than one thing at a time, you can still run an experiment, but you need to attribute all changes seen to all of the elements modified, with the statistical techniques at our disposal here. For example, if you replace a high-walled panel system in a workplace with an open plan with no cubicle enclosures, you could be in a situation in which not only can co-workers can see each other but also daylight moves from windows on one side of a space more fully into it, and former temperature regulation systems are compromised because there are now no enclosures impeding airflow. Changes that you see in whatever you are measuring before and after this change (such as employee perceptions of their own productivity) must be attributed to the entire set of environmental changes, not a single one, such as being able to see teammates.

We will be discussing experiments involving human experience/behavior specifically. It is also possible to discuss material-based experiments (e.g., tests of endurance and similar mechanical properties). Those experiments are run in the same ways as ones involving human experience or behavior.

The people who participate in an experiment should be as similar as possible to those that will ultimately use the space you are designing. Any differences could result in your study findings not being useful for informing the design process.

You can do an experiment within or outside a laboratory setting. Lab experiments have the advantage of restricting more of the elements in the environment that change, but not many practitioners (excluding acousticians and a few others) have access to a true lab.

It seems logical that you will be doing experiments in a live environment, in the same space (or sort of spaces) in which your findings will be applied. You will be painting the walls of a store that is equivalent to a store painted with the current palette (same yearly sales, same clientele, same product assortment, same sort of other shops adjoining, etc.) to test client reactions. In the test store, walls might be painted warmer tones than in the current store. In this retail environment, there is a readily apparent outcome for you to measure (sales per square foot). You can compare the sales per square foot in each environment, and if the only difference between them is the colors on the walls, you can attribute all of variations in sales to those different paint colors.

It is important to quantify what is changed and report the values tested—it is sloppy just say the walls were painted red (color specs need to be provided) or light levels were changed—quantification of differences in generally accepted measurements is required. Particularly when aspects of the environment that can be measured, such as lighting levels, are changed, its important to capture as much quantitative information regarding those aspects of the environment as possible. That way you can supply the data later to someone who can do more comprehensive analyses, or do them yourself after a class in statistics. These details also help in applying the info you have collected—it's a lot better to know that the light levels need to be at 100 lux or 1000 lux because that's what they were during the test, than just knowing that they need to be brighter or dimmer.

Often, the item to be studied and measured during an experiment will be identified in conversations with clients—they know what's important to them and what they'd like to see enhanced. The element that you choose to measure will be related to the design-related question you are trying to answer. If you are trying to determine if researchers can collaborate and concentrate individually in a space, make sure to collect information on collaboration and concentration; information on responding quickly to emergency situations or projection of organization brand is superfluous. Instead of sales per square foot, the retailer in the earlier example could have been interested in increasing sales to a particular income group. Zip code might be an unobtrusive way to measure those sales, so client sales clerks would then need to ask customers for their zip codes during the sales process. In this case, zip code is not a perfect reflection of income level, but it is an inoffensive way to collect information that is, in a general way, related to income. Healthcare facilities have a number of quantifiable outcome measures—from number of days in the hospital, to amount of pain medication or other treatments used, to number of times the nurse is called to the patient bedside. It's a lot harder to measure creativity in a space or mood—but it can be done. Refer back to the Steelcase example in Chapter 2 for inspiration.

Measurements of criteria of interest should be made as long as possible after the environmental test condition has changed or people in the test situation have had a real opportunity to experience it—not a fleeting exposure. If you have modified an aspect of a home kitchen to determine if it leads to more frequent family gatherings in that kitchen, you should not do the postchange data collection until several months have passed. By then, family members will have become familiar enough with the features of the space so there is no cause for concern that the family (or families in a multifamily complex) is simply visiting the kitchen because it is new and different. When scientists in labs are doing experiments, they set a period of time for an experiment to run based on a number of criteria derived from their careful review of the experimental literature. Since you are developing a space that people will use over an extended period of time, it is appropriate for you to collect data at the last possible moment that will still allow you to meet project deadlines.

It is also important to select items to analyze that are potentially variable in the space redesigned. If wall colors are being tested in a healthcare facility procedure room, for example, and the variable being measured is post-procedure pain medicine consumed, no meaningful data will be collected if the patient can be expected to be in the space for 30 minutes and the pain medicine delivered during the procedure does not begin to wear off for an hour. Similarly, if a new workplace is laid out to encourage employees to walk and burn calories, looking for changes in employee health before about a year, or so, has passed is not likely to be too useful. It will take firm employees multiple months to burn off enough calories at work so that there are any real changes in their health.

Experiments are generally related to quantitative data and not qualitative data. Changes are noted in something that can be clearly and unequivocally measured. It is possible to run an experiment where the data are collected using a qualitative tool, such as interviewing or content analysis. If this is the case, quantitative information derived from that qualitative material (counts of positive and negative statements about finding a place to talk with colleagues uninterrupted) can also be compared, and that quantification will add credibility to any changes discussed.

It seems most likely that any experiments that you run would be classified as *quasi-experiments*. In a true experiment, the people from whom you collect information are randomly distributed into the different test conditions—whether they see the regular colored walls or the warmer walls in that store is determined entirely by chance. If the color of the walls seen is not entirely randomly determined, the sort of study underway is called a quasi-experiment. In the store wall color example, a quasi-experiment is being conducted because the wall colors are not changed randomly for each individual participant; people walking by and through one store see one thing, and people walking through or by another store see another. People are not walking down those particular streets by chance—some other mechanism that might affect study results has determined the street visited. For our purposes and those of the basic statistical analyses we will conduct, we can ignore the differences between true and quasi-experiments.

If you run an experiment and get answers that are different from those that would be expected based on the body of research evidence, don't despair. First of all, make sure that your study is actually comparable to previous ones—do the people who participated in your study have different kinds of jobs or live in a different climate from those in the previous study, for example? It is also possible that you are correct and previous researchers have made an error—but you need to review all of your analyses and data collection procedures to be sure about that. It is also true that the world changes (albeit slowly), and both you and the previous researcher could have correctly conducted your experiments; differences observed in your results would thus be entirely appropriate. If no alternative explanations for your results are available and you cannot find an error in your process, still do not despair. People are complicated, and it could be that the difference between the findings you anticipated and those found are related to some aspect of human perception, behavior, or other factor that is just not recognized at this time.

As a final test to determine if the factor being modified is actually responsible for any changes in attitudes and behaviors seen, it is possible to return it to the state before any modifications were made and take additional measurements. If the levels on the variables of interest return to their previous reading, it is even more likely that the changes seen are indeed attributable to whatever was changed. Data collected can be analyzed using the statistical tests outlined in Chapter 5.

# A Story of Practice: Schematic Design

Information contributed through interview by: Conifer Research, Chicago, Illinois.

**Contributors:**
Megan Fath, Director of Design

Holly Roeske, Director of Operations and Planning

Carolyn Stuenkel, Ph.D., Director of Research

Adisorn Supawatanakul, Director of Advanced Technology and Development

Project: Conifer Research's story of practice: An ethnographic research method of identifying user behaviors to help clients "see their end users"

## THE METHOD

Conifer Research is a team of anthropologists, social scientists, strategists, and designers who work collaboratively to conduct user- and behavior-based observation techniques to capture and analyze customer or end-user behaviors, attitudes, and emotions as seen in real life—they help their clients see their end users.

Conifer's research method is based in ethnographic research—a study of human behavior in its natural setting that analyzes the connection between behavior and physical settings. From its observations, the team analyzes the data to identify patterns, conflicts, and insights that are later documented, modeled, and shared with its clients.

Conifer's scope of practice is broad, ranging from defining "cute" for a greeting card, or looking at how college students use textbooks or documenting commuters' navigation of public transportation. However, for this story of practice, Fath, Roeske, Stuenkel, and Supawatanakul describe how, for an architectural or interior design project, its process supports the schematic design phase of a project by generating insights into the behaviors of the end users of a space.

The research, Conifer notes, is a powerful tool in making distinctions between what people say they do in an environment and what they actually do. Its primary goal is to be the voice of the end user and amplify that voice for the designers of these spaces.

## GETTING STARTED

For each project, the team comes together to develop a unique protocol that establishes what methods of research to apply. Supawatanakul describes the process this way: "We start by defining the client's objectives. If the client is planning a move, we want to know, why is it moving? Is it about growth, a merger, or is the client trying to change its culture in some way?"

Next, the team establishes which user groups to include in the study. Often, it screens participants in advance. When the research has to yield specific information, the team will prototype its methods first to identify potential problems.

Having access to a range of people involved in different aspects of the environment is important, it notes. For example, in the case of a retail assignment, the team looks to have input from the customers, the workers, and even the maintenance crew. Often, Supawatanakul says, when working with architects and designers the time frame is short. Therefore, developing protocols that can be executed in a timely way is key.

Once the objectives are established, the team identifies the best methods to acquire the data. "There's never one approach; we look to combine multiple modes of data collection to yield the most useful insights," says Fath. Again, the scope of the project and time frame all factor into what protocols to use. Fath explains that if the time frame is short, a fixed video stream (when a camera collects data over a long period of time) may be unproductive because analyzing the recordings takes a long time. For Fath, the goal is to find ways to observe a range of events and understand the use cycles of an environment and, eventually, get to understand the users in the broadest context. Often, it's what she describes as a *backward engineering* approach to identifying what information will be useful later when applying the information to the design of the project (see Figure 6.9).

**FIGURE 6.9**
Once the research objectives are established, the team identifies the best methods to acquire the data and looks to combine multiple modes of data collection to yield the most useful insights.
*© Conifer Research*

# THE SELF-DOCUMENT METHOD

For a financial company, the team was looking to understand how office workers were managing the fluctuation of paperwork based on business cycles and workload. Rather than watch days of videotape, for this assignment the Conifer team asked subsamples of participants to self-document their workspaces at different time intervals. The team prepared a self-document kit, equipped with a disposable camera, a ruler, and a set of instructions and questions that essentially asked the sub-samples what type of work they were doing at specific times throughout the day and to measure the height of the papers stacked on the their desk at each interval.

Roeske points out that the hidden benefit to the *self-doc method* is that participants reveal what *they* perceive is important. An example she cites is asking participants to take pictures each time they meet with a coworker. "This is a powerful moment," she says. "It's the user's point of view, and suddenly we've uncoupled this discussion from the size of (or the numbers of seats in) a conference room, to seeing how users actually engage in discussion." When analyzing the data, the team may identify that the cafeteria or the coffee service counter is where employees are conducting the majority of meetings. This type of information generates important qualitative insights rather than merely quantitative data.

Roeske adds that when reviewing images with a client, Conifer often asks the participants to sort the images as a prompt for discussions (see Figure 6.10). Here, she notes, the stories behind why the images were taken, what was happening at the time, and what the participant was thinking are all very useful pieces of information that expose a level of insight and give the team an opportunity to probe on particular areas of interest.

# VIDEO AS A TOOL FOR MAPPING MOVEMENT AND SPACE UTILIZATION

For McDonald's, the team was looking to understand how people, information, and food moved in the test setting to optimize the setting for operational efficiencies and to develop best practices for the environment. The team identified the different zones that the employees occupied and positioned video recording devices to capture the activity over the course of several days. From observing the video, the team identified the different circulation patterns and what spatial zones employees occupied during different points of the customer service sequence. Next, the team identified when in the process the space was congested versus underutilized. With this information, the team prepared a series of diagrammatic maps that graphically illustrated the different conditions.

Roeske points out that with video, there are often multiple activities happening at once; therefore, planning what to diagram and map prior to setting up the video facilitates the process by creating a filter for the content evaluation (see Figure 6.11).

**FIGURE 6.10**
A photo sort provides the team with stories behind why the images were taken, what was happening at the time and what the participant was thinking. *© Conifer Research*

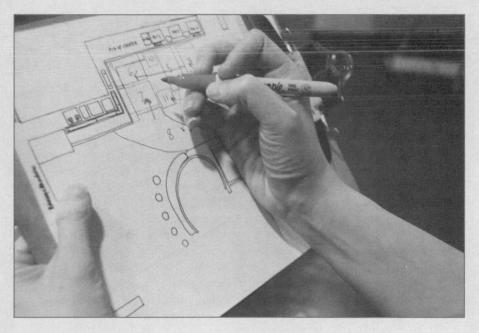

**FIGURE 6.11**
Planning what to diagram and map prior to setting up the video facilitates the process by creating a filter for the content evaluation.. *© Conifer Research*

# SITE OBSERVATION

For customer experience at McDonald's, Stuenkel wanted to understand customers' behaviors when ordering and waiting for food. Conifer employed four separate data streams over four days to understand waiting behaviors: observations, fixed video, short intercept interviews with customers, and finally, interviews with the crew.

The team spent two of the four days conducting real-time observation and analysis to observe patterns and ask customers about some of the behaviors observed. To help define the different spatial zones, the team used the existing 12-inch square floor tile in the space as an organizational grid and a way to ensure that each researcher's documentation was consistent. With that in place, the team observed where and how people wait. Because the team had fixed video from the observation days, it was able to create video collections overlaid with this zonal analysis to clearly illustrate, for the client, customers' waiting behaviors.

The data were both qualitative and quantitative. First, they quantified where people waited. Each time someone stood in a particular zone, he or she was counted. Based on the overall population who visited the restaurant, Conifer was able to calculate percentages of waiting patterns: 25 percent waited in the back, leaning with head on the wall, 10 percent waited by the vending machine, and so on. By observing and noting the different postures, the team was able to add qualitative assessments about what they were seeing. For example, leaning over a counter talking to a salesperson was an engaged encounter, while leaning against a wall and staring at the ceiling was disengaged.

# SURVEYS, INTERVIEWS, AND FOCUS GROUPS

As a qualitative research firm, surveys are rarely the method of choice at Conifer. Supawatanakul suggests that in the rare times that Conifer implements a survey, it intentionally constructs open-ended questions: "If a client comes to us and says they want to know how their employees are using conference spaces, we may reframe the question to say we want to understand how employees have meetings and we will ask where, when, and how those meetings happen."

Stuenkel recalls a recent assignment for a retail mall where the client insisted the team begin with a survey. They structured the survey in a way to have it serve as a recruiting tool for future methods. The survey uncovered data about the average visit duration to this mall, which was longer than the national average. To find out why, the team contacted several of the survey respondents and performed the next phase of the research called a *walk and talk* (see Figure 6.12). Here, the Conifer team walked through the mall with a subgroup of survey respondents. The team structured the exercise somewhat like a focus group. Team members asked questions while walking through the space, giving the participants the opportunity to pause and use the environment to point out responses. In the end, what they uncovered (and wasn't made explicit in the original survey responses) was that the mall's ancillary outdoor children's play area was highly valued by this subgroup and contributed to the longer-duration visits.

**FIGURE 6.12**
A *walk and talk* allows researchers to ask questions while walking through the space, giving the participants the opportunity to pause and use the environment to point out responses.
© *Conifer Research*

## ANALYSIS

Staggering the timing of the multiple modes of observation benefits the analysis process since it facilitates analyzing the data streams in smaller "bites" and gives the team additional opportunities to share the information with the client throughout in the engagement.

Fath explains that once the data streams are in place, the team analyzes the information by looking for patterns. If the data are photo-based, the team conducts what it calls a *sort*—clustering images by category.

For interviews and video, Conifer developed a proprietary software database that allows it to cull out pieces of video or moments of discussion and tag them with "themes" that are established for each project.

Next, the team objectively looks for things that repeat again and again or are aberrations (see Figure 6.13). As Fath explains, they look to uncover what is behind the information and drill down into why the patterns or aberrations exist.

**FIGURE 6.13**
In analysis, the research team objectively looks for things that repeat again and again or are aberrations. © *Conifer Research*

## SYNTHESIS

The final stage of the process is to synthesize the analysis (see Figure 6.14). Where analysis looks to break down the information into parts, the role of synthesis is to pull the findings together into a cohesive narrative. In this phase, the team will help the design team move beyond problem understanding to problem solving. The findings will be prioritized and framed to help translate these insights into design and development opportunities. In this transition, Conifer often hosts immersive, interactive client team workshops designed to deliver the findings, create user empathy, and generate concepts.

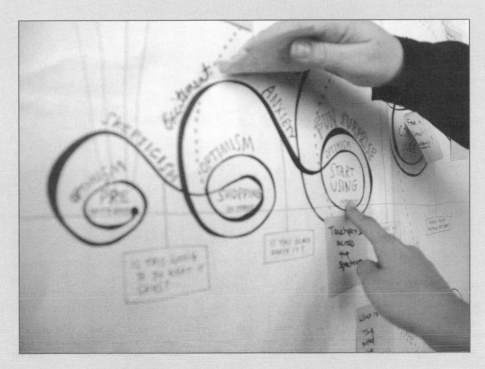

**FIGURE 6.14**
In the synthesis phase, the team will help the design team move beyond problem understanding to problem solving. *© Conifer Research*

## LESSONS LEARNED

Stuenkel notes that it is important to avoid contaminating the analysis. To accomplish this, the team keeps the days they are conducting research separate from the days they are analyzing research. In addition, she notes, good practice includes "sampling" the times of day, days of the week, and types of weather when doing research in spaces because these variables often affect people's behaviors and needs in very concrete ways.

Roeske advises finding ways to engage the participants and client throughout the process to create buy-in. Supawatanakul suggests that good upfront planning and clear communications of the objectives are key in establishing a smooth process. And above all, he says, since research projects create a lot of data, a good organization strategy for the data management is a must—especially when multiple team members and clients all have access to the information.

# A Story of Practice: Design Development

Information contributed through interview by Krueck & Sexton Architects

**Contributors:**
Krueck & Sexton Architects, Chicago, Illinois, USA

Information Provided by: Tom Jacobs, AIA, associate principal

Date of Completion: July 2004

Square Footage: 23,000 square feet

Location: Millennium Park, Chicago, Illinois

Project: Crown Fountain

Donor/Client: Henry Crown and Company, Chicago

Owner: Chicago Park District (Maintenance and Operation)

Artist: Jaume Plensa, Barcelona

Client Representative: U.S. Equities Development

Scope: Overall execution of the technical requirements and detail of the artistic vision of Jaume Plensa

Project Team: Krueck & Sexton, architects

   Halvorson & Kaye, structural engineers

   Advanced Structures Incorporated, façade consultant

   Environmental Systems Design, Inc., MEP consultant

   Crystal Fountains, water feature consultant

   Schuler & Shook, architectural lighting design

   Shen Milsom & Wilke, Inc., technology consultants

Vendors: L.E. Smith Glass Corporation, glass block manufacturer

   Barco Media, LED screen manufacturer

## PROBLEM DEFINITION

In 2001 Jaume Plensa, a Catalan (Barcelona) artist was awarded the commission to design the Crown Fountain in Chicago's Millennium Park (see Figure 6.15). The fountain is based on a concept of two opposing 50-foot-tall towers sitting atop a granite plaza. Each tower is a changing display of the faces of 1,000 Chicago residents. Plensa adapts a traditional fountain design where water flows from the mouths of gargoyles by having water flow from the mouths of the thousand Chicago residents. In an interview, Plensa is quoted as saying that the goal of the installation is to create a project that is "inspired by and created for the people, that will open up the souls of the city's inhabitants by serving as an archive of its people."

**FIGURE 6.15**
Jaume Plensa, a Catalan (Barcelona) artist, was awarded the commission to design the Crown Fountain in Chicago's Millennium Park. The fountain is based on a concept of two opposing 50-foot-tall towers sitting atop a granite plaza. Each tower is a changing display of the faces of 1,000 Chicago residents. The Chicago-based architecture firm Krueck & Sexton was selected to undertake the overall execution of the project.
© Hedrich Blessing

The Chicago-based architecture firm Krueck & Sexton was selected to undertake the overall execution of the project—to work through the complex, technical requirements of the project as well as the coordination of the specialty consultants assembled from across the United States. Tom Jacobs, associate principal, Krueck & Sexton, provided the content for this case study (see Figure 6.16).

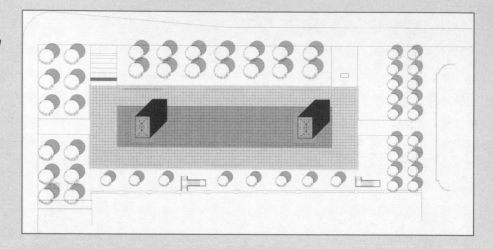

## OBJECTIVE

The Crown Fountain consists of two 50-foot high translucent towers constructed of glass brick that glow with internal light on all sides; 50-foot-high LED video screens are positioned within the two towers, projecting the faces of 1,000 Chicagoans. Water flows over the top and sides of the two towers and onto a 276-foot-long granite plaza (see Figure 6.17).

The objective of this case study is to present Krueck & Sexton's research-based strategy for developing the materiality, technical detailing, and validation for this one-of-a-kind building typology. This case will focus specifically on the material, structural, and detail development of the Crown Fountain and how this diverse project team transformed an artistic vision into a public venue.

## PROJECT SCOPE

Krueck & Sexton's work is heralded for its dedication to craftsmanship, material and detail that enables the firm's built work to express the values of modern design. Although the scope of this project was significantly different from a typical project for Krueck & Sexton—a work of art, not a building—Tom Jacobs points out how that became both the challenge and the attraction: "Jaume Plensa presented a vision and an artist's rendering. Our role was to take this work of art and devise a way for it to perform and last like a building, which, through proper detailing, would embody the artistic purpose and allow it to flourish. Our success would be measured by our ability to take advantage of the inherently transformative process from design concept to built sculpture."

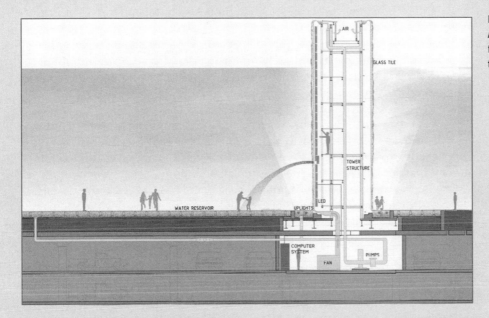

**FIGURE 6.17**
A section drawing of the fountain and infrastructure. © *Conifer Research*

## MATERIAL INVESTIGATION

The primary material for the structure was predetermined by the artist. Jacobs recalls that Plensa arrived at the first meeting with a handmade glass "master brick" for Krueck & Sexton to match. Plensa had experimented with different silica mixes at his studio in Barcelona for over a year to achieve the crystal-clear, water-white appearance of the brick. Krueck & Sexton needed to source a vendor who could produce 22,000 glass bricks that would conform to close dimensional and performance tolerances while being made by hand.

From there, the primary role of the assignment was to understand how to assemble and support the different components of this glass brick "membrane" into a structural and watertight system. Each glass brick was mortised into a continuous, stainless-steel T-grid frame with cementitious mastic composite that would capture each brick on all four sides.

The Krueck & Sexton team followed up with the consulting team to conduct controlled, scientific testing to establish the best mastic composite considering Chicago's specific environmental conditions. Due to internal refraction of light, the stainless-steel grid frame and mastic composite are invisible, and the glass brick membrane appears light and clear.

## THE RESEARCH STRATEGY

The team relied on two prime research approaches for this project: technical information and mock-ups.

Technical information was derived from the architects and the consultant teams. For example, information regarding the compressive strength of the glass brick components and how the performance may fluctuate based on changing temperatures or environmental conditions was readily available from the various consultants and product manufacturers.

To validate the findings and determine how to apply the information that was generated by the experts, Krueck & Sexton conducted a series of mock-ups. Jacobs explains this two-part research strategy by noting that the information that comes from the experts is just that—information. How an architect or designer evaluates the information for a specific use requires prototyping the use through mock-ups. It is this knowledge, combined with validation and judgment, that Jacobs considers the architect and designer's critical role in a research-based design process.

## MOCK-UP ONE—THE GLASS BRICK ASSEMBLY

The team's first mock-up, recalls Jacobs, was to evaluate how to take the separate glass bricks and assemble them into larger panels or a system of panels. The team considered two options: epoxy the glass bricks together, or create a tension ring that locks the glass bricks into place. Due to limited experience with its long-term performance and reliability, epoxy was dropped from consideration; the architects, along with the consultants, considered the latter a better strategy: a tension system that locks the panels in place. The approach was modeled after a similar and standard system developed for basement glass brick clerestory windows sold in home improvement stores.

The mock up was fabricated with wood blocks and a rigid tension band (see Figure 6.18). Jacobs recalls that all the important stakeholders assembled in Krueck & Sexton's main conference room. Once everyone was in place, the architects raised the panel system from a flat to vertical position. With all eyes on the system, the entire assembly exploded and bricks were lying all over the conference room floor.

Lesson learned? According to Jacobs, the first, while embarrassing, is that it is better to fail early and learn from the experience than fail late in the project when it is too late or costly to correct the problems. Had they relied solely on expert information and intuition, this discovery would have occurred onsite during the final installation. The second lesson learned, and the reason for the failure, is that the basement clerestory system was designed as a means to ship the materials to the installation (laying flat) and once the system is ready for install, the tension band is removed. The tension band, as the team later learned, only exacerbated the tendency for the panel to buckle and fail under lateral load conditions.

## MOCK-UP TWO—THE WATER FEATURE

Having a water feature consultant as part of the consultant team provided a mechanism to test different ways to address Plensa's vision for how the water would wash over the top and sides of the towers and how the gargoylelike effect of spouting water would be achieved.

According to Jacobs, the issue of water pressure was of greatest concern. Understanding that people would be walking near and under the fountain, it was critical to design a system that wouldn't knock someone over or cause someone to slip because of the force of the water. To test the water feature, consultant mocked up different water-volume conditions in a warehouse. Krueck & Sexton employees wearing boots, hats, and raincoats walked under each waterspout condition to determine the most suitable level of water pressure. In the end, the team concluded that, like a fire hose, having this volume and velocity of water coming out of a small spout was potentially dangerous. Not wanting to marginalize the visual effect, the team designed and followed up with additional testing of a showerhead system. The showerhead allows the same volume of water to flow, but instead of one spout, water flows from multiple spouts and therefore reduces the force of water and avoids potential accidents.

## MOCK-UP THREE—THE LED SCREEN

A fundamental challenge with the glass brick membrane had to do with the fact that the LED screens sits only three inches behind. Because the glass membrane takes on a significant amount of wind pressure (and suction), the backside of the membrane required a structural system that would transfer the load. Working with the structural consultants, the final solution was a metal structural element attached to the glass membrane that would penetrate through the LED wall and attach to the back structure of the tower.

The success of the LED system, however, relies on continuous, uninterrupted LED modules that sit atop one another to create a seamless image. Early in the process, the team consulted with several LED manufacturers who confirmed that, in theory, a LED module could be notched to accept a structural member. While in theory that was true, in reality, none of the manufacturers were prepared to fabricate a screen in this way.

To compensate, the team determined that it would need to pull the LED modules apart by a quarter inch to accept the structural members. The team also understood that as a result, horizontal lines would appear on the projected faces every couple of feet. Jacobs recalls that this was a "heart stopper" for the team. They mocked up the system to give the other stakeholders an opportunity to weigh in on the results. First the LED panels were separated to accept the structure and next they installed a sample of the glass brick membrane in front.

What happened next was not expected, and again points to the benefit of a mock-up. The thickness of the glass brick membrane softened and blurred the effect of the horizontal lines—so much so, says Jacobs, that they are imperceptible (see Figure 6.19). Here, Jacobs explains how the technical information of this particular mock-up told them one thing (lines would appear through the image), but the perception yielded a different result. "The reality is that the lines are there, but that's not what really matters. What matters is what you see and what you perceive. This mock-up taught us how important perception is—it was an extremely valuable lesson," says Jacobs.

**FIGURE 6.19**
In an alleyway outside the architect's office building, the team mocked up full-size sections of the LED screens with glass bricks positioned in front.
*© Krueck & Sexton Architects.*

## LESSONS LEARNED

According to Jacobs, the concern about having to realize someone's vision made the architects first hesitate to get involved in this project, but it also acted as the greatest lesson learned throughout the three-year process (see Figure 6.20).

**FIGURE 6.20**
Final installation of the towers with sections of glass brick being installed. © *Hedrich Blessing*

As Jacobs explains, architects and designers are often in Jaume Plensa's position of having to communicate the design vision. The Krueck & Sexton team came to understand that even when the vision was so clear to the artist, it still needed to be externalized so that all the stakeholders could understand it at the same level. What Jacobs came to understand is that communicating the vision so that it is understood by the entire team (internal and external) is just the first step that provides information. It's the next step, says Jacobs, that he came to appreciate as having even more value to the process,: to validate the vision. Information, he says, is just that—information. It's the synthesis of this information that transforms information into judgment, perception, and validation—what he considers as being key in effective design research.

Jacobs recalls the moment when he realized they had accomplished their goal with this project. It was a summer night, one week before the opening and the final testing of all the systems was taking place before the barricades were to be taken away. Jacobs called his family and invited them to come and see the project. "The kids were there, playing and dancing in the water. I was standing next to Jaume and he looked at the kids and said, 'It's working.'"

# CHAPTER 7

# The Goals of Implementation

*"A great building must begin with the unmeasurable, must go through measurable means when it is being designed and in the end must be unmeasurable."*

—Louis Kahn

## HOW RESEARCH INFORMS THE POST-OCCUPANCY EVALUATION (POE)

The built environment is a valuable source of information for design research, acting as a living lab for user-experience and design performance. The post-occupancy evaluation as a research initiative is focused on evaluating and measuring the performance of the built environment relative to the design objectives. The research tests and validates the design hypothesis; it is an opportunity for the design firm to learn from the results of the built project, to continue to improve the performance of the project, and to build on the body of knowledge produced throughout the design process.

After construction completion, users are given a period of time to familiarize themselves with their environments. Following the interval, the design team conducts user-perspective research in the form of surveys, focus groups, and interviews. These research tools open the lines of communication with end users and can uncover preventable issues, such as missing technologies or underused spaces or even when the space fails to meet user expectations. The opinions collected in the research allow designers to assess how well the actual design aligns with the client's needs, as well as to identify ways to improve the design and better familiarize users with their environment, validate organizational performance, diagnose and test innovative concepts, and measure and fine-tune energy performance.

The user's stated use is not always in accordance with the building's actual use. As a result, site observations are conducted to monitor and document actual use and establish comparatives with the project's stated design goals. The research clarifies the strengths and weaknesses of the space,

255

allowing the design team to allocate resources where needed. Additionally, the observations provide the design team with an opportunity to determine ways in which stakeholders can use the space more efficiently. The research results enhance the user experience of the existing design, as well as identify where design adjustments are needed.

*E Design just completed the design of a corporate headquarters. The client is interested in evaluating the effectiveness of their investment, as they hope to capitalize on the research accumulated over the course of the design process to inform future corporate campus projects. The client commissions E Design to perform a post-occupancy evaluation.*

*Six months after the client moved into their new home, E Design distributes a web survey to all of the building's users. The survey evaluates the user's satisfaction with the design, performance, technologies, and brand strategies. The results of the web survey are evaluated in relation to the participants' role, years with the organization, perceived satisfaction with the work-setting type and location on campus. The research pinpoints the strengths and weaknesses of particular design elements for different user types across the organization.*

*Next, the design team selects a sample population, reflective of the make-up of the firm, to participate in interviews. The open-ended format of the interviews allows for broader, unrestricted perspectives that are not limited to multiple-choice question and answers.*

Physical documentation, including electric bills, water usage, and human resource reports, provide ample data for the design team to analyze and assess the building's systems. The technical information allows designers to track performance results over a period of time, ensuring that client's operational needs are met, the building systems are performing efficiently, and the building's operators are properly trained.

*E Design hopes to research the performance of several design strategies implemented to decrease the building's environmental footprint. Upon move-in, the building's users are trained in the features of the building. The design team observes the user experiences of the new systems and uses the building's advanced energy monitoring systems to evaluate the strengths and weaknesses of the systems and training program. Six months following move-in, the design team compares the building's monthly electric and water bills with the firm's previous home and other similarly sized corporate campuses. The research results in an accurate picture of the usability and performance of the building's systems and the building construction that impacts these factors.*

The post-occupancy evaluation assesses the body of knowledge produced throughout the design process, testing design hypotheses as a means to inform future projects. The value of conducting a post-occupancy evaluation is seen in the monetary costs savings brought about by incorporating lessons learned and continuous improvements in the development, delivery, and occupancy of projects. Improved design performance resulting from thorough evaluations encourages ongoing and trusting relationships with clients, as both groups commit to progressively smarter design solutions.

## POST-OCCUPANCY EVALUATIONS

Post-occupancy evaluation is:

| Little known | 1 | 2 | 3 | 4 | 5 | Lot known |
|---|---|---|---|---|---|---|
| Quick | 1 | 2 | 3 | 4 | 5 | Not quick |
| Info straightforward | 1 | 2 | 3 | 4 | 5 | Info complex |
| Verbal | 1 | 2 | 3 | 4 | 5 | Numeric |
| How | 1 | 2 | 3 | 4 | 5 | Why |
| On-site | 1 | 2 | 3 | 4 | 5 | Off-site OK |
| Well-established | 1 | 2 | 3 | 4 | 5 | Innovative |
| Current | 1 | 2 | 3 | 4 | 5 | Future |
| Special | 1 | 2 | 3 | 4 | 5 | No special |
| Generally considered | 1 | 2 | 3 | 4 | 5 | Potentially considered |

[Score indicated by **bold**ing of number.]

*Post-occupancy evaluations* (POEs) are designed to provide evaluations and feedback on the project's performance from a variety of viewpoints. Often, the evaluations are conducted by the design team for internal benchmarking information with which other projects can be compared, or as a means to measure project success and improving the effectiveness of the design solution. A well-planned POE will collect useful information about the ramifications of design decisions and generate insights for use on future projects. A POE is a lot like an experiment—and, as a first step, deciding what can and should be measured is critical to success. To get the most out of a POE, it should be planned from the start of the project to establish the full and accurate evaluation of all of the ways the conditions changed between the two data collection periods.

Post-occupancy evaluations have historically been most likely to be prepared for workplaces, healthcare facilities, and schools, but there are POEs of multifamily living communities and other place-types. Individual homes are not generally studied with POEs. Retailers, however, carefully analyze the financial performance of different stores/restaurants and have been privately conducting their own post-mortems of their design projects since there have been stores and restaurants in operation.

To assess how the human experience of a space is impacted by a the design of a space, it is necessary to collect information before and after changes are made using exactly the same data collection tools (surveys, observations plans, etc.) in exactly the same ways (same set of people are asked to answer questions, same types of places observed, etc.), so that information collected before and after changes were made to a place can be compared (see Figure C.12 in the color insert). The tools used also need to be exactly the same so any apparent changes found can be attributed to the changes in the physical environment and not the tool. If the questions asked on the pre- and post-surveys are different and the environment has been changed, it is always possible that any variations seen in the data are attributable to changes in the survey and not to changes in the physical environment itself, for example.

POEs are a measure of space performance, and the more aspects of performance that can be investigated, the more useful it is as future spaces are being designed. Any of the research methods discussed in this book can be integrated into a post-occupancy analysis. When quantitative tools are utilized, such as surveys, the statistical software you are using can let you know if there are significant differences in the data, from pre- to post-redesign phase. If more qualitative methods are being used, such as discussion groups, the comparisons of pre- and post-redesign data will not be as numerically precise, unless data collected have been content analyzed and statistically assessed, but can still be confidently discussed.

A POE can be used exclusively by members of your research team or it can be shared with your client. If certain research tools are used—for example, surveys and interviews—it will be difficult to keep the findings private. Clients benefit from access to the information that used their employees' time to collect. Therefore, if your client will have access to POE findings; it is best to be prepared to discuss both the positive and negative findings. When scores on performance criteria decrease, it is always possible that the wrong design decisions were made, but changes in competitive conditions or other situations completely separate from the design of a space may also be responsible for differences found.

## Keys to Effective POE

There are two keys to an effective POE—you must measure the right things at the right time. The right times are a lot more straightforward to discuss—they are before users' experiences of their existing location have been distorted by the process of planning for a new facility and at least six months after the new facility goes into use. Studying users in a new space sooner than six months after a move in will not capture information about what the new space is really like—it will gather responses to relatively short-term issues—such as confusion about the location of the copying machines/printers or temporary (hopefully) problems such as the venting of cooking smells from the kitchen.

Deciding what to measure is much more challenging. The sorts of research questions that you will want to explore via a post-occupancy evaluation will be related to specifics of the design of that particular space, as well as general information about that sort of place in use. For a workplace, the criteria of interest are not only related to performing high-value jobs (ability to find a space that is visually and auditorily isolated to meet with teammates, concentrate on work tasks, speak spontaneously and briefly with other members of the work team, etc.), but also more generalized information about the experience of being at work, such as support for national and organizational cultures and the influence of environmental factors (e.g., glare) on work life.

What to measure should flow easily from the reason that a change is being/was made to the environment. If you are redesigning a workspace to make the people who work there more productive, how is productivity measured before any changes are made to the environment? It can (and should) be assessed using the same tools before and after the physical changes are made. Similarly, if the goal is to increase collaboration in a workspace, how has it been determined that collaboration needs to be improved? How is it measured now?

The goal of the POE for both the client and design team is to achieve feedback to measure and ultimately improve the effectiveness of the design delivery process and the management of the operations of the facilities.

## Nonverbal Messages

One of the most significant things that any space does is communicate nonverbally to the people in it. These nonverbal messages influence satisfaction with the environment, the job, and intent to remain in that job, for example. Therefore, measuring changes in the nonverbal messages sent before and after an environment is redesigned is important. Probing this topic with the same projective, image-based interview questions both before and after a space is modified will uncover the messages a space is sending. (See Chapter 5 for additional details about these techniques.)

Nonverbal messages are uncovered using uncommon research techniques. Often, determining what to measure requires deep thinking, as well. For example, in a famous healthcare study completed by Roger Ulrich, consumption of pain medicine in hospital rooms with two different views was compared.[1] In healthcare facilities, another common measure is how long patients in different sorts of rooms need to remain in the hospital. Studies in workplaces can avoid self-reports of time in the office (which can be biased) by determining if the company cafeteria is selling more of fewer lunches—if the quality/prices/and so on of those lunches has remained the same. For some redesigns, it might be more desirable to have more people in the office, and in other situations the reverse would be true. At a multifamily housing project, amount of vandalism can be used, in part, to determine satisfaction, with less vandalism tied to higher levels of satisfaction.

## Finding and Using Tools

Many of the general criteria you will want to measure before and after a change have been extensively studied in the past, and a little research on the Internet can turn up the most widely respected ways to measure these concepts—from job satisfaction to organizational commitment to perceived "restorativeness" of an environment (how psychologically restorative it is to be there). You can identify the respected tools in a field by doing an Internet search on the criteria you wish to measure, along with the word "test" or "measure," and reviewing the tools that turn up. Search to find the writers of the tool.

Finding a tool in a peer-reviewed journal or using tools developed by academics or professional researchers, particularly those with doctorates who hold teaching appointments at well-respected universities is a credible way to access relevant tools. This does not mean that these are the only people who can write good survey tools; it does mean that if people have these credentials, you can be more confident in the tool.

If using tools developed by others, the original authors should be acknowledged any time readers might assume that you have written the tool. You might need citations referencing the original author in project reports, for example. . In instances where the authorship is unclear, consulting with a lawyer in the local area is recommended, as rules could vary between jurisdictions.

Written surveys are the most common tools used in a POE, but there are other ways to assess how changes in a physical environment influence the experience of being in that space, some of which have been mentioned in earlier paragraphs of this section. You can observe shoppers in a store before and after it is modified, or interview them. You can use the same sorts of projective techniques and card sorts before and after a redesign. The important issue is pairing the data collection tool with the data collection objective. Since POEs have historically been used in environments such as workplaces where the desire is to collect as much information as possible from as many users as possible, even if that means that the data collected are not very nuanced or rich, written surveys have come to be associated with POEs.

Written surveys are also often the most cost-efficient way to collect data, particularly if the same survey can be used to gather information for several projects.

Using the same data-collection tools from one POE project to the next has advantages besides just saving money. If you can reuse a tool, you can start to build a database of information about people's responses to design changes that can inform future design decisions. Workplace designers are very concerned about changes in organizational culture or job satisfaction, for example, and your database can help reveal how these are affected when aspects of the physical environment are modified. Only information from similar projects should be included in the same analysis, however, since any changes seen must be attributed to all aspects of the environment that were changed. A workplace where people are moved from private offices to cubicles is very different from one in which they were moved to cubicles, large new windows to the exterior were built into the walls of the building, the color scheme was changed dramatically, sound masking was introduced, and more. If the sets of changes are too different, it is hard to anticipate differences that might be seen in future projects. Any patterns that can be found between legitimately similar events can be very useful when future design decisions are being made.

Since it can be a years between the first data collection and the final one, it is important to maintain an accurate record of other changes that space users would have experienced between the two data-collection periods. For example, if low-income multifamily housing has been built, have there been any changes in the way that public assistance is distributed between data collection periods? In an office design project, has there been a significant percent (say, more than 5 percent) change in the size of the workforce—either through adding new employees or laying off existing ones? Has the government started or stopped reimbursing patients undergoing a certain medical procedure, so that the size of the population of patients being treated in a particular health-care facility has changed dramatically?

## Example of Post-Occupancy Evaluation

Paco Underhill and his team at Envirosell have written easy-to-read but rigorous POEs of retail spaces—although they don't refer to their work using this term. Envirosell employees observe, for example, consumers' responses to a particular environmental condition, suggest a modification to their client, and return at a later date to determine shopper behavior after the change. *Why We Buy* by Underhill is full of specific examples of their work.[2] An excellent post-occupancy evaluation of an architectural office was conducted by Shepley and her colleagues.[3]

# CASE STUDIES

Case studies are:

| | | | | | | |
|---|---|---|---|---|---|---|
| Little known | 1 | 2 | 3 | 4 | 5 | Lot known |
| Quick | 1 | 2 | 3 | 4 | 5 | Not quick |
| Info straightforward | 1 | 2 | 3 | 4 | 5 | Info complex |
| Verbal | 1 | 2 | 3 | 4 | 5 | Numeric |
| How | 1 | 2 | 3 | 4 | 5 | Why |
| On-site | 1 | 2 | 3 | 4 | 5 | Off-site OK |
| Well-established | 1 | 2 | 3 | 4 | 5 | Innovative |
| Current | 1 | 2 | 3 | 4 | 5 | Future |
| Special | 1 | 2 | 3 | 4 | 5 | No special |
| Generally considered | 1 | 2 | 3 | 4 | 5 | Potentially considered |

[Score indicated by **bold**ing of number.]

Particular projects are distinctive in particular ways. Case study write-ups can capture those differences in content and process and preserve them for future reference. They can be postproject reports and as such become part of the knowledge base of the firm. The American Institute of Architects has developed a case study framework that you can consider as you outline the material that you will include in your report.[4] Each case study will be different, however, stressing the most important, interesting, and informative elements of a completed project—however you and your firm chose to define those terms.

A standardized online data-collection tool can streamline the process of developing a case study and make it more likely that needed information will be gathered in a timely manner (see Figure 7.1). People using the data-collection tool need the discretion to add additional information not requested by the tool, as needed, and to ignore sections that are not relevant to a particular project.

Case studies link current projects to prior knowledge and facilitate the development of future knowledge. Case studies are important reference tools, reporting information that can be useful in future projects—and projects can differ in ways that can't be anticipated when a standard format is adopted. In *Case Studies: The Study and Practice of Architecture, Development Checklist and Submission Guidelines*, the AIA outlines the sort of information that should be considered for inclusion in any case study.[5] Readers are referred to this document for a complete list of topics to include; only a representative sampling is presented here. The major topic areas, with a sample of the specific issues that AIA suggests may be relevant for a case study, follow:

**FIGURE 7.1**
Case studies can be customized on a project-by-project basis to collect information particularly pertinent to a project, such as use of wayfinding aids. *Photo: Augustin*

**"Project Abstract"**

    Significant identifying feature

    Important lesson learned

**"Project Perspectives"**

"Protocols: Web of Decision-Making"

    Important roles

    Decision chain

"Constituencies: Client Voice"

    Client aspirations (prioritized)

Constituencies involved (e.g., users, owners, neighbors, investors)

"Stories: Episodes of Practice"

    Case concepts

    Case personality

Anecdotal lessons

"Ideas: Innovation in Architecture Practice"

Innovations in service in technology

Innovation discouraged

"Measures: Individual, Practice, and Client Measures of Success"

Client's/users' measures of success

Firm's measures of success

Ethical issues

**"Project Analysis"**

"The Client"

Client's reasons for taking action (hiring architect)

Client strategies for project

Client values

Climate of working relationship

"Business"

Firm "vision, mission, goals, objectives, strategies, tactics"

Firm expertise and strategic alliances

Human resource strategies related response to project

"Design"

Drawings/photos linking aspirations to forms

Graphic analysis diagrams

"Delivery"

Project delivery methods

Agreements with clients

Risk management issues

Quality assurance strategies

Project management strategies

"Services"

Predesign services necessary

Design, construction, and project implementation services

Postconstruction operation and maintenance services

Allied and related professionals with important roles

"Resources"

Important organizations (e.g., could include community groups)

Particular special resources—material and human

Past experiences important

The AIA also suggests that people writing case studies consider including images, drawings, and photographs. These might be drawings that represent the project, photos that are important, and digital models.

It's a waste to write up case studies and not make them useful to people working on future projects. They should be organized using the principles in the knowledge management section of this book (Chapter 6).

Your firm may already do, for its own benefit, analyses of completed projects. Those analyses may already be case studies, in everything but name. The written format of a case study is not so important—participant narratives, prose, annotated presentation slides, or other methods. What is important is that information is preserved in a form that can be understood by others, even if the original team members are not available for discussion. It is useful if the standard section heads identified by the AIA (as modified by your firm to make them most useful) are included in whatever format you choose, so that future users can use standardized search terms to access information quickly.

The case study can include research done by others and can be collected in the course of the project being reported, as well as research done specifically for the case study. Since resources for writing case studies are often tight, as they are difficult to bill to clients, little case study–specific information will probably be collected. If it can be done, any of the research tools discussed in this text can be used.

A case study is different from a post-occupancy evaluation because it is not as technically rigorous.. A case study will inevitably contain some information gathered before an environment is created, because that information will have been used to guide the design process. In a POE study, the same tool must be used in the same way (e.g., same survey with exactly the same questions) before and after an environment is redesigned, while in a case study, this rigor may be relaxed (e.g., surveys may be distributed before and after an environment is modified, but the questions on the two surveys may not be exactly the same). Changes in the tools themselves or how they were used make drawing conclusions difficult—any differences in experience might be attributable to the environmental modifications or to the changes in the tools.

A case study is generally a report of events, and those events take place in the real world. The real world is messy, which complicates the process of drawing conclusions from case studies.

The people directly involved in research, client contact, and design decision making for a project should write the project case study—and one person or a very small group of people might serve in all three of these roles. These people need to make a conscious effort to share the subtle but important bits of information that may have become tacit to them—these might be the most valuable components of the study for people later doing comparable projects.

If time allows after the conclusion of a project, it can be really useful to determine why conclusions derived in different case studies are consistent or inconsistent.

Benchmarking is in many ways like developing a series of mini–case studies. It is described in detail in a side bar in the introduction to this book. Numbers collected for comparison in different circumstances require context in order to be truly useful, and that context can come through the case study format.

If they are available, case studies done by other firms make interesting reading. They can broaden your knowledge of important issues. Case studies are available, for example, at the AIA website and may be accessible through government websites, as well.

## Example of Case Study

For detailed examples of completed case studies, review the examples provided at the American Institute of Architects' website (www.aia.org).

## ENDNOTES

1. Roger Ulrich, "View though a Window May Influence Recovery from Surgery." *Science*, vol. 224 (1984), 420–421.

2. Paco Underhill, *Why We Buy*: *The Science of Shopping* (New York: Simon and Schuster, 2000).

3. Mardelle Shepley, Kelly Zimmerman, Mary Boggess, and You Lee, "Architectural Office Post-Occupancy Evaluation," *Journal of Interior Design*, vol. 34, no. 3 (2009), pp. 17–29.

4. The American Institute of Architects, Case Studies in the Study and Practice of Architecture: Development Checklist and Submission Guidelines (Washington, DC: The American Institute of Architects, 2001). Available at www.calpoly.edu/~sede/pdf/AIAcasestudy.pdf.

5. Ibid.

# A Story of Practice: Post-Occupancy Evaluation

Information contributed by: Keelan Kaiser, Chair Department of Architecture, Judson University, Elgin, Illinois

**Contributors:**
Project: Harm A. Weber Academic Center

Location: Judson University, Elgin, Illinois

Design Architects: Short and Associates Architecture of Record: Burnidge Cassell Associates (PSA-Dewberry/BCA as of March 2009)

Prepared by: Keelan Kaiser, AIA, NCARB, LEED, Chair, Department of Architecture, Judson University

David M. Ogoli, Ph.D., Judson University

Malcolm Cook, Ph.D., Loughborough University, Leicestershire, United Kingdom

## CONTEXT

One important form of architecture and design research is the post-occupancy evaluation (POE). The POE seeks to evaluate building performance and is typically developed based on at least two approaches: building energy performance and resource management, and perceptions of user comfort and satisfaction. The quantitative and qualitative approaches necessary to document these two areas of evaluation require different sets of expertise. The energy performance, measurement, and calculations fall in the quantitative arena of building forensics and research. The user-related evaluation falls more in the arena of the behavioral sciences research. The former requires the collection of utility consumption and building automated systems information, tracked longitudinally over time—usually several years to account for weather variations. The latter requires user survey instruments and careful assessment of findings so that accurate conclusions can be developed.

The POE is a difficult process for funding because it is a service that falls outside the conventional contractual arrangements of client and architect. The POE has merit in communicating value to future clients, based on demonstrated performance in previous ones. However, POE studies are typically funded within the academy, with some of the most notable contemporary work explored by the University of California–Berkeley in the United States and the Usable Building Trust in the United Kingdom. Because of numerous recent accounts of poor-performing LEED certified buildings in the United States, POE is effective as a means of testing actual building performance against design-case energy-model predictions. Because energy models are notoriously inaccurate, verification is practically a requirement so that users might know with certainty how their facility is performing. This might mark an alternative form of community outreach by collegiate architecture and design programs.

## ABSTRACT

The Weber Center at Judson University is a mixed mode, naturally ventilated building in a continental climate (cold winters, hot summers), with initial occupancy in August 2007. The following post-occupancy evaluation compares the design objectives and building performance expectations against the first year of actual energy consumption. The POE contrasts the building performance with general user satisfaction and perceptions of comfort through the use of user surveys and interviews. The innovations involved in this building, particularly mechanical strategies atypical in contemporary practice within this climate and region, have introduced some interesting problems that have been documented in the post-occupancy evaluation process, while confirming many of the original intentions of the design.

## INTRODUCTION

The Weber Center, designed by Short and Associates (design architect) and Burnidge Cassell Associates (record architect), is a first of its kind in the continental climate region of Chicago, Illinois (see Figure 7.2). The result of a winning entry in a 2001 invited-design competition for a new School of Art, Design and Architecture combined with a central library, the four-story building occupies approximately 88,000 gross square feet on the Judson University campus in Elgin, Illinois. Construction commenced in 2005 and was completed in July 2007 with final commissioning and occupancy in August 2007.

## VENTILATION AND ENERGY STRATEGIES

The facility employs a hybrid natural ventilation strategy that reduces heating and cooling loads during swing months of the spring and fall, and uses night flushing accompanying a high thermal mass of precast concrete. Other passive strategies, including modest passive solar and shading, in conjunction with significant daylighting, reduces loads on heating, cooling, and lighting. An extensive landscape architecture complements the new facility with on-site stormwater management and native prairie and habitat restoration.

**FIGURE 7.2**
The Weber Center is a mixed mode and naturally ventilated building at Judson University. The authors compare the design objectives and the building performance as part of a post-occupancy evaluation (POE). *Photo: Authors*

Fifty percent of the carbon emissions generated by electricity usage of the building is offset through a local renewable energy certificate agreement (see Figure 7.3). Preconstruction modeling was conducted early in the design stages and included computational fluid dynamics modeling (De Mont University Institute of Energy and Sustainable Development), as well as experimental and theoretical modeling of key aspects of the building integrated photovoltaic and natural ventilation in the south façade (BP Institute for Multiphase Flow University of Cambridge). The preliminary modeling provided the basis for design decision making by the record architects and particularly their consulting mechanical engineers, KJWW.

Because the facility houses a professional architecture school and a central library, it provides a remarkable learning context that positions sustainable building as a core architectural education priority.

A proposed energy savings of 42 to 47 percent over a conventional academic building was presented by Short and Associates during the competition
selection process in 2001 and was considered one of the most promising values
to the institution. The competition jury, composed of a cross-section of users,
administrators, and trustees of the university, perceived that these savings
were valuable not only economically but also philosophically as an institution.
Ultimately, the prospect of the institution building an architecture school that
would be "one of a kind" because of its environmental approach was the kind
of distinction the jury responded to and ultimately why the Short and Associates scheme was selected.

The process of design and construction was not without its challenges.
Neither the record architect nor the construction manager/general contract-
ing firm had built a high-performance building to date, and neither had any
previous experience working with a naturally ventilated building. The entire
design team was required to collaborate through what was a steep learning
curve. During the fundraising stage between 2001 and 2003, the design team
pursued many design iterations in order to align the specific programmatic

requirements with the energy scheming. Certain programs were in conflict with the energy scheming. One example is the humidity caused by naturally ventilated air and the need to protect library books from high humidity.

Ultimately, a precast concrete structure that was exposed to the interior and insulated and sealed on the exterior was developed (see Figures 7.4 and 7.5).

The building employs two primary types of natural ventilation circuits. The central library/architecture studio block employs an edge in/center out type (see Figure 7.6). The academic wing employs an edge in/edge out type.[1] The two types function independently of one another in the complicated mixed program of open library and cellular academic functions.

**FIGURE 7.4**
A precast concrete structure that is exposed to the interior and insulated and sealed on the exterior was developed. *Photo: Authors*

**FIGURE 7.5**
Image of the precast concrete structure with return air stacks during rough framing of the building. *Photo: Authors*

**FIGURE 7.6**
Image of the precast
concrete structure with
supply and return air
ducts. *Photo: Authors*

Fresh air is drawn into the building through the ceiling plenum at the
ground level (see Figure 7.7). Intake filters, screens, and automated dampers control the intake air at this area of the building envelope. Hot water unit
heaters occupy the ground-level plenum space for tempering of air during
the swing seasons, when outdoor temperatures are between 42 to 60 degrees
Fahrenheit. Air is then supplied through the four-story structure through a
glazed central atrium (see Figure 7.8).

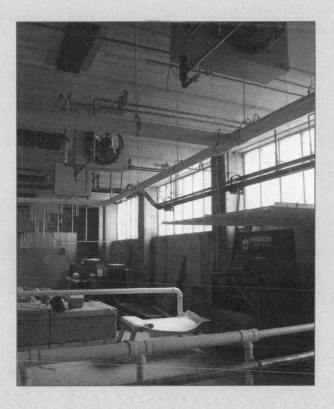

FIGURE 7.7
External fresh-air intake supplies the lower-level insulated ceiling plenum. *Photo: Authors*

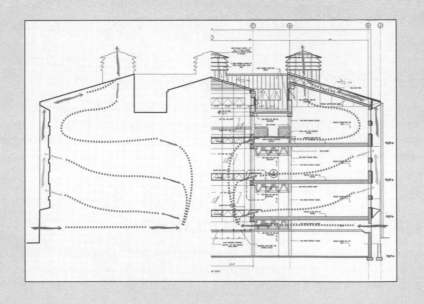

FIGURE 7.8
Airflow diagram through intake supply, central atrium, individual floor plates, and roof exhaust at library/architectural studios.

Originally created by Burnidge Cassell Associates but modified for graphic purposes by the authors.

The stack elements that pull the ventilation throughout the building are applied to the exterior of the precast structure in most situations and exhaust air above the roof in three multidirectional termini types (see Figure 7.9).

## ENERGY PERFORMANCE YEAR ONE

One component of this evaluation is the overall energy performance over a 12-month period between February 2008 and January 2009. This date range provides the most accurate and complete 12-month data set available during the first 18 months of operation. The data were drawn from the building management system and compared against utility bills for accuracy.

## ENERGY COST BUDGET PREDICTIONS

The mechanical engineers prepared energy cost budgets for the building, comparing a base case against the design case. The software used to calculate the energy cost budget was Trace 700 v6.1.1. These budgets estimated a conventional ASHRAE 90.1 total annual base case energy consumption of 7423.3 MBtu, including 5621.0 MBtu in electricity and 1802.3 MBtu in gas. The design case energy consumption total was estimated at 6061.7 MBtu, with 5026.4 MBtu in electricity and 1035.3 MBtu in gas. The anticipated electricity savings were modeled at 10.6 percent, while gas savings were modeled at 42.6 percent for a total predicted energy savings of 18.3 percent over the base code (see Table 7.1).

| | ASHRAE Base Case Energy (MMBtu) | HWAC Design Case Energy (MMBtu) | % Difference from Base Case |
|---|---|---|---|
| Electricity | 5621.0 | 5026.4 | 10.6% |
| Gas | 1802.3 | 1035.3 | 42.6% |
| Total | 7423.3 | 6061.7 | 18.3% |

**TABLE 7.1**
Annual Energy Use Budget: Base Case versus Design Case, % Difference

The predicted gas savings were comparable to the original design goals of the Short and Associates scheme (42–47% savings in the earliest design modeling in 2001).[2] The electricity savings were not as easy to achieve in the design case model. There were three specific barriers, according to the mechanical engineers:

1. Programmatic flexibility in the spaces required increased density of plugs and fixtures.

2. Most of the automatic lighting was value engineered out of the project due to budget constraints and predictions that manually operated fixtures by aware users might yield better performance.

3. Some of the savings originally anticipated by reduced fan use were not realized. As a result, the design case anticipated a modest 18.3 percent savings.

## 1.2 HWAC ACTUAL ENERGY USE

Collecting data from the building management system during the months of December 2008 through December 2009, an estimated total energy consumption of 6203.7 MBtu was tracked during the 12-month period of February 2008 through January 2009 indicating a reasonably accurate energy use prediction during the first year. The actual usage differs from the predicted usage by approximately 2.3 percent. Compared to the base case energy model, HWAC operated with a 16.4 percent energy reduction (see Table 7.2).

**TABLE 7.2**
Annual Energy Use Comparison: Base Case versus Actual Use, % Actual Energy Difference

|  | ASHRAE Base Case Energy (MMBtu) | HWAC Design Case Energy (MMBtu) | % Difference from Base Case |
|---|---|---|---|
| Electricity | 5621.0 | 3324.7 | 40.9% |
| Gas | 1802.3 | 2879.1 | 159.7% |
| Total | 7423.3 | 6203.7 | 16.4% |

The building performance in electricity is quite good, while there appears to be a chronic issue in gas consumption.

Comparing the actual energy use with the design case shows an understandably narrower margin of energy reduction in electricity use, and further spike in gas use. This resulted in a 2.3 percent increase in overall energy use (see Table 7.3).

**TABLE 7.3**
Annual Energy Use Comparison: Design Case versus Actual Use, % Actual Energy Difference

|  | ASHRAE Base Case Energy (MMBtu) | HWAC Design Case Energy (MMBtu) | % Difference from Base Case |
|---|---|---|---|
| Electricity | 5026.4 | 3324.7 | 33.9% |
| Gas | 1035.3 | 2879.1 | 278.1% |
| Total | 6061.7 | 6203.7 | 102.3% |

Although the total energy use amount seems good at first glance, it should be noted that the design case energy predictions were far below the 2001 estimates of 42 to 47 percent overall energy savings. The revelation of actual gas use against the modeled predictions has prompted diagnosis of the problem by the mechanical and commissioning engineers. Some preliminary considerations include leaky dampers or building envelope, damper operating errors, boilers not running as efficiently as design, the system waiting too long to switch from natural to mechanical mode, and the possibility of poor energy modeling due to the uniqueness of the building. More work fine-tuning the system is underway as a result of this POE.

## THE IMPORTANT ROLE OF THERMAL MASS

One performance factor central to the operation of this facility is the presence of a significant amount of internally exposed precast concrete for use as thermal mass. In a mixed-mode building of this kind, this is an important mechanism for maximizing the period of natural ventilation to reduce the cooling load. This is accomplished by a combination of exposed thermal mass, night flushing, and mechanized supply and exhaust damper. Although it remains unclear the degree of energy savings due to night flushing for passive tempering of supply air, it is clear that the system is moving air through the building as intended.

The following overviews of temperature measurements and comparisons over three typical seasons and periods of time demonstrate the stabilizing power of thermal mass in passively affecting the heating and cooling loads of the HWAC.

During summer months, the continental climatic conditions require air conditioning to control the temperature and moisture of the incoming air (see Figure 7.10). During these periods, the air temperature inside the HWAC is controlled to within the range of approximately 72 to 76 degrees Fahrenheit.

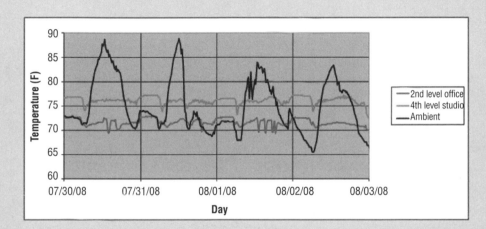

**FIGURE 7.10**
During the summer months, the climatic conditions require air conditioning to control the temperature and moisture of the incoming air.

During the swing months of spring and fall, where little or no air conditioning is used for the majority of operating hours, the combined temperature of the air entering the space as well as temperature of the surrounding thermal mass determines the temperature inside the building (see Figure 7.11).

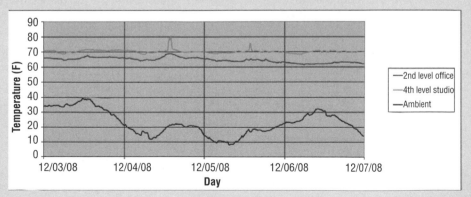

**FIGURE 7.11**
The winter months engage the mechanical system more fully, and analysis indicates a conventional comparison of internal and external temperatures.

The winter months engage the mechanical system more fully, representing a more conventional comparison of internal and external temperatures. The role of the thermal mass is neutralized as air temperatures are stabilized due to constant mechanical treatment of air.

Internal air temperature lags behind the ambient temperature due to the thermal mass of the building, thus providing passive cooling during the early hours of the following day and reducing the need for air conditioning. Note that the temperature perceived by the occupants (the operative temperature) could be lower than the (air) temperatures if the surrounding surfaces are cooler than the incoming air temperature. This is likely to be the case following successful night ventilation.

Substantial work remains to efficiently manage the building systems to realize both energy savings and to ensure adequate user comfort. The original design set points of 70 to 77 degrees Fahrenheit were reduced and narrowed to 69 to 74 degrees Fahrenheit due to user comfort concerns. Periodic user complaints about warmth, humidity, and/or airflow rates during the summer illuminate the need for further refinements in operations.

## ENERGY USE CONCLUSIONS

The energy use by the HWAC facility during the first year of operation was approximately 70.5 KBtu per gross square feet per year and approximately 17.7 MBtu per person per year, based on an average occupancy of 350 users. Although both estimates are of limited value because of the complexity of the programmatic uses and hours of operation, they do provide initial benchmarks for usage rates for future comparisons.

Future energy use calculations will focus on comparative studies of similar building type and scope (e.g., De Montfort University Queens building et al.) as well as more detailed studies of building performance, particularly in the swing months where HWAC is expected to deliver its most notable performance of minimizing mechanical cooling needs and the summer where night flushing promises some performance benefit.

## USER PERCEPTIONS

The second component of the study draws from user awareness of energy conservation measures in the HWAC and user perceptions of comfort. Questions related to comfort were administered through a survey. The survey was collaboratively generated with a colleague in social sciences and sought to capture base perceptions broadly defined as awareness, comfort, behavior, and assessment. Each question used a different scale, ranging from three to five points, distributed via e-mail through an interactive digital form (see Table 7.4). The completed surveys were e-mailed to the authors for tabulation.

| Scale | Comfort | Vote |
|:---:|---|---|
| +2 | Very satisfied | |
| +1 | Satisfied | |
| 0 | Neutral | |
| −1 | Slightly uncomfortable | |
| −2 | Very uncomfortable | |

**TABLE 7.4**
Sample Voting Graphic,
Five-Point Scale

To establish an understanding of the degree to which building users are aware of their environment, we shaped questions that measure awareness of energy conservation concepts as they relate to the built environment. We assumed that a range of awareness would result based on the user knowledge, level of education, or staff role. Questions probed knowledge of energy consumption in buildings and carbon emissions, conservation goals of the building, technologies employed within the building, actual energy savings, and their own behavior. From these responses, we expected to gain a better understanding of the building users, their awareness of energy conservation as a broad subject, and their specific concern for this particular building performing well.

These questions were followed by inquiries regarding building systems awareness. They included inquiries regarding knowledge of the unique mechanical system at work in the building, whether or not they were aware of the building making automatic adjustments (e.g., audibly noticing dampers opening and closing), and a perception of whether the system was operating properly in their area of survey (see Table 7.5).

| Very Aware | Aware | Unaware |
|---|---|---|
| 42.4% | 35.3% | 22.3% |

**TABLE 7.5**
Sample Voting Graphic,
Five-Point Scale

One area of intense user awareness is that the building is changing throughout the day. Actuators open and close dampers, airflow rates change periodically, and lights turn on when entering offices. On the one hand, 65.2 percent of respondents reported being "very aware" of mechanical systems changes throughout the day. On the other hand, the same percentage of respondents was unaware of actual energy savings for HWAC to date—a nod to the need for more attention to informing users of building performance.

## USER COMFORT

User comfort is more ambiguous and requires further investigation. Anecdotal information suggests general satisfaction with the building thus far in its operation, with some notable exceptions. Temperature regulation seems difficult in many spaces; set points are spread wide, resulting in spaces not maintaining steady temperatures from day to day. Airflow regulation in specific areas, like the main classrooms, is disruptive at times, due to changes in airflow or slight howling in the ducts as air moves through. The most vexing problem to date, however, is the acoustic issue that plagues the new building. The exposed precast concrete thermal mass has its consequences—a very acoustically live building.

However, building users are very satisfied with perceptions of comfort, health, and wellness related to daylighting: 56.5 percent of respondents noted that they were either satisfied or very satisfied with daylighting in their spaces.

Although many of the noted items can be adjusted, some require significant adaptations. Still, for this initial survey at least, user comfort as a whole seems moderately good (see Table 7.6).

**TABLE 7.65**
**Overall Comfort Using HWAC**

| Very Satisfied | Satisfied | Neutral | Slightly Uncomfortable | Uncomfortable |
|---|---|---|---|---|
| 19.9% | 34.8% | 16.1% | 21.1% | 8.1% |

## User Behavior

The survey also attempted to measure the degree to which the building users changed their behavior as a result of working within the HWAC. Early in the design of the facility, numerous conversations with the designers touched on user comfort and user ranges of comfort. Because of the nature of uses involved in the building—a library and academic classrooms, studios, and offices—a calculated risk was taken to begin operations with a wide range of set points, beyond the conventional ASHRAE requirements. Unfortunately, the outdoor temperature and humidity levels in August 2007 at initial occupancy were brutal, users were not comfortable, and set points were tightened, as noted previously. As the building has continued in operation from those early adjustments, the authors of this evaluation attempted to measure user adaptation to the unique demands of the building. The evaluation looked at whether users were layering clothing more than previously to modulate their own comfort. It also looked at whether users were more tolerant of the wider temperature set points because of being aware of the potential energy savings benefits. In this evaluation, it was discovered that the building changed the general behavior of about half the users (see Table 7.7).

**TABLE 7.5**
**Sample Voting Graphic, Five-Point Scale**

| Yes | No | N/A |
|---|---|---|
| 47.8% | 42.4% | 9.8% |

With more investigations into this subject planned for the future, the authors plan to investigate the users modulating their spaces with small space heaters in the winter and desktop fans in the summer, understanding that these are barriers to energy performance and would not be necessary if discrete cellular spaces were performing optimally for user comfort.

## Assessment and Values

The final question set in the survey addressed the degree to which users appreciated a connection between their health and wellness and the built environment of HWAC. Questions probed user perceptions of relationships between health and wellness regarding fresh air, daylighting, energy efficiency, and knowledge of the technologies deployed. We found that survey respondents did make a soft connection between their own perceptions of health and wellness and the features of HWAC.

| Very High | High | Neutral | Low | Very Low |
|-----------|------|---------|-----|----------|
| 8% | 32.2% | 35.7% | 11.3% | 13.0% |

TABLE 7.8
Value Health and Welfare
Aspects of HWAC

From a perspective of tracking values of users, one can see that though increased air changes and daylighting, both increase health and wellness as a general principle, the respondents were soft in linking them together in this case. For example, only 34.8 percent of the users perceived that their health and wellness was highly improved because of the natural ventilation and 39.1 percent of the users perceived that their health and wellness was highly improved because of the daylighting in the building. The mean scores are just slightly above neutral. It remains unclear whether these rankings reflect a lack of education on health and wellness issues or the building is not explicit in its value-added role.

## CONCLUSION

It is clear that the first 18 months of operation of the HWAC facility have yielded mixed results. One immediate value of this study was the identification of poor performance in the category of gas consumption. The subsequent trouble shooting of the deviations between the energy model and actual performance are of immediate value to the owner. This is a testimony to the value of measurement and verification exercise taking place post-commissioning when the performance of a building can be studied over time. Without this research study, the excessive gas consumption of the building might have continued for some time without notice.

It is also clear that the daylighting strategies for this have yielded success in terms of energy consumption even though some automated controls were sacrificed during value engineering. A valuable follow-up to this study is the monitoring of the lighting loads or the building isolated from the rest of the electric loads to evaluate how the design case modeling of 1.75KW/s.f. compares to actual usage.

For the future: Additional follow-up studies should track the first one to three years of natural ventilation mode operation. These studies would yield valuable information regarding the cost benefit of including the hybrid natural ventilation system. It remains unclear whether this system is competitive with conventional geothermal, for instance. Since both systems are more or less mutually exclusive (in that they both benefit from energy savings in swing months), geothermal might be a more successful design strategy in the continental climate. More study into the subtleties of the strengths and weaknesses of these and other renewable energy strategies seems warranted before the hybrid natural ventilation model can be called a legitimate approach in this climate.

In addition, what is unclear is whether building user education was underestimated at initial occupancy of the HWAC, and more concentrated work remains to be conducted in this area. Although it is encouraging to observe that building users in general do feel moderately comfortable and have adapted, or not, to the unique nature of this building, energy usage might drop further and user perceptions of comfort might increase with a more robust user education/information program.

## ACKNOWLEDGMENTS

The POE authors thank KJWW engineer Wade Ross for his assistance in evaluating some of the data contained in this evaluation and Dr. Marsha Vaughn, Judson University Department of Social Sciences, for assistance in editing the environmental comfort survey. Finally, the authors commend the work of Judson University graduate students Matt Ackerman and Ken Nadolski in assisting with the preparation of data for this evaluation.

## ENDNOTES

1. K. Lomas, "Architectural Design of an Advanced Naturally Ventilated Building Form," *Energy and Buildings vol.* 39 (2007), pp. 166–181; K. Lomas, M. Cook, and D. Fiala, "Low Energy Architecture for a Severe U.S. Climate: Design and Evaluation of a Hybrid Ventilation Strategy," *Energy and Buildings* 39 (2007): 32–44.

2. C.A. Short and K. Lomas, "Exploiting a Hybrid Environmental Design Strategy in a U.S. Continental Climate." *Building Research & Information* 35(2): 119–143.

# CHAPTER 8

# How to Maintain and Access Research Findings

RESEARCH, KNOWLEDGE, AND INSIGHTS ARE VALUABLE. They enhance the worth of the firm and your own professional reputation—if you respect them and build them a suitable home. A knowledge management system retains and provides access to this source of competitive advantage in our knowledge-based economy. It is also a unique attribute of a particular firm, and the specifics of the information, knowledge, and insights retained distinguish one firm from another. Efficient and effective access to the collective knowledge of a firm has a direct relationship to company income.

On a practical level, knowledge management systems allow several people to move forward on a project simultaneously because they externalize some information from individuals, which is key as teamwork becomes more important in the workplace. When people share information, the costs of having each person separately attempting to answer the same questions are reduced, a consistent approach is taken across all team members, and information that the organization has already paid to collect is reused at no real additional cost to the firm. Time not spent developing the same knowledge required on previous projects is freed up for valued activities, such as developing creative design solutions. Wicked, cyclical problems, which are the usual sort of issues designers need to deal with, are solved using intelligent knowledge management systems.

Throughout this chapter, we'll refer to a library. A *library* is a resource center staffed by people who are experts at accessing thought-enhancing and -provoking resources and sharing them in a useful way with others. You can bring that library metaphor to life at your firm.

Successful libraries are intuitive and effortless to use. People want to visit them because doing so is a rewarding experience. Successful knowledge management systems at design firms are developed by their users, for their users. Just as designers need to do their own research for the client, the designer, and the firm to effectively bring the knowledge gained to design insights, designers must develop their own information systems. When they do, the materials they need and value are captured and maintained in a way that is useful to the only population that *must* dip into it—the firm's design community (see Figure 8.1).

An effective design library not only has raw resources (such as books and material swatches) but also a system that organizes these items (analogous to the Library of Congress system in a public library) and a way to access and review them (such as a check-out or circulation system).

**FIGURE 8.1**
Knowledge management should be customized by each firm to meet its needs, with information organized using search terms that are meaningful to employees. © *iStock-photo.com/sase*

# RAW RESOURCES

Design libraries can be thought of as organizational memories—they live beyond individual projects and even particular employees. The research done and the insights gained in the course of those projects and by those employees need to be preserved.

The material that you and your organization maintain will evolve as you learn about how your organizational culture and individual personality effectively reuses information gathered in the past.

Initially, in addition to records (notes, videos, etc.) of client meetings and visioning sessions, retain items such as the following in electronic format:

- Articles from scholarly publications (On a range of topics, from social science to material science; articles and similar items need to be electronically scanned for inclusion.)

- Articles from professional publications

- Articles from popular/consumer publications

- Radio and television segments (These are generally available from broadcasters' websites; best if section of tape of interest is mentioned in introduction to resource.)

- Expert interviews conducted by the firm (including contact information for the interviewee)

- Insightful reviews of projects done by your firm or other firms (These can be in several forms, including precedent and case studies.)

- Literature reviews conducted by firm employees

- Primary research conducted by firm employees (The data, statistical analyses, and write-up can all be useful later.)

- Thought or white papers written by employees for internal or external distribution, along with any supporting materials

- Documentation of design or other processes of note (e.g., benchmarking, post-occupancy evaluation, client billing)

- Project-related drawings (CAD and otherwise)

- Project-related photographs

- Inspirational, non–project-specific drawings

- Inspirational, non–project-specific photographs

- Project-specific books

- Inspirational, non–project-related books

- Information about materials

- Material samples (Images of materials should be stored electronically but samples themselves need to be retained in physical form. Photographs of all items on file can aid in the quick review of all options.)

- Models built (stored as with material samples)

No list of suggested items will ever be complete if it is done by a firm outsider. What you retain should be consistent with the organizational culture and mission of your firm.

Take the perspective of a topic virgin when deciding which materials to retain. Although as a project ends a detail might not seem useful, that same detail might be of value to someone without your previous exposure to a topic or project in the future—so don't edit it out of the report being archived or throw it away.

As the design process speeds up, it has become virtually impossible for any employee to create materials solely for the purpose of retaining them in a design library. Also, few firms have resources to actually build a library or spend a lot of time cataloging items into it. Use the evolving and user-friendly content management systems or wikis to structure your system. During the life of this book, many will be available, so none is suggested.

Wikis are particularly useful because they have been developed to allow content to be entered by any reader, even readers with no technical background. Any wiki created should be accessible only to firm employees—making it available to others not only decreases its competitive advantage but may also require the editing of particular documents for "nonfirm" eyes. A Google search on "wiki" will provide the information required to implement one of these collaborative software sites.

Employees need a real and significant reward for taking the time to think about the materials that they have access to that might be of interest to others and to post these items where they become available to all. The best rewards are not financial but those that indicate personal respect and are consistent with an organization's culture. To encourage entries into the firm's wiki system, respected company officers should positively refer to specific entries in public forums. To succeed, a design library must record information respected by the firm and participation in the project entry process must be rewarded by firm culture.

Much of the most important knowledge in a firm resides solely in the heads of its employees, either as tacit knowledge or as explicit knowledge that has never been applied in a firm context, so it has not been recorded in a format that can be shared. Tapping into this system electronically can be quite straightforward. A daily e-mail to all employees, with requests for particular sorts of project-relevant knowledge and insights, can collect this information. The mailing must be quick to read and people with material to share must be able to do so in a way that does not distort their workday— a quick phone call to the info seeker is not onerous, but needing to produce a comprehensive report and transmit it is. A system (even hash marks on a tally sheet maintained by the receptionist) that records who has responded to a request for information and provides employee meaningful rewards (such as upgrades to at-home work-stations or paid time off or company-paid museum memberships) encourages participation and indicates firm respect for those contributions. A similar list of outside experts can be maintained if there is money available to pay for their services.

## ORGANIZATIONAL SYSTEM

Save what you have found useful. And save it under several different category headings. Category headings should be terms that you actually use, day-to-day, in your work. A listing of the headings in use should be kept current and available to everyone for reference. The way that you organize the knowledge and insights retained by your firm is what creates the true value for it—a random collection of facts, and so on makes much less of a contribution than a structured system with intuitive, incisive, and clever subject headings.

Multiple headings should be used because the same material can be useful in different situations, which will bring different subject headings to mind. There are often several different kinds of material that can be retrieved from one single item, and different people trying to access the same item will find different elements of it salient for search.

An example is in order. Imagine that an interview has been conducted with a psychologist who is an expert on retail design. The subject headings you use in your "card catalog" to access this information could include:

- Speaker's name

- Speaker's professional affiliation

- Speaker's profession

- Date of interview and interviewees name

- Names of specific built projects mentioned

- Major social science topics discussed (e.g., privacy, social identity, need for uniqueness)

- Major design-related topics discussed (e.g., symmetry, material use, project phase)

- Project-type specific information (e.g., fixturing, wayfinding signage, and dressing room design)

- Other major topics discussed (e.g., biological, chemical, environmentally responsible practice; breakdowns within these categories are also useful)

- Other topics that might be of use later for some random reason (e.g., increasing size of clothes and how that influences display practices, a farmers' market practice that could find its way into other retail channels, a random client related fact that could be useful in a future proposal)

Not all of these sorts of headings will be useful in any particular situation. They are provided to inform the subject heading choices that you make.

Organizing a material library can be straightforward if only physical properties of materials are considered, but more other ways to categorize samples and notes about materials can be very useful. Faller, Scaletsky, and Kindlein recommend that materials libraries be organized by both tangible and intangible properties (see Figure 8.2).[1] *Intangible properties* include the emotional responses or cultural and other associations generated by a product and its sensory features. These sorts of categorization systems need to be developed on firm and regional bases, and the specific terms selected for use need to be well explained in a glossary. Some examples of organizing categories suggested by the Faller research team include (in the sensorial category): smooth/rough, hot color/cold color, odorless/aromatic. Associative sort terms they suggest include: time, origination, and physical state. Emotional categories discussed by Faller and his teammates include calm, curious, happy, pleased, optimistic, perky, sentimental, and their opposites—anxious, indifferent, sad, frustrated, nostalgic, ashamed, boring. Interpretive categories mentioned include: disposable/durable feminine/masculine, funny/serious, unfriendly/friendly, classic/modern, formal/informal, and public/restricted.

Free tools to help you organize material available as this book goes to press include Zotero (www.zotero.org) and EverNote (www.evernote.com).

## ADDITIONAL CONSIDERATIONS

One of the most effective ways to manage knowledge at a firm is to retain the people in the firm responsible for generating that knowledge initially. In both tough and buoyant economic times it can be difficult to keep experienced employees, but doing so is important for the firmwide knowledge continuity. This is particularly significant for tacit knowledge management.

Workspaces can be designed to encourage casual mixing among groups of employees that can ultimately culminate in knowledge sharing—and the more heads that knowledge gets shared into, the more likely that one of them will be around at a future time when that information needs to be shared.

Although money is often tight at design firms, hiring a person to manage knowledge resources is money well spent. A person with a background in library science is very familiar with state-of-the-art knowledge management practices and technology. As the resource manager becomes more familiar with firm culture, he or she can deploy specific skills more effectively. If resources are not available for a full-time employee with these skills, consultants and continuing service providers can be hired or an established firm employee can attend related continuing education classes.

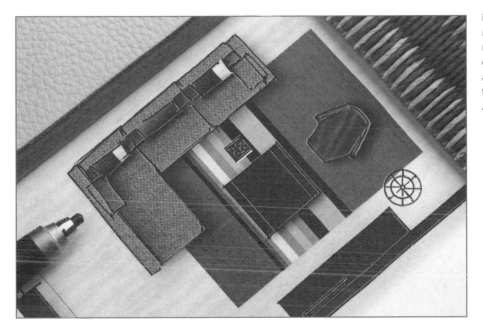

**FIGURE 8.2**
Materials can be organized in libraries based on both their tangible and intangible properties. © iStockphoto.com/Mr-Eckhart

## CORE CONCEPTS

What a firm has learned in the past is important for the future of the organization; it provides a unique competitive advantage. Although retaining and organizing company-specific information is a habit that needs to be established and encouraged, the effort to do so is justified. Effective knowledge management systems, responding to firmwide culture and mission, ultimately sustain themselves with minimal input of additional firm personnel or financial resources.

# ENDNOTES

1. Roberto Faller, Celso Scaletsky, and Wilson Kindlein, "Structure for a Material Informational Database: A Material Selection Tool for Project Development." (Presented at the Design and Emotion Society Conference, Chicago, IL, October 4–8, 2010.)

# Doing Design Research

DOING DESIGN RESEARCH IMPROVES and adds value to the practice of design by establishing a body of knowledge that informs the outcome of the designed environment: the who, what, where and why of a particular environment. Design informed by research meets space users' needs. It facilitates desired activities and mental processes: stores are shopped and objects purchased; patients heal and staff is committed; students learn. In spaces where design is supported by research, workers are creative or collegial or both, as desired. People restock exhausted stores of mental energy. These are spaces that provide value to clients and satisfaction to the design team. They are good for society because they enhance individual and group well-being. Research makes spaces successful.

Successful spaces are sustainable, using Alexander Garvin's comprehensive six-factor definition of sustainability.[1] Spaces that dovetail with user needs aren't continually being redesigned because they are, for some reason, "just not right." That makes them sustainable in the way we are used to thinking about the topic—but Garvin's definition goes far beyond green policies.

Garvin says that successful public gardens share six sustainability attributes. It is easy to see that his discussion of public gardens can be applied to spaces in general. Design research ensures that each sustainability attribute is reflected in the final form of a space created.

The six aspects of sustainability recognized by Garvin are as follows:

1. *Social sustainability*. Thoughtful design means that people can satisfy a variety of needs in the space as a whole, from folk dancing to meditation.

2. *Functional sustainability*. Built-in flexibility means that as needs change, the space can support them—long-term use requires this.

3. *Environmental sustainability*. This is the "respect for the planet" definition that is familiar.

4. *Financial sustainability*. Return on investment (e.g., whether measured in sales or tax dollars) must be sufficient to justify action.

5. *Political sustainability*. A space needs advocates if it is going to continue to exist.

6. *Aesthetic sustainability*. Successful spaces continue to provide new pleasurable experiences to users.

Successful spaces provide pleasure through use now and in the future, In the terms of Chapter 2, they comply, communicate, challenge, continue, and comfort. They are places whose design has been informed by research.

## ENDNOTE

1. Alexander Garvin, *Public Parks: The Key to Livable Communities* (New York: W.W. Norton and Company, 2011).

# ADDITIONAL SOURCES OF INFORMATION FOR DESIGN RESEARCHERS

Amedeo, Douglas, Reginald Golledge, and Robert Stimson. *Person Environment Behavior Research: Investigating Activities and Experiences in Spaces and Environments.* New York: The Guilford Press, 2009.

Augustin, Sally. *Place Advantage: Applied Psychology for Interior Architecture.* New York: John Wiley & Sons, 2009.

Berg, Bruce. *Qualitative Research Methods for the Social Sciences* (5th ed.). New York: Pearson, 2004.

Booth, Wayne, Gregory Colomb, and Joseph Williams. *The Craft of Research* (3rd ed.). Chicago: University of Chicago Press, 2008.

Coombs, Ted, and Roderico DeLeon. *Google Power Tools Bible.* Hoboken, NJ: John Wiley & Sons, 2007.

Fowler, Floyd. *Improving Survey Questions: Design and Evaluation.* Thousand Oaks, CA: Sage Publications, 1995.

———. *Survey Research Methods* (3rd ed.). Thousand Oaks, CA: Sage Publications, 2002.

Groat, Linda, and David Wang. *Architectural Research Methods.* Hoboken, NJ: John Wiley & Sons, 2007.

Hektner, Joel, Jennifer Schmidt, and Mihaly Csikszentmihalyi. *Experience Sampling Method: Measuring the Quality of Everyday Life.* Thousand Oaks, CA: Sage Publications, 2006.

Jankowicz, Devi. *The Easy Guide to Repertory Grids.* Hoboken, NJ: John Wiley & Sons, 2004.

Jordan, Patrick *Designing Pleasurable Products: An Introduction to the New Human Factors.* New York: Taylor and Francis, 2000.

Kuniavsky, Mike. *Observing the User Experience: A Practitioner's Guide to User Research.* New York: Morgan Kaufmann Publishers, 2003.

Preiser, Wolfgang, and Jacqueline Vischer. *Assessing Building Performance.* New York: Elsevier, 2005.

Rose, Gillian. *Visual Methodologies: An Introduction to the Interpretation of Visual Materials* (2nd ed.). Thousand Oaks, CA: Sage Publications, 2007.

Scott, John. *Social Network Analysis: A Handbook* (2nd ed.). Thousand Oaks, CA: Sage Publications, 2006.

Solcy, Lawrence, and Aaron Smith. *Projective Techniques for Social Science and Business Research.* Milwaukee, WI: The Southshore Press, 2008.

Sommer, Robert, and Barbara Sommer. *A Practical Guide to Behavioral Research: Tools and Techniques* (5th ed.). New York: Oxford University Press, 2002.

Steinberg, Steven, and Sheila Steinberg. *Geographic Information Systems for the Social Sciences: Investigating Space and Place.* Thousand Oaks, CA: Sage Publications, 2006.

Zaltman, Gerald. *How Customers Think: Essential Insights into the Mind of the Market.* Boston: Harvard University Press, 2003.

Zeisel, John. *Inquiry by Design.* New York: W.W. Norton, 2006.

# INDEX